Great Lakes Ships We Remember

A Photo-History of Selected Great Lakes Ships

Great Lakes Ships We Remember

Volume I

Revised Edition

Rev. Peter J. Van der Linden

Editor

IN COOPERATION WITH:

John H. Bascom
Rev. Edward J. Dowling, S.J.
Peter B. Worden
Dr. Richard J. Wright
Marine Historical Society of Detroit

Published by
FRESHWATER PRESS, INC.
Cleveland, Ohio U.S.A.
http://www.lakeboats.com

ISBN 0-912514-24-8

"And the beauty and mystery of the ships,
and the magic of the sea."

"My Lost Youth"
Henry Wadsworth Longfellow

WE REMEMBER . . .

Down through the ages, the fascination and romance of ships has captivated the thousands who have watched the leviathans plow through calm or troubled global waters. Great Lakes ships, as well as the men who have labored aboard them, have had their enthusiasts since La Salle's GRIFFON first sailed these inland waters. We remember these ships, old and new, and now recall in story and pictures some of the fascination we have felt for them.

Many of these stories originally appeared in the monthly bulletin of the Detroit Marine Historical Society, *The Detroit Marine Historian.* We have embellished, edited, and added photographs to these in hope of bringing to the public the many interesting and intriguing facts and histories of some of the Great Lakes' vessels. We have selected these ships as a representative group, and do not claim to include all the thousands of vessels which have sailed these inland waters. All photographs used have come from several of the many collectors in the Great Lakes area. The facts and figures come from various government publications and insurance firms, and some of the details only the survivors of the shipwrecks themselves could tell. We have endeavored to produce a volume that should be fascinating to the uninitiated, and informative to the enthusiast.

We dedicate this work to the sailors who, over the past two hundred years, have labored aboard the thousands of ships of every description on the Great Lakes. Especially, we would like to remember the many men who have lost their lives on the icy waters or have gone down with their vessels. The ships that are recounted herein would not have sailed these saltless seas were it not for their dedication.

The people who worked on this project deserve a word of praise, too, for without their dedication to history this would never have been completed. First, to the original writers, who saw the "Ships That Never Die" project of the Detroit Marine Historical Society "off the ground" more than 30 years ago, go our thanks for their inventiveness. To those no longer with us, who contributed to the original project, goes our hope that clear sailing is their happy lot. They are: Tom Dancey, Captain Frank Hamilton, Captain Geoffrey Hawthorne, Fred Landon, William A. McDonald, Neil Morrison, John Poole, Rev. Franklin C. St. Clair, Kenneth E. Smith, Captain W. J. Taylor and W. R. Williams.

The writers of the monthly columns which appeared in the *Detroit Marine Historian* are: Leonard Barr II, John H. Bascom, Dana Thomas Bowen, Milt Brown, Rev. E. J. Dowling S.J., Dave Glick, Wes Harkins, Jim Howick, Al Jackman, Gary Kazor, Bill Luke, Emory Massman, Russ Mortinger, Jim Roach, Ralph Roberts, Victor Scrivens, Paul Sherlock and Rev. Peter Van der Linden.

Thanks go, too, to those who have given pictures and drawings from their private collections to be used in this volume: John H. Bascom, John N. Bascom, Duff Brace, Rev. Edward J. Dowling, S.J., Rev. Raymond Donahue, Jim Kidd, Claude Lockwood, Ralph Roberts, Ken Thro, the late Ed Wilson, Peter B. Worden, and Dr. Richard Wright. Others, including *Lake Log Chips,* the Toronto Marine Historical Society, the Valley Camp Museum at Sault Ste. Marie, Michigan, and the Canal Park Museum at Duluth, Minnesota, who have been most helpful in promoting this volume.

Special thanks go to the committee which followed this book to its conclusion amid a series of trials: Rev. Edward J. Dowling, S.J., pre-eminent historian of the Lakes; John H. Bascom of Toronto, who worked ceaselessly, especially on the Canadian ships portrayed; Peter B. Worden, who assisted in compilation of material and printing photos, the Staff of Freshwater Press, Inc., and the Staff of the Great Lakes Research Center at Bowling Green University, with its able director, Dr. Richard Wright. Lastly, to Mrs. Donna Sobas, who typed the manuscript, and to Mrs. Betty Yura of the faculty of Bishop Borgess High School, Detroit, and John N. Bascom of Toronto, Ontario who were so kind as to proof read the manuscript, and to Suzette Worden and Tim Blackwell who proof read the galley proofs.

We thank the many members and friends who pointed out errors in the first printing and who provided new, additional material to substantially improve this second edition.

Rev. Peter Van der Linden
Editor

EXPLANATION

The ships depicted in this revised edition book were creatures of engineering art. The following explanations about the dimensions and statistics of these vessels should be understood to follow accurately the chronology of each individual ship story.

Unless otherwise noted, the length of a vessel is that length found in the official documents of the country in which the vessel was constructed. The length dimension nearly universally used in these documents is *length between perpendiculars*. This is defined as "the length of the vessel as measured on the Summer load line from the foreside of the stem to the afterside of the rudder post." Other lengths which apply to vessel statistics and which typically are used in the maritime field are: 1) *keel length*, which is the length of the vessel measured along the keel plate, and 2) *overall length*, which is the extreme length of the vessel as measured from its forward most to aftermost perpendicular extensions. The beam and depth of the vessel as shown refer to the greatest breadth measured over the frames and the moulded vertical hold depth measured on the center line of the vessel amidships, respectively. *IN ALL CASES, THE TECHNICAL INFORMATION SHOWN WITH EACH VESSEL STORY IS THE ORIGINAL STATISTICAL DATA WHEN THE SHIP WAS PUT INTO SERVICE, WITH THE EXCEPTION OF ANY SUBSEQUENT OFFICIAL NUMBERS. ANY SALIENT SUBSEQUENT CHANGES TO THIS ARE NOTED IN THE TEXT.*

Each ship is given an official number when first documented in a country. The vessel might have many different names in its lifetime, but the official number rarely changes unless she is transferred to another nation, in which case she is given a new official number according to the system used in that particular country.

The types of engines used in various steam and diesel vessels have particular significance to an enthusiast of the shipping world. Each engine is a little different than the next. The dimensions of each engine are given for sake of completeness. The diameter of cylinders used can vary during a ship's lifetime. The engine can be re-bored to make it more economical, thus changing the diameter. The stroke is the vertical distance that a piston takes to make one up or down movement. If an engine is a "triple expansion" (the most popular) type, it will have three cylinders, the low pressure, the intermediate, and the high pressure. The steam flows from the high pressure cylinder to the low, giving added power with each stroke. Propulsion machinery data are, of course, not shown in this book for non-self-propelled vessels such as barges and schooners.

The hull numbers are noted because they are a means of determining just how many ships a shipyard built during its lifetime. The numbering will differ from one firm to another, but most keep an accurate record of the ships they have built. Although uncommon, some yards preferred not to assign hull numbers and, where this is the case, the data line is omitted.

Gross registered tonnage applies to vessels, not to cargo. It is determined by dividing by 100 the area, in cubic feet, of the vessel's closed-in spaces. A vessel ton is 100 cubic feet. This tonnage is determined by hull inspectors of the classification society for each ship. This may change from time to time in a ship's life according to the measurement system and governing rules under which the calculation is made. The tonnages listed are taken from the American and Canadian records found in the annual reports issued by these nations. The American vessels will be in the "Merchant Vessels of the United States," the Canadian in the "List of Shipping."

Launch dates, when available, have usually come from articles appearing in daily newspapers when the vessel was christened. Specifications of the engines and other dimensions were traced back through the various classification society records such as "Lloyds Register of Shipping," "The Record" of the American Bureau of Shipping, older issues of "Inland Lloyds," "Beeson's Marine Directory" and "Underwriters Insurance" records. Today, such statistics may be found in "Greenwood's Guide to Great Lakes Shipping," an annual publication by the publishers of this volume.

To any enthusiast or "Boat Collector," everything about a ship is of utmost importance. So that the reader may see the effort of pleasureful research that goes into a hobby such as this, we have attempted to share herein all we know about any given vessel's history. Particularly interesting sidelights have been added whenever possible.

Renaming of ships often causes difficulty. To make it easier to understand the time sequence and order in which the ship was given various names, the first name a ship is given in official records is listed as the "a" name. Each successive name and the date it is changed are mentioned. The second name, therefore, becomes the "b" name, etc. Some ships were originally destined to be named one way but were given a name change before the official records were made. These cases are noted wherever possible.

ABERDEEN

ABERDEEN at dock

ABERDEEN,
b) Gladys H.

BUILT: James Davidson,
West Bay City, Michigan
LENGTH: 211'
BREADTH: 35'
DEPTH: 16'6"
GROSS REGISTERED
TONNAGE: 1,045
REGISTRY NUMBER: US 106975

The large wooden three-masted schooner ABERDEEN was typical of most such vessels built toward the end of the "days of sail," strictly utilitarian and designed to be towed rather than sailed. She was built in 1892 for the Davidson Transportation Company.

In the early spring of 1897, her ownership was changed to the Minch interests of Cleveland, Ohio. Successively, she was operated by the Minch-controlled Minch Transit Company, Nicholas Transit Company, and Kinsman Transit Company, all within the space of a year.

In June, 1899, the large vessel was sold to Henry J. Pauly of Milwaukee. After three years service for him, ownership was transferred to S. G. Jenks of Port Huron, Michigan. Her American enrollment was closed on April 6, 1906, when she was sold Canadian (C. 126469; 212' × 35' × 16'6"; 919 gross tons). She enjoyed another brief stint in American ownership, 1907–1910, with William H. Hackett and Son, of Clayton, New York.

In 1910, she left American ownership for good, being sold to the Quebec Transit and Forwarding Company of Quebec, who renamed her GLADYS H. Generally engaged in the unglamorous job of carrying coal, she was acquired by the George Hall Coal Company of Canada, Ltd., in 1918. Sincennes-McNaughton Line, Ltd. of Montreal purchased her in 1923, and in 1927 her last owners, the Consolidated Oka Sand and Gravel Company, also of Montreal, operated her. The registry of the GLADYS H. was closed on November 19, 1930, thus ending a profitable thirty-eight year career spanning all five of the Great Lakes, plus the St. Lawrence River trade.

ADMIRAL

ADMIRAL,
b) J. K. Dimmick,
c) Edward U. Demmer

BUILT:	Detroit Shipbuilding Company, Wyandotte, Michigan
HULL NUMBER:	133
LENGTH:	423.9
BREADTH:	51.9
DEPTH:	28
GROSS REGISTERED TONNAGE:	4,651
REGISTRY NUMBER:	US 107523
ENGINES:	22″, 35″, 58″ diameter × 42″ stroke Triple expansion
ENGINE BUILDER:	Shipyard

ADMIRAL 1907

J. K. DIMMICK 1919

EDWARD U. DEMMER 1922

In 1900, the American Steamship Company, M. B. McMillan owner, contracted for a coal-fired steel bulk freighter, which served her owner well during the first two decades of her life. She was renamed J. K. DIMMICK in 1913, but continued to serve in the movement of iron ore, coal, grain, and stone in interlake commerce for Mr. McMillan until being sold on April 12, 1920 to the Minnesota Transit Company. At this time the ship was given its last name, EDWARD U. DEMMER. As the DEMMER, this vessel was sold to the Milwaukee-Western Fuel Company during 1922 and operated by D. Sullivan & Company.

1923 was a season on the Great Lakes plagued with much fog. It is amazing that there were not more disasters in that season, for only two ships were lost, neither catastrophe being attended by loss of life. The EDWARD U. DEMMER became one of these victims on May 20, 1923 when she collided with the ore carrier SATURN of the Interlake Steamship Company fleet forty miles southeast of Thunder Bay Island in Lake Huron. The DEMMER sank in a matter of minutes but all of the crew were able to escape. Dense fog surrounded both vessels on that day in May and traffic was proceeding with caution. Whistle signals apparently were misunderstood and the inevitable resulted, ending the career of this bulk freight vessel.

One of the more serious hazards to Great Lakes shipping has been the dense, "pea-soup" fog that prevails in the Spring and Fall of the year. Today, with radar and radio-telephone communications vastly improved over even 10–15 years ago, such an accident as that which befell the DEMMER is rare. However, seamen still regard fog as a major enemy and are required to navigate their vessels with extreme care during those periods of the season when it is prevalent.

ADRIENNE

ADRIENNE

The wooden steam yacht ADRIENNE was built in 1884 for S. I. Leighton of South Haven, Michigan. In 1887, still listed in her original port of enrollment, Grand Haven, Michigan, she went through a dimension change (74'5" × 16'6" × 7'). By 1899, her ownership had changed to Maria Crysler of Harbor Springs, Michigan, and the following year to W. E. Crysler. During this period, she undoubtedly was used in the resort business in and around Little Traverse Bay.

In 1900, Mr. Crysler renamed the jaunty craft SEARCH-LIGHT. In 1906, she was sold to O. E. Wilbur of Charlevoix, Michigan, and went through another rebuild (94'8" × 19'5" × 6'5"; 95 gross tons). The details of her last few years are somewhat clouded. She was sold to W. D. Hamilton of Chicago, Illinois, where she ran to Lincoln Park with SILVER SPRAY. To Chicagoans, the SEARCHLIGHT was perhaps best known for excursion trips around Chicago harbor and to well-known Lincoln Park where summer picnics were popular and trips on board the vessel were inexpensive. In 1914, a Mr. M. Martinek of Chicago became her owner and the following year, her home port was changed to Duluth, Minnesota. She was dropped from documentation in 1916 and is presumed to have been dismantled.

SEARCHLIGHT

ADRIENNE,
b) Searchlight

BUILT:	L. A. Leighton, South Haven
LENGTH:	74
BREADTH:	16.6
DEPTH:	7
GROSS REGISTERED TONNAGE:	63
REGISTRY NUMBER:	US 106249
ENGINES:	16" × 16" Non-condensing
ENGINE BUILDER:	St. Joseph Iron Works, St. Joseph, Michigan

AGNES

ISLE ROYALE

This vessel was of wooden construction and was launched as a barge in 1879. Built for the account of John A. Wansey, the ship was promptly sold upon completion to Crockett McElroy of Marine City to be run as a ferry and excursion vessel on the St. Clair River. To suit this purpose, an engine was installed during the 1879–80 winter. Cabins for the vessel were built at the Dunford and Alverson Drydock at Port Huron, Michigan and installed.

In 1884 she was sold to Cooley, Larague and others of Duluth, Minnesota. These men operated the Duluth and North Shore Line. Upper cabins and passenger berths were installed at Duluth and, on April 14, 1884, the vessel was renamed ISLE ROYALE. Ready for her new owners, she was put into service on the passenger and package freight run between Duluth, Isle Royale and Port Arthur, Ontario.

John Malone, keeper of the Managerie Island Lighthouse, Lake Superior wrote in his diary on July 30, 1885: "Re Steamer ISLE ROYALE. She is a poor boat to depend on at any time. She is always breaking down. She is the only steamer running in the vicinity of this lighthouse." On August 11, 1885 his entry read: "I learned today that the Steamer ISLAE ROYALE (*sic*) of Duluth was lost off Washington Harbor on the 26th (July). Sprung a leak and went down, all hands saved." At the time of her demise, she was enroute from Port Arthur to Duluth and was valued at $10,500.

The lighthouse keeper was prophetic in the entry of his diary just four days after the ISLE ROYALE's actual sinking. She was built for the river trade and the rougher life battling Lake Superior proved too much for her. Wooden vessels were prone to spring a leak now and then due to changes of weather and sea conditions, but Lake Superior was not the place to be caught when that happened. Luckily, the ISLE ROYALE was only two miles off her namesake island when she went down.

AGNES,		*BREADTH:*	18.2
b) Isle Royale		*DEPTH:*	6.9
		GROSS REGISTERED	
BUILT:	John A. Wansey,	*TONNAGE:*	55
	Alexander Anderson's Yard,	*REGISTRY NUMBER:*	US 29909
	Marine City, Michigan	*ENGINES:*	unknown
LENGTH:	91.8	*ENGINE BUILDER:*	unknown

ALABAMA

ALABAMA as a Goodrich liner out of Chicago

ALABAMA Kirby Liner

BUILT:	Manitowoc Dry Dock Company, Manitowoc, Wisconsin
HULL NUMBER:	36
LENGTH:	250
BREADTH:	45.5
DEPTH:	26.1
GROSS REGISTERED	

TONNAGE:	2,626
REGISTRY NUMBER:	US 207138
ENGINES:	Triple expansion 23″, 38″, 62″ diameter × 36″ stroke
ENGINE BUILDER:	Toledo Shipbuilding Company, Toledo, Ohio

The steel passenger and freight steamer ALABAMA was built in 1910 for the Goodrich Transit Company. She was launched on December 18, 1909, and went into service the following spring. Perhaps this vessel will best be remembered for her prowess as an icebreaker for the Lake Michigan cities which she served. Extra heavy hull plating made the ALABAMA the most reliable winter boat on the Lakes. Whenever a ship was stuck in the ice on Lake Michigan, the ALABAMA was called to help release her. Ice conditions around the Lakes vary from year to year, but ports often remain clogged after more open waters have cleared. Here the ALABAMA was used to her best.

The Goodrich line was dissolved in 1933 and the ALABAMA was owned successively by the following companies: in 1934, by the Chriscarala Corp.; in 1937, by Earl J. Kirby; in 1940, by Paxton Mendelson; in 1944, by the Georgian Bay Line; in 1945, by the C&B Transit Company; in 1945, also, by the Blue Water Steamship Company; in 1946, back to the Georgian Bay Line; in 1962, by John W. Magill; and since 1964 by the Stender Marine Construction Company.

The ALABAMA lay idle at Holland, Michigan from 1946 to 1960, and in 1961 her cabins and engines were removed. The cut-down hull was redocumented as a barge and a crane was added in 1964. Her service as a barge continues but she is remembered as a palatial passenger vessel with excellent speed and fabulous accommodations by the people who had so enjoyed her hospitality over the years.

ALABAMA arriving at Detroit

ALABAMA as a Georgian Bay Liner

ALABAMA as a barge at Detour, Mich.

ALASKA

ALASKA Anchor Line

BUILT:	Gibson & Craig, Buffalo, New York in 1871	*GROSS REGISTERED* *TONNAGE:*	1,288
LENGTH:	212.6	*REGISTRY NUMBER:*	US 105135
BREADTH:	32	*ENGINES:*	24″, 51″ diameter × 36″ stroke
DEPTH:	13.9		Steeple compound
		ENGINE BUILDER:	Perry & Lays

ALASKA in the St. Clair River

Between 1870 and 1873, four similar iron hulls for the package freight trade were built for the Erie and Western Transportation Company, commonly known as the Anchor Line. These were the ALASKA, CHINA, INDIA and JAPAN. Unlike ALASKA, the other three also provided passenger accommodations. All these ships had long and interesting careers of better than 30 years, with the top performance for longevity being made by the ALASKA, 76 years. It is interesting to note that the Anchor Line passenger ships CHINA, INDIA and JAPAN were regarded as triplets (sister ships).

For forty years the Steamer ALASKA served on the company's trade routes between Buffalo, New York, and Chicago, Illinois, and Duluth, Minnesota, handling package freight. In 1911 she was sold to James O'Conner of Tonawanda, New York, who engaged the Empire Shipbuilding Company of the same city to convert the vessel into a bulk freighter. The work was performed with dispatch and the ALASKA began her new role on the Great Lakes. In 1914, she passed into the ownership of the Mullen Coal Company of Detroit, Michigan who primarily used the vessel for the movement of coal. This activity waned in the 1930's

however, and even though now only a storage barge, the fine, old steamer fell into near disuse, lying idle behind Mullen's coal fueling pier at Sandwich, Ontario, until she was finally towed by the tug ATOMIC to Hamilton, Ontario, in July, 1948 where her hull was cut up for scrap. The old timer had been sold to Canadian owners back in 1936 but she had apparently never been documented as a Canadian vessel. Used only as a storage barge, the vessel spent her last days in relative obscurity as can be seen from the photographs of the ship taken just after World War II.

Iron hulls were not very common on the Great Lakes, but the ones that did see service on these waters were uncommonly durable. The transition from wood to steel vessels on the Lakes was quicker because of the availability of iron ore and the steel-making plants in the region. When the forests were almost exhausted, the age of steel had already begun and the use of iron in shipbuilding was limited. The ships were carrying the necessary iron ore directly to the mills on the lower Lakes, where shipbuilders had a distinct advantage over coastwise ports in developing the steel vessels that soon came from their launching ways in droves.

ALASKA as a lumber-hooker in 1912

ALASKA as a barge at Mullen's Coal Dock

ALASKA a stern view in her last years

ALASKA
(1878)

The wooden sidewheel steamer ALASKA was built in 1878. She received the engine, pilothouse, and smokestack from the Revenue Cutter JOHN SHERMAN, built in 1863. Her trial trip was conducted on July 2, 1878, under Captain John Edwards, and the following day she departed for Cleveland, Ohio. She was owned by John Clark (3/4) and Walter O. Ashley (1/4), and was intended to run from Put-in-Bay, via Cleveland, to Buffalo, connecting with the JAY COOKE from Detroit, at Put-in-Bay. Twenty-nine staterooms off the main cabin, done in white and oiled cherry, provided accommodations. A beautiful winding mahogany stairway at one end of the chandeliered grand salon gave access to the upper deck.

In about 1886, the jaunty paddle steamer was placed on the Detroit, Put-in-Bay, Sandusky run under the locally renowned Captain Albert J. Fox. On this run she departed the foot of First Street in Detroit on Mondays, Wednesdays, and Fridays, at 8:30 a.m. arriving back the same day at

10:30 p.m. In April, 1889, ownership changed to Walter O. Ashley (5/20), Alice E. Atcheson (3/20), Florence C. Ashley (3/20), Ashley and Dustin (3/20), all of Detroit, and William H. McFall (6/20) of Sandusky.

On the evening of May 7, 1889, after tying up to the Michigan Central depot wharf in Detroit, the ALASKA was discovered to be on fire. She burned to a total loss, her place being taken by GAZELLE and then PEARL. Her hull was sold to the Au Sable Transportation Company, enrolled at Port Huron, and was converted to a two-masted, schooner-rigged barge (318 gross tons, 302 net tons). Her engine went into the steamer FRANK E. KIRBY, then building, which became known as "the Flyer of the Lakes."

Charles N. Carleton and John E. Mills purchased the old barge at a United States Marshall's sale on January 6, 1891, and towed her as part of the Mills Transit Company, of Marysville, Michigan. In 1895, Larkin, Stickey and Cram of Saginaw, Michigan, bought the hull and converted her

ALASKA as a passenger steamer

to a propellor-driven lumber hooker (165′2″ × 29′ × 10′6″; 339 gross tons). The engine from the tug JIM PULLAR (US 77146) was placed in her (high pressure non-condensing, 16″ × 20″, built in 1880 at Lockport, N.Y., by Pound Manufacturing Company; 250 indicated h.p.). In this role, she went through a succession of American owners; Fred L. Swart, Port Huron; L. Ludington, Alpena, Michigan; William H. Sanborn, Alpena, before being sold to Canadian owners. She was removed from documentation at Port Huron on May 15, 1906 (C. 117174).

Her new Canadian owners, W. J. Pulling, et al., of Windsor, Ontario, continued her in the lumber trade. On December 23, 1910, bound from Owen Sound, Ontario, for Windsor, she lost much of her deck load of lumber in strong Georgian Bay weather. After finding shelter at Tobermory, she burned to a total loss there the following day.

ALASKA as a steam barge at Alpena

BUILT:	John P. Clark, Springwells (Detroit), Michigan	*GROSS REGISTERED TONNAGE:*	510
LENGTH:	165′2″	*REGISTRY NUMBER:*	US 105798
BREADTH:	29′	*ENGINES:*	Beam Condensing
DEPTH:	10′6″	*ENGINE BUILDER:*	Fletcher & Harrison, Hoboken, New Jersey (1863)

ALGOMA

ALGOMA just after arrival at Owen Sound.

ALGOMA in the Weitzel Lock

The Canadian Pacific Railway Co., Montreal, had this steel freight and passenger vessel built in 1883 for Upper Lakes Service. She crossed the Atlantic loaded with coal. Her passenger cabins were added at Port Colborne, Ontario. To get through the St. Lawrence and Welland Canals, she was cut in two at Cantin's shipyard in Montreal and rejoined at Union Dry Dock Co. in Buffalo. She began regular service from Owen Sound, Ontario, to the Lakehead (Fort William and Port Arthur, Ontario) on May 11, 1884.

On November 5, 1885, under command of Captain John Moore, she left Owen Sound on her usual run. On November 7, upbound on Lake Superior with a southeast gale and blowing snow, she struck Greenstone Rock on Isle Royale. She broke in two just forward of the engine room and the forward end foundered in deep water. Thirty-eight lives were lost. The engines and boilers were removed in 1886 and were eventually placed in the MANITOBA which was built as a replacement at Owen Sound in 1889.

BUILT:	Aitken and Mansell, Kelvinhaugh (Glasgow), Scotland	*GROSS REGISTERED TONNAGE:*	1,773
LENGTH:	270	*REGISTRY NUMBER:*	C 85766
BREADTH:	38.1	*ENGINES:*	Fore & Aft Compound 35″ and 70″ diameter × 48″ stroke
DEPTH:	23.3	*ENGINE BUILDER:*	David Rowan & Co., Glasgow, Scotland

ALGOMA—Str. ISLE ROYALE at right

What was left of the vessel on the rocks

ALGOSOO

The steel bulk freighter SATURN was built in 1901 for the Gilchrist Transportation Co., Cleveland. She was acquired by Algoma Central Railway, Sault Ste. Marie, Ontario, in 1913, and renamed J. FRATER TAYLOR (C. 130776). A partial rebuild was completed at Midland, Ontario, in 1919. She was given her last name, ALGOSOO (1), in 1936, and was operated by Algoma Central until 1965; during their ownership she travelled nearly 2,000,000 miles and carried more than 14,000,000 net tons of cargo. For her last trip, she loaded grain at the Canadian Lakehead for Sorel, Quebec in November 1965. While coming down Lake Superior, she was in trouble off Whitefish Point when her cargo shifted in very heavy weather. The U.S. Coast Guard Cutter NAUGATUCK went to her aid from the Soo. In the Spring of 1967, she left Sorel under tow and arrived at Bilbao, Spain, for scrapping on May 24, 1967.

SATURN in 1905

J. FRATER TAYLOR in the St. Mary's River.

ALGOSOO downbound at Mission Point

Saturn,		*BREADTH:*	48
b) J. Frater Taylor,		*DEPTH:*	28
c) ALGOSOO (i)		*GROSS REGISTERED*	
		TONNAGE:	3,373
BUILT:	American Shipbuilding	*REGISTRY NUMBER:*	US 117023
	Company,	*ENGINES:*	22″, 35″, 58½″ diameter × 42″
	Lorain, Ohio		stroke
HULL NUMBER:	306		Triple expansion
LENGTH:	346	*ENGINE BUILDEER:*	Shipyard

ALGOSOO in the St. Clair River

AMAZON

AMAZON in the Soo Locks—Str. GERMANIC at left

Built in 1897, the barge AMAZON was generally towed by one of the wooden Corrigan freighters. After 1902, when her sister steel barge, the AUSTRALIA, was converted into a steamer, AMAZON usually was her consort. In 1908, when she belonged to the Australia Transit Company, the steel barge was given an engine which had been built in 1889 for the Corrigan wooden freighter ITALIA, which had once towed the AMAZON up and down the Lakes. The denuded ITALIA then received another engine.

In 1915, the vessel passed into the Pioneer Steamship Company, Hutchinson & Company, managers. She operated for this fleet until the beginning of World War II, carrying various bulk freight cargoes and visiting many different ports. Her duties were not exceptional, and she handled them with little trouble. In 1942, AMAZON was traded to the United States War Shipping Administration (USWSA) in exchange for new tonnage. The USWSA leased her to the Gartland Steamship Company, managed by Sullivan, in 1943. At the end of the hostilities, she escaped the fate

of her other trade-in companions at the scrapyard, and continued to operate under the Gartland flag until 1949. After laying in Buffalo for a time, the T. H. Browning Steamship Company took over the lease during the Korean conflict and operated the vessel until 1954 in Browning colors. The hull was finally scrapped at Lackawanna, New York, in 1954.

She had served her various masters well, both as a barge and a steamer. Her conversion in 1908 at Cleveland by the American Shipbuilding Company gave her an engine of proven ability and maintained the ship's economic viability for nearly another half century. Her gross tonnage was changed at this time to 3,702. The huge triple expansion engine was too much for the old wooden ITALIA, but fit just perfectly in the AMAZON. The durability of the old wooden hulls was limited, and the engines from these craft often saw more service than the hulls. This is not the case in modern vessels, where the hulls of durable steel often outlast the engines.

As a barge in 1906

BUILT:	Chicago Shipbuilding Company, South Chicago, Illinois	*GROSS REGISTERED TONNAGE:*	3,599
HULL NUMBER:	29	*REGISTRY NUMBER:*	US 30089
LENGTH:	376	*ENGINES:*	19″, 30″, 50″ diameter × 42″ stroke
BREADTH:	46.2		Triple expansion
DEPTH:	22.4	*ENGINE BUILDER:*	Dry Dock Engine Works, Detroit, Michigan—1889

Locking down in 1920 with Str. MUNCY

In the Detroit River

AMAZON in Browning Colors

AMAZON during her last years

AMERICA

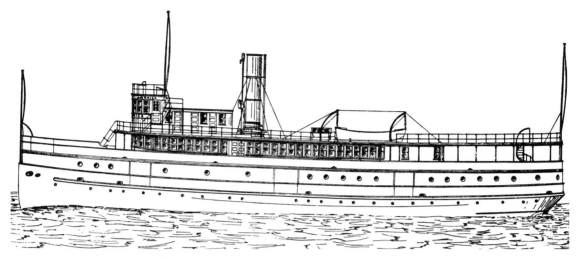

AMERICA in outboard profile

AMERICA on Lake Michigan, Michigan City harbor

BUILT:	Detroit Dry Dock Company, Wyandotte, Michigan	*GROSS REGISTERED TONNAGE:*	681
HULL NUMBER:	127	*REGISTRY NUMBER:*	US 107367
LENGTH:	164.6	*ENGINES:*	15″, 24″, 38″ diameter × 24″ stroke
BREADTH:	31		Triple expansion
DEPTH:	11	*ENGINE BUILDER:*	Dry Dock Engine Wks., Detroit, Mich.

22   In 1898, the steel passenger ship AMERICA was built for E. C. Dunbar of Chicago, Illinois, to use in the Lake Michigan trade. During the summer months, the AMERICA ran excursions to Michigan City, Indiana, making a stop at Calumet Harbor, South Chicago, to pick up passengers from the south side of Chicago.

In 1903, she was sold to the Booth Fisheries Company and was transferred to her new owner's Lake Superior line, The United States and Dominion Transportation Company, for whom the AMERICA operated between Duluth and Port Arthur on the north shore.

In 1911, she was lengthened to 182.6 feet (937 gross tons) to accommodate the increased traffic. A familiar sight to Duluthians, the AMERICA was admired a great deal. Especially popular were the excursions during the hot summer months up the north shore where the cool breezes of the wide expanse of Lake Superior would enthrall her patrons. She was a fast boat, and was assigned the delivery of the U.S. Mail to ports from Duluth to Port Arthur, Ontario.

Her 30 years of service came to an abrupt end on June 7, 1928, when she accidentally stranded on Isle Royale in Lake Superior, and proved a total loss. Her crew and passengers were saved, but her hull was abandoned to the underwriters. Her wreck was visible for many years after the accident until the forces of nature rendered her invisible from above the water. However, in recent years, skin divers have found her a source of extreme interest as they dive on her remains, picking up souvenirs from the many she left behind. Some of the "treasures" are insignificant, but are held in great esteem by the young people who dive on her. Any brass fittings, light fixtures, china, crockery, and utensils make handsome remembrances of the ships that have sailed the Lakes in bygone days. They are avidly sought by enthusiasts on both sides of the border. However, in recent years, the governments of the States and Province of Ontario have become interested in the wrecks to save them for posterity. A project to make underwater parks of areas where many wrecks litter the bottom is under study. Divers of the future could then see the past as it is preserved under the clear waters of Lake Superior.

In Duluth Harbor

AMERICANA

In 1907 the Lake Erie Excursion Company decided to initiate its service between downtown Buffalo, New York, and a favorite amusement park and picnic area in Ontario known as Crystal Beach, located on the north shore of Lake Erie. To implement this idea, it ordered the construction of this vessel.

The typical run for the AMERICANA was from the foot of Main Street in Buffalo, out the north harbor piers and across the eastern end of Lake Erie to Crystal Beach where a suitable pier had been constructed to moor the vessel. Literally thousands of Buffalonians would use this vessel during the summer months to escape from the city and relax on her decks and enjoy the outdoors upon arrival at Crystal Beach.

In 1910, a second vessel was added, the steamer CANA-DIANA. Both ships thrived on this popular route. The owners reorganized the company in 1927 under the new name Buffalo & Crystal Beach Corporation. In 1929, the AMERICANA was sold for off-lakes use to the Meseck Steamship Company of New York, leaving only the CANA-DIANA to travel the route to Crystal Beach.

The AMERICANA was active on the East Coast until 1953, carrying sightseeing passengers around the New York City area. Her dimensions were changed slightly by Meseck in that her length between perpendiculars was reduced to 203 feet. A few cabins were enclosed, but basically, the vessel ran on saltwater very much as she had done on Lake Erie and her appearance was changed little.

The ship met the fate of so many excursion vessels which fell victim to the decline of vessel passenger business concurrent with the rise in use of the family automobile. In the fall of 1953 she was towed to Baltimore, Maryland, and was cut up for scrap.

Few excursion vessels remain on any of the inland waterways of North America today, but those which served the public are still remembered as faithful and beautiful, in their means of allowing some pleasant moments aboard ship and away from the heat of summer in and around many major cities. The route of AMERICANA and CANA-DIANA from Buffalo to Crystal Beach was finally abandoned in 1958.

AMERICANA outbound at Buffalo

AMERICANA with a small crowd

BUILT:	Buffalo Drydock Company, Buffalo, New York	*REGISTRY NUMBER:*	US 205096
HULL NUMBER:	213	*ENGINES:*	20″, 32″, 50″ diameter × 36″ stroke
LENGTH:	209.7		Triple expansion
BREADTH:	45	*ENGINE BUILDER:*	Detroit Shipbuilding Company (engine division), Detroit, Michigan
DEPTH:	15.8		
GROSS REGISTERED TONNAGE:	969		

ANDASTE

ANDASTE in the locks at Cascades on the Soulanges Canal

BUILT:	Cleveland Shipbuilding Company, Cleveland, Ohio
HULL NUMBER:	16
LENGTH:	266.9
BREADTH:	38.1
DEPTH:	17.9
GROSS REGISTERED TONNAGE:	1,573
REGISTRY NUMBER:	US 106926
ENGINES:	Triple expansion 17″, 29″, 47″ diameter × 36″ stroke
ENGINE BUILDER:	Shipyard

ANDASTE late in her career

ANDASTE in 1919

The Steamer ANDASTE was an unusual vessel. Along with the CHOCTAW, it was built in 1892 for the Lake Superior Iron Company. The ANDASTE was a straight-back steel freighter, similar in design to the whaleback type of ship designed by Alexander McDougall but with straight sides and a conventional bow. The ships were painted red to hide the unsightly stains which were left on the ships' sides as a result of their sharp tumble-home. These stains were caused by the dripping rinse of red iron ore cargoes. The decks were washed down after the ore cargo had been loaded in the holds of the ship and the residue washed out down the scuppers (holes in the side of the ship near the deck which allow water to flow off the deckside).

Cleveland-Cliffs Iron Company operated the ANDASTE in the upper lakes trade carrying iron ore and coal; the iron ore downbound to the lower lake mills, the coal upbound to the railroads of the Mesabi Iron Range. Sometimes the vessel would carry an occasional cargo of grain to the elevators at Buffalo, New York. In her later years, the ANDASTE was used to carry pig iron. In 1920, the ship was shortened to 246.9 feet which allowed her to operate in this trade through the Welland and St. Lawrence River canals.

In 1925, the ANDASTE was sold to Leatham D. Smith of Sturgeon Bay, Wisconsin, and converted to a sandsucker. This owner used her as a sand dredge until 1928 when she was sold to the Andaste Steamship Company of Cleveland, Ohio. This firm was managed by the Construction Materials Company of Chicago, Illinois. Unfortunately, the ANDASTE saw only limited service for this firm. She was lost with all hands on September 9, 1929 between Grand Haven, Michigan, and South Chicago, Illinois, on Lake Michigan. Twenty-five persons lost their lives on this little vessel as she was overcome by the elements. The AN-DASTE's exact ending remains a mystery. With no one to tell of her dying moments, we too, remain in doubt of her final struggle and the ultimate end of the men who sailed her.

ANDASTE in 1928

ALEX ANDERSON

BUILT:	Alexander Anderson, Marine City, Michigan
LENGTH:	193
BREADTH:	37.2
DEPTH:	13.7
GROSS REGISTERED TONNAGE:	738
REGISTRY NUMBER:	US 106928

ALEX ANDERSON at the Soo

This three-masted wooden schooner, later a tow barge, was built in 1892 and named after her builder, Mr. Alexander Anderson, a prominent St. Clair County shipbuilder. The ANDERSON was one of the larger schooners built. For many years she ran for the Mills Transportation Company of Marysville, Michigan, in the lumber trade.

On March 13, 1916, this schooner was sold to the Sullivan Transportation Company, an affiliate of Moore-McCormack Lines in New York City. She was taken to the East Coast via the St. Lawrence River, along with the Steamer GETTYSBURG and the wooden schooner ARENAC, leaving Marine City in August, 1916.

About 3:30 a.m., when about 20 miles off Seal Island Light, near Sable Island in the Gulf of Maine, the group ran into a 50–60 MPH windstorm on October 1, 1916. The GETTYSBURG, the towing steamer, began to leak badly and pound in the heavy seas. When she could no longer make headway and her hold filled with six feet of water, the GETTYSBURG cast off her two barges, the ANDERSON and the ARENAC. The steamer called for help, picked up the crew off the ARENAC, and headed for the nearest shelter.

The Steamer SAGAMORE heard the distress signal and rescued Captain Carr and the crew of the ANDERSON, taking both it and the ARENAC in tow. Still struggling in the seas, the SAGAMORE managed to tow the barges toward shelter. However, when the cargo of pulpwood on the ANDERSON shifted, and she snapped the towline, the SAGAMORE had to give up and leave that barge to the elements. The old barge drifted and finally sank beneath the waves on Sunday, the 2nd of October. (For the story of the ARENAC, see the report on this vessel elsewhere in this book.)

Being repaired at Marine City

ANN ARBOR NO. 4

The Ann Arbor Railroad was the original owner of this carferry and ran it from Frankfort, Michigan, the western terminus of the railroad, across Lake Michigan to Manitowoc and Kewaunee, Wisconsin, and Manistique, Michigan, to connect with the Green Bay & Western and Soo Line Railroads, respectively. She was launched on October 20, 1906 amid joyous cheers and the traditional bottle of champagne.

As the years progressed and the traffic across Lake Michigan increased, new carferries were built to supplant the older vessels. The ANN ARBOR NO. 4 was retired from service and used as the spare boat when the others of the fleet had to go to the shipyard for inspection or repairs. One serious accident occurred in the career of this vessel. On St. Valentine's Day, February 14, 1923, the ship encountered a severe storm which had been building during the previous day. The cargo of railroads cars became dislodged from their fastenings and crashed around the deck. The plight of the vessel became serious as the pumps could not hold back the waters which surged in over her stern as the captain attempted to return to Frankfort. By miraculous luck, or perhaps more by the captain's uncanny sense of direction, they made their way back to the protection of the outer harbor where the vessel hit the pier and sank. The crew had to cross the slippery jetty to reach land, but all came back safely. The ship was subsequently repaired.

In 1937, the ANN ARBOR NO. 4 was sold to the Michigan State Highway Department and was converted to carry 85 automobiles across the Straits of Mackinac from St. Ignace in Michigan's Upper Peninsula to Mackinaw City in the Lower. At Manitowoc, Wisconsin, where the conversion was accomplished, the vessel was painted white and the railroad tracks removed. She was renamed CITY OF CHE-BOYGAN. This was the first of the larger carferries across the Straits, and the vessel served well with her later sisters until the Mackinac Bridge, spanning the gap between the two peninsulas, was completed in 1958.

Edward Anderson & Company purchased the vessel along with the larger CITY OF MUNISING and intended to make them floating potato processing plants. The engines were removed in 1958, and the old lady was moored at Washington Island, Wisconsin, in upper Lake Michigan. The third name of her career was assigned, EDWARD H. ANDERSON, and the vessel was duly registered under the Washington Island Storage Corporation in 1961.

When the business for which the vessel had been purchased fell off, the hull was sold for scrap. Together with the CITY OF MUNISING, the ANDERSON departed the port of Quebec bound for scrapping in Italy under the tow of the tug SEETRANS I on October 18, 1973, just two days short of 67 years after she first touched the waters of the Lakes. In early 1974, the vessel and her tow arrived at Sevona, Italy, where the ANDERSON was cut up.

ANN ARBOR NO. 4 Arriving at Sturgeon Bay

ANN ARBOR NO. 4 on the Frankfort pierhead in 1923

ANN ARBOR NO. 4,
b) City of Cheboygan,
c) Edward H. Anderson

BUILT:	American Ship Building Company, Cleveland, Ohio	*BREADTH:*	52
		DEPTH:	19
		GROSS REGISTERED TONNAGE:	1,884
HULL NUMBER:	436	*REGISTRY NUMBER:*	US 203695
LENGTH:	259	*ENGINES:*	Triple expansion (2) 14″, 22½″, 38″ diameter × 32″ stroke
		ENGINE BUILDER:	Shipyard

ANN ARBOR NO. 4 as rebuilt

CITY OF CHEBOYGAN at the Straits of Mackinac

EDWARD H. ANDERSON as a potato storage barge

ARENAC

ARENAC at the Soo

The ARENAC was originally a wooden schooner, and later became a tow barge which was built in 1888 for Pack, Fish and St. Clair. She was designed for use in the lumber trade and carried cargoes for numerous owners on the Lakes. These were A. B. Comstock of St. Clair, Michigan, Sinclair of Duluth, Minnesota, O. W. Blodgett of Duluth, and the Pringle Barge Line of Detroit, Michigan. This vessel was a familiar sight on the St. Clair and Detroit Rivers.

Along with the schooner ALEX ANDERSON and the Steamer GETTYSBURG, the ARENAC was sold to the Sullivan Transportation Company of New York, an affiliate of the Moore-McCormack Lines in 1916. The World War I need for hulls had forced many Eastern seaboard companies to seek vessels wherever they could. Many lake boats were taken to salt water for the war effort to carry cargoes in the Coastwise trade. The ARENAC outlived the ANDERSON, which was lost in a gale on October 1–2, 1916 in the Gulf of Maine, and served on the East Coast until sold in 1923 to Cuban interests. What happened to her after that date is unknown.

BUILT:	Simon Langell, St. Clair, Michigan
LENGTH:	178.6
BREADTH:	34.5
DEPTH:	12.7
GROSS REGISTERED TONNAGE:	521
REGISTRY NUMBER:	US 106549

ARIEL

The small wooden passenger ferry ARIEL was built in 1881 and was enrolled at Detroit on December 17, 1881 to Hiram Walker for service across the Detroit River as part of his Walkerville and Detroit Ferry Company. She ran on the same route from the foot of Joseph Campau Avenue to Walkerville, Ontario, until 1922, serving the public with only an occasional would-be suicide attempt or other near-drowning victim to break the monotony. She received a new boiler in 1902 (Scotch—11′ × 11′—built by Desmer and Ritchie, of Detroit).

From 1922 to 1926, the State of Michigan Highway Commission engaged her as the first of their fleet connecting Upper and Lower Michigan at the Straits of Mackinac. To accomplish this, they sheathed her hull in iron. As larger vessels were placed in this service, the ARIEL was judged expendable because of her small size.

Accordingly, in 1926, she was sold to the Port Huron and Sarnia Ferry Company, to transport persons and vehicles across the St. Clair River. She was rebuilt at this time (95′9″ × 28′9″ × 11′1″; 168 gross tons, 86 net tons). In 1936 she came under the jurisdiction again of the State of Michigan, this time with the State Bridge Commission. With the completion of the new Blue Water Bridge, the ARIEL again was considered surplus. She lay idle at Port Huron from about 1938 to 1944, when she was towed to Detroit. After a stay at Dubois Street, she was moved to St. Jean Street where, during the winter of 1947–48, she was capsized by a severe wind. There she was dismantled— within sight of her first route sixty-seven years earlier.

ARIEL in drydock at Detroit

ARIEL in the St. Clair River

BUILT:	Detroit Dry Dock Co., Wyandotte, Michigan	*GROSS REGISTERED TONNAGE:*	201
LENGTH:	95′	*REGISTRY NUMBER:*	US 106032
BREADTH:	28′	*ENGINES:*	Non-condensing H.P. 20″ Diameter × 24″ Stroke
DEPTH:	11′	*ENGINE BUILDER:*	Frontier Iron Works, Detroit, Michigan—1881

ARLINGTON

F. P. JONES in the St. Mary's River in 1915

GLENCADAM in the ice in 1922

F. P. Jones,	
b) Glencadam,	
c) ARLINGTON	

BUILT:	Detroit Shipbuilding Co., Wyandotte, Michigan	*DEPTH:*	21
HULL NUMBER:	192	*GROSS REGISTERED TONNAGE:*	1,870
LENGTH:	244	*REGISTRY NUMBER:*	C. 138219
BREADTH:	43	*ENGINES:*	Triple expansion 18″, 29″, 48″ × 40″
			Two coal fired Scotch Boilers 12′ × 11′6″
		ENGINE BUILDER:	Detroit S.B. Co.

Built in 1912 for the George Hall Coal Co., Ogdensburg, New York, she was originally named F. P. JONES (US 211084). During 1918–19, she operated for the United States Shipping Board in deep sea service, but was returned to the Hall Co., in 1919.

In 1920, she was sold to James Playfair, Midland, Ontario, and placed in the Glen Transportation Co. Ltd., a Playfair-Mathews consortium, as b) GLENCADAM for use in the Caribbean sugar run. For this service she was fitted with sampson posts and derrick booms. Her boilers were converted to oil fuel, the ship's double bottom being used as fuel tanks. Her ports of call in the Caribbean did not provide longshoremen so a dog house was fitted on her deck amidship providing accommodations for her own longshoremen. With her ballast tanks being used for fuel oil, the problem of not enough ballast became apparent. To take the place of water ballast, her empty coal bunker was filled with 100 tons of stone. In spite of these alterations, she was not successful as a sugar carrier and returned to the Lakes.

Her first winter back on fresh water was spent in Collingwood where her derricks were removed, the stone was removed from her coal bunker and her boilers were reconverted to burn coal. In 1925, she was sold to the Mathews Steamship Co. Limited, Toronto, and renamed c) ARLINGTON. The Mathews fleet went into receivership in 1931 and during 1932 and 1933 the fleet was chartered to Toronto Elevators Ltd. although ARLINGTON did not operate. Late in 1933, the fleet was sold to Colonial Steamships Ltd. which was formed by Capt. Scott Misener. In 1936, she was sold to her final owners, Burke Towing and Salvage Co. Ltd. of Midland, Ontario. They operated her mainly in the grain and pulpwood trade on the Upper Lakes. Her end came during a severe gale on Lake Superior on May 1, 1940 while downbound with grain. Sixteen members of her crew were picked up by the steamer COLLINGWOOD, accounting for all but one of those on board. Captain Fred "Tatey Bug" Burke went down with his ship.

ARLINGTON towing barge SALVUS

ARROW

ARROW in Lake Erie

ARROW (right) with R. B. HAYES and A. WHERLE, JR. at Sandusky

	ARROW,	*DEPTH:*	9'5"
	b) H-165	*GROSS REGISTERED*	
		TONNAGE:	365
BUILT:	Detroit Dry Dock Co.,	*REGISTRY NUMBER:*	US 107155
	Wyandotte, Michigan	*ENGINES:*	Beam Condensing
HULL NUMBER:	119		40" Diameter 108" Stroke
LENGTH:	165'3"	*ENGINE BUILDER:*	Fletcher & Harrison,
BREADTH:	28'		Hoboken, New Jersey—1868

The steel sidewheel steamer ARROW was launched on January 5, 1895. She was built for the Sandusky and Island Steamboat Company of Sandusky, Ohio, to run from that community to the Lake Erie islands. She remained a fixture on this route until 1922. Her Fletcher and Harrison engine came from the steamer JAY COOKE (US 13780). In 1911, she received a new fire-box boiler (9'6" × 15'11") from the American Ship Building Company of Lorain, Ohio.

On October 14, 1922, the ARROW was gutted by fire at her Put-in-Bay dock. She was replaced by the sidewheeler CHIPPEWA, formerly the revenue cutter WILLIAM P. FESSENDEN, purchased from the Arnold Transit Company.

After an extensive rebuild, the ARROW was sold in 1923 to the North Shore Steamship Company (John L. Batley, Manager) of Chicago, Illinois, to run from Chicago to Waukegan. While laid up in the north branch of the Chicago River in 1931, she again was visited by a serious fire, finishing her as an excursion ship.

The burned-out hulk was towed to Sturgeon Bay, Wisconsin, where she was further stripped. She was removed from documentation in 1934. In 1936 she again was documented, this time as a barge (333 gross tons, 333 net tons), owned by Charles W. Armentrout, of Monroe, Michigan.

In 1938, Benjamin O. Colonna, of Norfolk, Virgina, purchased the barge and she left fresh water forever. With the great demand for tonnage brought on by World War II, the old hull was sold, in 1942, to Honduran buyers. They placed a diesel engine in her and she was renamed H-165. After four years in the banana trade, she was wrecked, on October 26, 1946, on Barrier Reef, nine miles NNE of Hunting Cay Light, Honduras.

ARROW after a fire in 1922

ARROW as rebuilt

ASIA

The wooden steamer ASIA was built as a combination package freighter and passenger vessel for J. C. Graham and Sylvester Neelon, both of St. Catharines, and George Campbell of Windsor, Ontario, in 1873. These gentlemen formed the Windsor-Lake Superior line of steamers. The Beatty family soon became interested and operated the business in connection with their Northwest Transportation Co., Ltd., Sarnia. Along with SOVEREIGN, the ASIA operated between Windsor, Sarnia and Duluth from 1873 to 1881.

On July 9, 1881, ASIA stranded in the St. Mary's River and settled with her bow in shallow water. Salvaged and repaired at Sarnia, she returned to her former run. However, she also made several trips carrying construction materials for the Canadian Pacific Railway to the North Shore of Lake Superior. She was then chartered to the Great Northern Transit Co., Ltd., to replace the MANITOULIN, which burned off Shoal Point, Manitowaning, Ontario, on May 18, 1882. Near midnight on September 14, 1882, ASIA cleared Owen Sound under the command of Capt. J. Savage, heavily laden and with about 100 passengers aboard. On the morning of September 15, 1882, she was overtaken by a severe gale from the west which prevented her from making the port turn at Killarney. She finally foundered stern first south of the Bustard Islands. Only two passengers survived.

ASIA at her dock in Duluth

BUILT:	Melancthon Simpson, St. Catharines, Ontario	GROSS REGISTERED TONNAGE:	662
LENGTH:	136.9	ENGINES:	Unknown
BREADTH:	23.7	ENGINE BUILDER:	Unknown
DEPTH:	11.4		

ASSINIBOIA

ASSINIBOIA at Owen Sound

ASSINIBOIA ready to leave

BUILT:	Fairfield Shipbuilding & Engineering Co., Ltd. Govan, Scotland	*GROSS REGISTERED TONNAGE:*	3,880
HULL NUMBER:	452	*REGISTRY NUMBER:*	C. 125984
LENGTH:	336	*ENGINES:*	23½", 34", 48½" & 70" diameter
BREADTH:	43.6		× 45" stroke
DEPTH:	26.9		Quadruple expansion
		ENGINE BUILDER:	Shipyard

ASSINIBOIA in the St. Mary's River

This steel passenger and freight vessel was built in 1907 for the Canadian Pacific Railway's Upper Lakes Service. She was launched on June 25, 1907, being sponsored by Mrs. Bosworth, wife of one of the C.P.R. vice-presidents. ASSINIBOIA ran her trials on the Clyde on August 28, 1907, and sailed for Canada in ballast from the Tail of the Bank on August 30th.

Upon her arrival at Quebec, she was placed in drydock and cut in two for her passage through the St. Lawrence and Welland Canals. The two sections arrived at the yard of the Buffalo Drydock Company early in November 1907 and were rejoined. ASSINIBOIA left Buffalo for Owen Sound on November 18 and arrived there on November 24. Interior fittings and furnishings were installed over the winter and she left Owen Sound on her first voyage to Port Arthur and Fort William on July 4, 1908, under the command of Capt. E. B. Anderson.

ASSINIBOIA ran to the Canadian Lakehead for her entire active career, although the eastern terminus of the line was changed from Owen Sound to Port McNicoll in 1912. Her interior fittings were considerably improved during the winter of 1915–16. She was converted from coal to oil fuel over the winter of 1953–54, at which time her four original Scotch boilers were replaced by two Foster-Wheeler water-tube boilers.

The C.P.R. lake line ceased carrying passengers at the end of the 1965 season but ASSINIBOIA continued in service as a package freighter until the close of navigation in 1967. Laid up at Port McNicoll, she was sold in 1968 to Donald Lee of Port Lambton, Ontario, and towed to Point Edward, Ontario. Lee sold her to the Assiniboia S.S. Corp. of Philadelphia, Pennsylvania, and she made the trip from the lakes to the Delaware River under her own power in August and September, 1968. It was intended that ASSINIBOIA be converted for use as a floating restaurant but before work commenced, she burned to a total loss on November 11, 1969. The hull was cut up for scrap in 1970.

ASSINIBOIA

ATLANTIC

This palatial wooden side-wheel passenger boat was built in 1849 for Captain Eber B. Ward. She was chartered by the Michigan Central Railroad to serve as a connecting link between the terminus of the New York Central Railroad at Buffalo, New York, and the Michigan Central Railroad at Detroit, Michigan. At that time, it was the most traveled route of immigrants on their way to the West, and the need for fast passenger ships to accommodate the rush of people who wanted to settle the mid-western states was great.

The ATLANTIC was one of the fastest steamers afloat on the Lakes at the time and the sleek vessel made one record after another as she plowed her way between the two cities. (The record time established by this vessel was 16-1/2 hours, which is still quite respectable even today).

During the early hours of August 20, 1852, the ATLANTIC was bound from Buffalo to Detroit with a passenger list of 600, mostly immigrants. A few miles off Long Point, Ontario in Lake Erie at about 2:30 a.m., she collided with the freight propellor OGDENSBURG of the Northern Transportation Company which was bound from Cleveland, Ohio, through the Welland Canal to Ogdensburg, New York, with a cargo of wheat. The night was hazy but not foggy. The ATLANTIC tried to cross in front of the OGDENS-BURG but failed to make it safely. The ODGENSBURG slashed into the ATLANTIC just forward of the "larboard" (left) side of the wheelhouse. Thinking there was no great damage, both vessels proceeded on their way after being locked together for a brief time. Since the OGDENSBURG had reversed her engines just prior to the crash, it was thought at first that no serious damage had been done.

Both vessels continued on in darkness, but the ATLAN-TIC had been holed below the waterline and soon the fires under her boilers went out and she started her plunge into the deep. The passengers and crew began to panic, many jumping overboard to certain death. The OGDENSBURG, having proceeded only a short distance, heard the cries and shrieks of terror and turned back to the aid of the stricken ship. Some 250 were picked up by the OGDENS-BURG and brought to Erie, Pennsylvania, while other survivors awaited rescue on flotsam and the remaining life boats from the ATLANTIC. About 130 of the 600 passengers and crew were drowned. The exact number will never be known because of insufficient records kept at the time of the ATLANTIC's departure. The negligence of the crew of the ATLANTIC was blamed for the disaster, which at that time was one of the worst ever. The crew had failed to launch lifeboats on time, had not tried to prevent panic, and had negligently proceeded to get underway after the collision, not attempting to determine the extent of the damage before it was too late.

Many attempts to raise the sunken vessel were made in the following years but these were unsuccessful. In 1873, some valuables were recovered, but no further attempts were made because of the depth of surrounding waters.

ATLANTIC as drawn by Samuel Ward Stanton

BUILT:	Jacob Wolverton, Newport, Michigan	*GROSS REGISTERED TONNAGE:*	1,155
LENGTH:	265.7	*ENGINES:*	Vertical beam 60″ Diameter × 132″ Stroke
BREADTH:	33	*ENGINE BUILDER:*	Hogg & Delamater, New York, N.Y.
DEPTH:	13.6		

BANNOCKBURN

The steel canaller BANNOCKBURN was built in 1893 for the Montreal Transportation Company. This was the fabled "Flying Dutchman" of the Great Lakes. The original Flying Dutchman was an old-time ocean sailing vessel that mysteriously vanished and was never heard from again. Salt water tars claim to have seen the old Dutchman riding majestically and calmly along the waves on wild and stormy nights. When the "Flying Dutchman" is seen, sailors interpret the vision as an ill omen.

The BANNOCKBURN was not an old time man-of-war, but a relatively modern steel freighter. Through pilot house windows, sailors on the Lakes have said that they have looked across the tossing waters of Lake Superior and watched the three masts and tall stack of the BANNOCK-BURN ride past in misty majesty. So goes the tale.

It was a cold morning late in the season of 1902 when the BANNOCKBURN cleared Port Arthur, Ontario, for the lower Lakes. Late that evening, the upbound passenger steamer HURONIC of the Northern Navigation Company reported passing the BANNOCKBURN as the former pushed westward across a quiet lake. Though no storm was reported on that or succeeding nights, the BANNOCK-BURN vanished completely. No other ship ever saw her and for more than a year no wreckage was found. Some 15 months later, a lifebelt bearing the name of the missing ship was found on the shore. Around 1927, a quarter of a century afterward, a lifeboat's oar was found with the name BANNOCKBURN faintly legible. None of the many conjectures advanced to explain the event can account for the lack of floating wreckage. November 21, 1902 is a date

that will live on in memory as the beginning of the fabled "Flying Dutchman of the Great Lakes."

Around the tradition of the "Flying Dutchman," the English sailor-novelist, Captain Frederick Marryat, penned a classic story called "The Phantom Ship" wherein the riddle and mystery are solved theoretically, and the novel ends with the triumphant words. . . "and the Phantom Ship sailed the seas no more." But on the Great Lakes, especially Lake Superior, the BANNOCKBURN sails on. The story still remains one of the most vivid tales told around the warm fireplaces of Lake sailors during the winter months. Twenty men lost their lives back in 1902, but their plight lives on in legend even today.

BUILT:	Sir R. Dixon & Company, Middlesborough, England
LENGTH:	245
BREADTH:	40.1
DEPTH:	18.4
GROSS REGISTERED TONNAGE:	1,491
REGISTRY NUMBER:	B. 102093
ENGINES:	21″, 34″, 56″ diameter × 39″ stroke Triple Expansion
ENGINE BUILDER:	Northeastern Marine Engineering Company, Ltd., Newcastle, England

BANNOCKBURN with the GOVERNOR SMITH at Port Dalhousie

BAYANNA

ARAGON at the Soo

Aragon, b) **BAYANNA**		**GROSS REGISTERED**	
BUILT:	Detroit Dry Dock Co., Wyandotte, Michigan	*TONNAGE:*	1,450
HULL NUMBER:	123	*REGISTRY NUMBER:*	US 107228
LENGTH:	247.7	*ENGINES:*	17″, 27½″ & 46″ diameter × 36″ stroke
BREADTH:	42.6		Triple expansion
DEPTH:	14.8	*ENGINE BUILDER:*	Dry Dock Engine Wks., Detroit, Mich.

ARAGON unloading sand at Windsor

This veteran steel freighter was built in 1896 for the Argo Steamship Co., Cleveland. She went to salt water in 1903, but was returned to the Lakes trade in 1921 by Prindiville & Co., Chicago. She stranded on Wickett's Point, Lake Ontario, November 7, 1921, corn-laden from Chicago to Montreal, and was abandoned to the underwriters. The ship was salvaged by John E. Russell in 1922, and later sold to International Waterways Navigation Co., Ltd., Montreal, and converted to a scraper-type self unloader in 1927 (C. 150811). Ownership passed to Eugene Lefebre, Montreal, in 1935. In 1937, she was acquired by the Sterling Construc-

tion Co., Ltd., Windsor (Essex Transit Co.). She was sold in 1943 to Tees Transit Co., Hamilton, Ontario, and finally sold in 1946 to Bayswater Shipping, Ltd., Brockville, who renamed her BAYANNA.

In 1960 she received the texas, wheelhouse and stack from the scrapped COLLIER. She stranded near Deseronto, Ontario, in the Bay of Quinte on December 7, 1962 and was abandoned as a total loss. Although salvaged by P. E. LaRose, Williamsburg, Ontario, on December 10, 1963, she was gutted by fire in May 1964 and scrapped later that year at Deseronto.

ARAGON downbound in the Detroit River

BAYANNA westbound in the Soulanges Canal

BAYFIELD

The tug GENERAL U.S. GRANT was built in 1864. Her first enrollment was issued on May 21, 1864 to Harvey Booth of Grand Island, New York. She was readmeasured in May, 1865 (113.7' × 20.8' × 10.35'; 131.28 tons). On July 7, 1866, her enrollment was transferred to John Demass and George C. Codd, both of Detroit, Michigan. She remained under this Detroit ownership until June 10, 1872, when she was removed from American registry "because vessel was sold foreign, date of sale unspecified."

The date could not have been too "unspecified" because the tug was registered at Montreal the following day as the S.S. EDSALL, owned by L. A. Smith of Port Hope, Ontario. In October, 1876, she was sold to Andrew Wilson of Toronto. Four years later, on November 22, 1880, James Murray of St. Catharines, bought the tug and transferred her registry to Toronto.

On May 17, 1884, the tug appeared with a new name, BAYFIELD (C61153), having been purchased from Murray

two weeks earlier by the Minister of Marine and Fisheries. Her Canadian measures were 110' × 18'5" × 9'3", 150 gross tons; 94 registered tons. Under this name she became well known through her use as a survey steamer by the Canadian Government.

She was "sold out of service" on March 31, 1903 to E. J. "John" Harrison of Owen Sound, Ontario, who modestly renamed her HARRISON. On March 13, 1909, he gave the forty-five year old tug her fifth and last name, CHURCHILL. She reportedly was sold in 1910 to a "Mr. Shipman" of Sault Ste. Marie, Ontario but apparently this sale never materialized. Harrison remained her owner until she was removed from Canadian registry on December 29, 1937, because the "vessel believed out of existence; supposed to be sunk near Bruce Mines, Ontario." If indeed this was the case, her demise must have been at least a few years prior to 1937.

General U.S. Grant, b) Edsall, c) BAYFIELD, d) Harrison, e) Churchill

BUILT:	William Crosthwaite, Buffalo, New York	*GROSS REGISTERED TONNAGE:*	210.85/95
LENGTH:	113'	*REGISTRY NUMBER:*	US 10283
BREADTH:	21'	*ENGINES:*	One Cylinder
DEPTH:	9'6"		28" Diameter × 30" Stroke
		ENGINE BUILDER:	D. Bell Steam Engine Wks., Buffalo, New York

BAYFIELD as a tug

C. F. BIELMAN

In 1892 the wooden bulk cargo vessel C. F. BIELMAN was built for the Stewart Transportation Company of which Mr. C. F. Bielman of Detroit was owner. Originally the vessel had three masts, but in later years carried only two.

In 1896, the BIELMAN passed into the ownership of George Peck and carried a wide variety of cargoes. In 1902, the boat entered the fleet of the McLachlan Transportation Company owned by Henry McMorran of Port Huron, Michigan. The vessel often towed a schooner-barge behind her, carrying cargoes of pulpwood which were extremely lucrative for lake carriers at that time.

The Reid Wrecking Company of Port Huron and Sarnia, Ontario took over the vessel in 1918 and repowered it with a double steeple compound engine built by the King Iron Works of Buffalo, New York, to increase the vessel's speed.

The cylinders of this engine were: 18″, 18″, 52″, 52″ in diameter with a 42″ stroke. The BIELMAN returned to service under the flag of the Spokane Steamship Company which was managed by Captain Reid of Port Huron and had been rebuilt with eight hatches over only one cargo compartment. This was done to provide unobstructed movement in the hold when carrying autos.

After many years of successful service, the BIELMAN was retired after the season of 1926. It was largely dismantled at Port Huron and then towed up Lake Huron to Great Duck Island and sunk. Her skeleton can be seen today at low water. The BIELMAN is remembered as a faithful workhorse around Port Huron and Sarnia where she spent most of her career.

C. F. BIELMAN in 1903

BUILT:	F. W. Wheeler Company, West Bay City, Michigan	*GROSS REGISTERED TONNAGE:*	2,056
HULL NUMBER:	92	*REGISTRY NUMBER:*	US 126887
LENGTH:	291	*ENGINES:*	Triple expansion 20″, 33″, 54″ diameter × 42″ stroke
BREADTH:	41		
DEPTH:	19.8	*ENGINE BUILDER:*	Frontier Iron Works, Detroit, Michigan

CLARENCE A. BLACK

The steel bulk freighter CLARENCE A. BLACK was built in 1898 for the Northern Lakes Steamship Company. When scarcely a year old, she was purchased by Henry W. Oliver, who was acting for Andrew Carnegie and was assembling a fleet to transport ore for Carnegie's steel mills. Despite efforts by the Rockefeller interests to block them, Oliver and Carnegie succeeded in acquiring seven freighters altogether, and these formed the first Pittsburgh Steamship Company in mid-1899.

Six more freighters, the famous "College" group, brand new from shipyards, and named after prominent Eastern colleges, joined the fleet in 1900. The hassle between Rockefeller and Carnegie was ended early in 1901 when the new United States Steel Corporation (Elbert H. Gary and J. Pierpont Morgan) purchased them both. Thus the giant "steel trust" fleet with 112 ships known as the Pittsburgh Steamship Company came into being.

For 45 years the CLARENCE A. BLACK sailed as a "tin stacker." Traded to the U.S. Maritime Administration in 1942 in exchange for new tonnage, she continued to be operated by the Pittsburgh Steamship Company for the duration of World War II. At the end of the conflict, she was laid up in Erie Bay on Lake Erie and towed to Hamilton, Ontario in 1946 for scrapping.

Some vessels on the Lakes lead rather sheltered lives. They are not involved in any headline-making stories; they are not the causes for disasters; they are not unlucky ships. Such a vessel was the CLARENCE A. BLACK, who did her job without fanfare or repercussion, but when the time came to aid others in distress, she was on the scene. This was the case in the spring of 1942 after another ship of the fleet, the EUGENE J. BUFFINGTON, had run full-speed onto Boulder Reef in Lake Michigan. With the aid of the Great Lakes Towing Company's FAVORITE, the BLACK was lashed alongside the broken BUFFINGTON, which was then taken to South Chicago for repairs.

CLARENCE A. BLACK in the Detroit River

BUILT:	Cleveland Shipbuilding Company, Lorain, Ohio	*GROSS REGISTERED TONNAGE:*	4,521
HULL NUMBER:	31	*REGISTRY NUMBER:*	US 127300
LENGTH:	413.4	*ENGINES:*	22″, 35″, 58″ diameter × 40″ stroke
BREADTH:	50.2		Triple expansion
DEPTH:	24.5	*ENGINE BUILDER:*	Shipyard

CARL D. BRADLEY (2)

CARL D. BRADLEY in the Detroit River

BUILT: American Shipbuilding Company, Lorain, Ohio
HULL NUMBER: 797
LENGTH: 623.2
BREADTH: 65.2
DEPTH: 30.2

GROSS REGISTERED TONNAGE: 10,028
REGISTRY NUMBER: US 226776
ENGINES: Steam Turbine
ENGINE BUILDER: General Electric Company, Schenectady, New York

At the Soo

50   The Bradley Transportation Company of Rogers City, Michigan, had the largest self-unloading steel steamer on the Great Lakes built in 1927 and named her CARL D. BRADLEY after the President and Director of the firm. She served in the limestone and coal trades her entire career on the inland seas and set many cargo records in the process. The self-unloading type freighter was not rare on the Lakes at that time. That type of carrier had been in existence since the turn of the century but it had been perfected in the BRADLEY. She was by far the largest carrier on the Lakes at that time as well as being the largest self-unloader. It was a proud day for the citizens of Rogers City when she first steamed into port on her maiden voyage. The majority of her crew were from that small Northern Michigan port and the ship proved her worth to her owners over the next quarter century of her existence.

Her days of service came to an end in a violent storm on Lake Michigan on November 18, 1958. She had left the lower Lake Michigan port of Gary bound for Rogers City in ballast and was buffeted by gale force winds almost immediately after her departure. Heavy seas washed over the bow but the BRADLEY held course towards the northern part of the Lake. At approximately 5:30 that evening she broke in two and sank almost immediately off Gull Island.

Just before going down she had sent out distress signals which were heard by the Coast Guard and a German motor vessel in the vicinity. Both the motor vessel and a US Coast Guard cutter rushed to the position last broadcast and began the search for survivors. Only two men were rescued from the thirty-five crewmen aboard.

This was the most severe loss of life on Lake Michigan since the violent gales of the Armistice Day Storms of November 11, 1940. Later investigations and televised photos of her wreck on the bottom of the lake proved the BRADLEY had split in two before she sank. The mighty ship had suffered so severely from the huge seas in the last hours of her existence that she buckled and plunged to the bottom in only a few minutes.

Thus ended another career of a gallant ship and the lives of her captain and crew. The city of Rogers City was overwhelmed with grief. Most of the crewmen were residents of that small town and almost every family was involved. The entire Great Lakes community was shocked at the loss of the BRADLEY and the stories of her final days in service and of the bereaved town circulated for many weeks thereafter. In these days of extreme care for the safety of ships and men, the story of the BRADLEY could hardly be believed.

CARL D. BRADLEY under the Ambassador Bridge

CHARLES H. BRADLEY

CHARLES H. BRADLEY above the Soo Locks

This old lumber hooker was built in 1890 for the C. H. Bradley Lumber Company. The firm was a prospering enterprise in Bay City at the time, and this vessel was a much needed addition to its fleet. The design of the ship was typical of the steam lumber barges of the time, and, because of her powerful engine, this vessel could tow as many as three schooner-barges behind her.

In 1896, she was transferred to the O. W. Blodgett Lumber Company of the same city and did yeoman service for this firm, which was commonly known as the Bradley Transportation Company. The ship was designed so that she could carry the greatest number of planks at a convenient rate with easy and efficient unloading capacity for the stevedores. The BRADLEY was just the right depth to enable the men to unload her with ease, if this might be the term to use, because these vessels were all unloaded by hand. As many as three days were allowed to unload the ship and often the weather determined the extent of the time used to discharge the heavily laden vessels.

The danger of fire was always uppermost in the minds of the sailors and shore personnel when they worked these sturdy but vulnerable vessels. On October 9, 1931, after many years of service, the BRADLEY, too, met the fate so many of her compatriots had suffered in the past. She burned to the water line at Portage Lake, Michigan on the Keweenaw Peninsula that juts into Lake Superior. The hulk lay where it burned and her remains were never removed. The bitter end of the lumber transportation business on board Lake vessels was imminent. She and her consorts had lived successful lives, but progress supplanted them with self-propelled trucks and other vehicles to carry what little remained of the giant lumber tracts of Northern Michigan to the cities to the south. What was left of the lumber hooker fleets at the time of the BRADLEY's demise disappeared completely within a decade, and the very last wooden vessel engaged in this trade, the I. WATSON STEPHENSON, was retired in the early 1940's.

October 1931 Portage Entry, Lake Superior

BUILT:	F. W. Wheeler Shipbuilding Company, West Bay City, Michigan
HULL NUMBER:	75
LENGTH:	201
BREADTH:	37
DEPTH:	13.6
GROSS REGISTERED TONNAGE:	804
REGISTRY NUMBER:	US 126653
ENGINES:	24″, 48″ diameter × 40″ stroke Fore & Aft Compound
ENGINE BUILDER:	S. F. Hodge & Company, Detroit, Michigan

BRITAMOIL

This steel petroleum products tanker of "canal" dimensions was built for the British-American Oil Company of Canada in 1931. Her original name was an abbreviated form of her original owner's name, hence BRIT . . . AM . . . OIL.

Designed for service on the Great Lakes and coastal areas, she traded between British-American marine terminals, carrying a variety of petroleum products. In her later years, she was operated for British-American by the Gayport Shipping, Ltd., of Toronto, Ontario. The transfer in 1946 was to simplify the general operations of the Lakes' marine division of the Company.

In August of 1959, the entire British-American fleet (with one exception, B. A. PEERLESS) was sold to the Hall Corporation of Canada, and at this time BRITAMOIL was renamed ISLAND TRANSPORT. This was the first usage of this name in the fleet. The vessel was operated by Hall until December 17, 1960, at which time she was laid up at Port Weller, Ontario, her inactivity destined to last 2-1/2 years. Then, in April of 1963, she was purchased by Messrs. D'Alesio and Castaldi of Livorno, Italy. After undergoing a refit at Port Weller Dry Docks, she was renamed ELBA

on May 5th of the same year. ELBA, with Livorno as her new port of registry, left Port Weller on May 9, 1963 for the Mediterranean where the ship was to transport fuel oil between Italian Coastal ports. In 1968, her owners were P.G. & M. Castaldi of Italy. In 1975, she was sold to Cabotagi S.p.A. and in 1978 to Navalcarena S.p.A. As of this writing, she is still sailing those waters.

The business of transporting oil by water is not a novel one, but carrying it in bulk cargoes is relatively new. Prior to 1890, oil products were carried on board ship in barrels. At the turn of the century, after the petroleum industry expanded with the discovery of oil in the Sarnia, Ontario area, carriers for bulk oil products became a necessity on the Great Lakes. Early steel petroleum tankers were built in the shipyards of the Lakes in the 1890's, but these were intended for ocean-going service. Tanker barges were constructed for the Standard Oil Company and hauled to the East Coast ports through the Welland and St. Lawrence River Canals. The prototype of the Canadian tanker, similar to the BRITAMOIL, was constructed in the early 1900's. From then on, the tanker fleets expanded on both sides of the border, culminating with the giant carriers of the present day.

BRITAMOIL downbound in Lake St. Clair

ISLAND TRANSPORT (1) in Lake Huron

BRITAMOIL,
b) Island Transport (1),
c) Elba

BUILT:	Furness Shipbuilding Company, Ltd. Haverton-on-Tees, England
HULL NUMBER:	199
LENGTH:	258
BREADTH:	43.3
DEPTH:	18

GROSS REGISTERED TONNAGE:	1,931
REGISTRY NUMBER:	C. 157039
ENGINES:	17″, 28″, 46″ diameter × 36″ stroke Triple Expansion
ENGINE BUILDER:	Northeastern Marine Engineering Company, Ltd., Newcastle, England

ELBA at Port Weller

B. B. BUCKHOUT

B. B. BUCKHOUT in 1907

The two-masted wooden schooner-barge B. B. BUCK-HOUT was launched in April, 1873 for Mr. Buckhout's own account. She received her first enrollment from the Port Huron, Michigan, customs house on May 23rd of that same year. In 1884, she was purchased by A. C. McLean and W. H. Bridges, both of Bay City, Michigan. During the winter of 1887–1888, her rig was changed from two to three masts as she continued in the lumber trade for which she had been built. Also in 1888, she received a new bottom and was recaulked. In 1900, Mr. McLean became sole owner of the BUCKHOUT. In 1906, she was sold to Shannan & Garey Lumber Company of Bay City, for whom she continued hauling lumber until 1912.

The year 1907 proved to be quite an eventful one for this old lumber barge. On July 22nd, while in tow of the propellor HOMER WARREN with two other schooner barges, she stranded about ten miles west of Whitefish Point,

Lake Superior. Much of her lumber cargo, bound from Two Harbors, Minnesota, for Bay City, Michigan, had to be lightered. She finally was released on July 25th. The strain to her hull undoubtedly played a part in her next mishap that year. On August 31st, in tow of the wooden propellor TEMPEST, and bound from Blind River, Ontario, for Saginaw, the old vessel needed assistance to keep herself afloat. Four blasts of the steamer's whistle alerted the Thunder Bay Life Saving Service crew who relieved the BUCKHOUT's exhausted crew at the pumps. The schooner made the safety of Alpena harbor before settling. On June 29, 1912, she was dropped from American registry and sold to Rixon, Ainslie, Stoddart Company, Ltd., of Owen Sound, Ontario (C 126059; 155′ × 28′8″ × 10′; 341 registered tons). Her end came sometime prior to 1923 when her registry was closed.

BUILT: W. S. Campbell,
East Saginaw, Michigan
LENGTH: 158.2
BREADTH: 28.8
DEPTH: 10
GROSS REGISTERED
TONNAGE: 351
REGISTRY NUMBER: US 2857

B. B. BUCKHOUT last in line—Str. HOMER WARREN the Towing Steamer

At the Soo

RALPH BUDD

In 1905, the Western Transit Company, part of the New York Central Railroad, ordered a steel package freighter from the Great Lakes Engineering Works yard at Ecorse, Michigan. The company named this ship SUPERIOR.

The end of the railroad-controlled steamship lines came in 1915. All the various companies' package freight vessels were then transferred to other owners. The SUPERIOR went over to the newly organized Great Lakes Transit Corporation. For this firm she operated successfully as the RALPH BUDD (renamed in 1926) until a near fatal accident compelled the company to abandon her to the underwriters. On May 15, 1929, she ran ashore in a storm on Saltese Point on the Keweenaw Peninsula in Lake Superior. No loss of life occurred, but the ship was deemed a constructive total loss, so severe was the damage to her hull. She was recovered, however, released and rebuilt by the salvagers, J. T. Reid & Sons.

She was sold to the Great Lakes Transit Company, Ltd., a Canadian firm out of Midland, Ontario; (C. 154862). The BUDD appeared in the same colors as those of its former owners and sailed for this firm until 1938, when it was sold to the Upper Lakes & St. Lawrence Transportation Company, Ltd., of Toronto. Although a package freighter in her early life, she now engaged in the bulk freight trade, carrying grain from the Canadian lakehead to lower lake ports.

During her stay with Upper Lakes Shipping, she usually towed one of the whaleback barges, ALEXANDER HOL-LEY or #137. Her powerful engines enabled her to tow one barge, and she could tow two of them on occasion. The parade of steamers with tow-barges on the Lakes came to an end shortly after the opening of the St. Lawrence Seaway in 1959, when supplanted by the 730 foot steel giants that traverse the new canals of the St. Lawrence River. The BUDD was renamed L. A. McCORQUODALE in 1959 and in her final years was given two deck cranes in hope that she could once again compete in the package freight business. She was retired at the close of the 1963 season and was scrapped at Hamilton, Ontario in 1966.

SUPERIOR in the St. Mary's River

Superior,
b) RALPH BUDD,
c) L. A. McCorquodale

BUILT:	Great Lakes Engineering Works, Ecorse, Michigan
HULL NUMBER:	70
LENGTH:	382
BREADTH:	50
DEPTH:	30
GROSS REGISTERED TONNAGE:	4,544
REGISTRY NUMBER:	US 202329
ENGINES:	$20^{3}/_{4}''$, 30″, $43^{1}/_{2}''$, 63″ diameter × 42″ stroke Quadruple expansion
ENGINE BUILDER:	Shipyard

RALPH BUDD with whaleback 137

RALPH BUDD top view

58

L. A. McCORQUODALE at Point Edward with BRYN BARGE

In Lake Huron

BURLINGTON (1)

BURLINGTON in the St. Clair River

BURLINGTON (1),
   b) Juneau,
   c) Back Bay

BUILT:	Great Lakes Engineering Works, Ecorse, Michigan
HULL NUMBER:	36
LENGTH:	244
BREADTH:	43.2
DEPTH:	27
GROSS REGISTERED TONNAGE:	2,285
REGISTRY NUMBER:	US 204945
ENGINES:	16¾", 24", 35", 51" diameter × 36" stroke Quadruple expansion
ENGINE BUILDER:	Shipyard—1907

BURLINGTON at Detroit

JUNEAU on the coast

60

The bulk and package freight steel canallers were a breed peculiar to the old Welland and St. Lawrence River Canals. Because of their ability to fit the length of the canal locks, 263 feet, these ships served the Great Lakes and St. Lawrence River valley for over a century. With the advent of the St. Lawrence Seaway in 1959, a new breed of "canaller" has come into existence, the 730 foot bulk carrier, the maximum size vessel permitted in the new St. Lawrence Seaway System. The story of the BURLINGTON, built in 1908, concerns one of the few American canallers built to fit the earlier canals and locks.

The Rutland Transit Company, a Central of Vermont Railroad subsidiary, ordered a few canal-sized steamers after the turn of the century to supply its railroad divisions and retain control over its shipping routes which had been established in the 1880's. When the U.S. Government forced divesture by the railroads of their shipping interests in 1915, the BURLINGTON was sold to the Alaska Steamship Company which purchased the vessel in October of that year. She was renamed JUNEAU in 1915 and was taken overseas during World War I to serve on the coast during that conflict. On March 15, 1923, the vessel was purchased by the Gartland Steamship Company and brought back to the Great Lakes. The vessel was then renamed BACK BAY.

In her service on the Lakes, she resumed her former trade through the canals, this time in the scrap steel trade. In 1924, she was converted to a crane ship at Calumet Shipbuilding and Dry Dock Company, Chicago, Illinois, to enable her more easily to handle the cargoes of scrap steel. In this trade she served until World War II when the U.S. Maritime Administration took over her control. Again she was converted for ocean service at Ecorse in 1942, and taken through the canals for Wartime service across the Atlantic to Great Britain. In 1943, the boat once again came to the Lakes under the operation of the Gartland Steamship Company.

After the war, BACK BAY was no longer considered operable and she was sold for scrap by the U.S. Maritime Commission to the Washburn Wire Company and scrapped by them on the Seekong River near Phillipsdale, Rhode Island, in February of 1950.

BACK BAY at Cleveland

CADILLAC (2)

STEEL KING (1) in 1916

STEEL KING was a steel bulk freighter built in 1902 for the Gilchrist Transportation Company. Her sister ships were the F. M. OSBORNE and E. N. SAUNDERS. It is a unique coincidence when three ships, identical sisters, are built at the same time and place for the same new owners, and end their days together in the same place. This is what happened to these three. The other two were renamed once, while the STEEL KING had two later names.

Along with her sisters, the STEEL KING operated for the Gilchrist fleet from 1902 until 1912 when all three vessels were sold to James Davidson of Bay City. They were operated and managed by his son-in-law, George A. Tomlinson, until the winter of 1914–15, when they were purchased by the Cleveland-Cliffs Steamship Company to replace obsolete tonnage and to increase their new owner's capacity

in the defense effort of World War I. During the winter of 1916–17, STEEL KING became CADILLAC (2).

In 1923, the STEEL KING was reconstructed at River Rouge by the Great Lakes Engineering Works, and her gross tonnage was changed to 3,586. Here she received a new pilot house and other modifications. The OSBORNE and SAUNDERS were renamed MUNISING and NE-GAUNEE respectively.

Twice, in 1945 and again in 1949, the old sisters were laid up, and fears were spread that they would soon be scrapped as were other wartime trade-ins. Finally, Cliffs dropped their charters in September 1953 and the three sisters sailed to Buffalo under their own steam to be laid up for good. In 1954, their days ended together, the three vessels being scrapped at Buffalo, New York.

Steel King (1),
b) CADILLAC (2),
c) Chacornac

BUILT:	American Shipbuilding Company, Lorain, Ohio
HULL NUMBER:	316
LENGTH:	380
BREADTH:	50
DEPTH:	28

GROSS REGISTERED TONNAGE:	4,308
REGISTRY NUMBER:	US 117134
ENGINES:	22″, 35″, 58″ diameter × 40″ stroke Triple Expansion
ENGINE BUILDER:	American Shipbuilding Company, Cleveland, Ohio

CADILLAC at Detroit

CHACORNAC in Lake St. Clair

CHACORNAC in the Locks at the Soo

Downbound with iron ore

CAMBRIA (1)

CAMBRIA in 1906 at the Soo

CAMBRIA (1),
b) Lakeland

BUILT:	Globe Iron Works, Cleveland, Ohio
HULL NUMBER:	12
LENGTH:	280
BREADTH:	40
DEPTH:	20
GROSS REGISTERED TONNAGE:	1,878
REGISTRY NUMBER:	US 126420
ENGINES:	24″, 38″, 61″ diameter × 42″ stroke Triple expansion
ENGINE BUILDER:	Globe Iron Works

CAMBRIA in 1907

In 1887, the steel bulk freighter CAMBRIA was built for the Mutual Steamship Company, managed by M. A. Hanna & Co. This beautiful but rather small ship sailed the lakes for nearly three decades and had quite an interesting career.

In 1901, the newly organized Great Lakes vessel subsidiary of United States Steel Corporation, the Pittsburgh Steamship Company, took over the entire Mutual fleet. The steamer CAMBRIA was included in the transaction. With the arrival of many 600-foot vessels, the smaller CAMBRIA soon became obsolete. The vessel was sold to the Port Huron & Duluth Steamship Company and rebuilt as the passenger and freight vessel LAKELAND at Milwaukee, Wisconsin, in 1910. Palatial cabins were added to make her as handsome a vessel for her new owners as she had been a practical carrier in her prior duties as an ore carrier.

In 1917, ownership changed to the Northwestern Steamship Company, of Port Huron, Michigan. In 1921, LAKELAND was sold again to the Tri-States Steamship Company of Port Huron. During these years the ship served on a trade route from Port Huron to Duluth, Minnesota, with stops at Mackinac Island, Sault Ste. Marie, Michigan, and the Lakehead ports of Port Arthur, Fort William and Duluth-Superior.

In addition to the normal run she was often chartered to various other companies for special trips. Business also was sought for her freight carrying capacity. On one trip with general cargo and new automobiles aboard late in the season of 1924, LAKELAND was on Lake Michigan when she suddenly sank under mysterious circumstances near Sturgeon Bay, Wisconsin, on December 4th. The mystery of her sinking was not resolved at the time but all of her crew had time to take to the life boats and none was lost in spite of the cold wintry day when LAKELAND met her fate. The LAKELAND had been a suitable ship for both her trades, and the unfortunate circumstances of her demise did not diminish the appreciation her officers, crew, passengers and owners had for the excellence of the ship's handling ability in storms and heavy weather.

LAKELAND in the locks

Ready for business at Muskegon

Steaming up the St. Clair River

CAMPANA

North,
b) CAMPANA

BUILT:	Aitken & Mansel, Glasgow
HULL NUMBER:	64
LENGTH:	240.8
BREADTH:	35.3
DEPTH:	20.7
GROSS REGISTERED TONNAGE:	1185.40 (in 1880)
REGISTRY NUMBER:	C. 51646
ENGINES:	Compound surface condensing 30″ & 50″ × 33″ (shown as 26″ & 52″ × 33″ in 1881)
ENGINE BUILDER:	David Rowan & Co., Glasgow, Scotland

CAMPANA in the locks

CAMPANA was built as NORTH in 1873 as a freighter for the South American cattle trade. She was not originally under British registry. In 1878, while operating to the River Plate, the ship was chartered to transport 700 mules from Brazil to South Africa. She arrived safely but as her supercargo disappeared with a large sum of money, the vessel was ordered sold to pay the debt. Under these circumstances, the ship was registered at Cape Town on May 19, 1880 under ownership of Isabella Ohlsson, wife of Anders Ohlsson of Cape Town, Merchant.

Registry was transferred from Cape Town to London, England on March 31, 1881 with owner shown as James Casey of 10 Philpot Lane, London, Engineer.

The vessel was sold in June 1881 to Alexander M. Smith of Toronto who remained her registered owner until his death on January 19, 1895. She was next registered at Quebec, P.Q., on November 4, 1895 in the name of Charles Peter of Toronto, Merchant. Peter sold the hull on November 25, 1895 to the Quebec Steamship Co., Ltd. Quebec; revised

tonnage at that time was 1681 gross. When A. M. Smith (of Smith and Keightley) acquired her in 1881, she was cut in two and brought to the Upper Lakes for service on the Collingwood-Lake Superior run to fill in as a replacement for the burned CITY OF WINNIPEG of the Canada Lake Superior Transit Company. Renamed CAMPANA, she was converted from a freighter to a combination package freighter and passenger carrier at Owen Sound during the winter of 1881–82. When the ship came out in 1882, she was chartered to the Canadian Pacific Railway and remained in their service until superseded by MANITOBA which began operation in 1890. In 1893 CAMPANA operated to the Worlds Fair at Chicago. She remained in service in the Lakes until sold to the Quebec Steamship Company in 1895 for service between Montreal, Quebec and Prince Edward Island. She stranded and broke in two on the Wye Rock at Point St. Michel on the north shore of the St. Lawrence on June 17, 1909. The wreck was abandoned as a total loss.

CAMPANA with a good crowd leaving Sarnia

CANADIAN SIGNALLER

CANADIAN SIGNALLER at the Soo

A steel bulk freighter built in 1919 for the Canadian Government Merchant Marine at a cost of $814,926, CANADIAN SIGNALLER was originally intended for salt water service. Similar in design to the American "Lakers" of World War I, these sturdy craft saw service all over the world. All the Canadian vessels of this type were named after various trades and prefixed by the word "Canadian," a practice that has been revived recently by Upper Lakes Shipping, Ltd.

During the early 1920's, she operated in the Canadian Grain Trade. The vessel was sold in 1925 to James Playfair's Canada-Cuba Line and renamed EMPEROR OF HALIFAX. This venture was not a success and she was sold again to an associate of Playfair's, Frank M. Ross of Montreal, in 1928. Somewhere in the history of this vessel, she was supposed to be renamed LAKE TAMARAC but no record of this name appears in any of the Lloyds Registers of Shipping. Ross in turn sold her in 1929 to Alfred J. Buckingham. On September 3, 1929, the vessel was sold again, this time to Norwegian Interests and renamed SKJOLDHEIM (A/S "SKJOLDHEIM", Christiansand, Norway). The ship was renamed POLYANA and served for A. S. Hank until 1941 when she was lost on a voyage from Sunderland, England to Freetown. In the early morning of April 25, she was attacked by U103; Captain Schulze, and sunk in the German guadrant EH 9356, 24N/27W at 0038 hours.

CANADIAN SIGNALLER, b) Emperor of Halifax, c) Skjoldheim, d) Polyana

BUILT:	Collingwood Shipbuilding Co., Collingwood, Ontario	*GROSS REGISTERED TONNAGE:*	2,415
HULL NUMBER:	63	*REGISTRY NUMBER:*	C. 141479
LENGTH:	251	*ENGINES:*	16″, 27″ & 44″ diameter × 33″ stroke
BREADTH:	43.6		Triple expansion
DEPTH:	26.1	*ENGINE BUILDER:*	Shipyard

CAROLINA

The iron steamer HARTFORD was built in 1892 for the Hartford and New York Transportation Company of Hartford, Connecticut, to run between New England ports and New York. However, she was seized in 1897 by the United States government for running contraband guns to insurgents in Cuba.

The vessel was assigned to the United States Army Quartermaster Corp for use as a hospital ship during the Spanish-American War, and was renamed the TERRY. In April, 1901, she was sold to the Chicago and Muskegon Transportation Company (the Barry Line), of Muskegon, Michigan, and came to the Great Lakes as HARTFORD. That same year, she was placed on the Muskegon-Chicago route and renamed CHARLES H. HACKLEY (1304 gross tons), carrying passengers and freight.

On April 6, 1905, she was sold through a United States Marshall's sale to Thomas Hume, of Muskegon, and two weeks later integrated into the Hackley Transportation Company, also at Muskegon. She then resumed her former route. Following the burning of Goodrich Transit Company's ATLANTA in 1906, the HACKLEY was acquired by that firm as a replacement. The Goodrich Line renamed her CAROLINA.

She continued under Goodrich colors until the financial picture darkened in the 1930's. Then, on May 10, 1933, she was sold at a public auction at Chicago to William F. Price, of the First Union Trust and Savings Company of Chicago. The following year, the Chriscarala Corporation of Chicago, became her owner. They laid up the CAROLINA at Sturgeon Bay, Wisconsin. In 1937, she was cut down to her main deck. She went out of documentation in 1940. Reportedly she was sold to John Roen and scrapped at Sturgeon Bay about 1942.

CHARLES H. HACKLEY at dock at Muskegon

CAROLINA underway

Hartford, b) USS Terry, c) Hartford, d) Charles H. Hackley, e) CAROLINA

BUILT:	Neafie & Levy, Philadelphia, Pennsylvania	*GROSS REGISTERED TONNAGE:*	1,337
LENGTH:	220′	*REGISTRY NUMBER:*	US 96172
BREADTH:	40′	*ENGINES:*	Fore and Aft Compound (2)
DEPTH:	13′		20″–40″ Diameter × 48″ Stroke
		ENGINE BUILDER:	Shipyard

W. J. CARTER

W. J. CARTER loading lumber

The wooden steam barge W. J. CARTER, a lumber hooker, was built in 1886 for W. J. Carter and J. R. Cook. One of the workhorses of the Lakes, the W. J. CARTER operated for numerous companies and diverse managers engaged in the lumber and coal trades. In 1896, the vessel belonged to J. E. Danaher; in 1902 to Captain J. B. Hall; in 1904 to John W. Greenwood and in 1908 to the Churchill Lumber Company of Alpena, Michigan under the management of F. G. Kimball. For this large enterprise it ran until 1913, when it was sold to Finn and Olsen Freighting Company of Ogdensburg, New York. In 1918, the CARTER went to the Ogdensburg Steamship Company and in 1919 to the St. Lawrence Coal and Freighting Co. On April 20, 1920, it was sold to Robert Hicks Coal and Towing Company of Cobourg, Ontario, and transferred into Canadian Registry (C. 141764).

During a gale on Lake Ontario on the afternoon of July 28, 1923, the CARTER, laden with coal from Oswego, New York, to Cobourg, Ontario sprung a leak and foundered 20 miles south of Point Peter. Her crew of eight men and one woman took to the lifeboats and tried to ride out the storm. They were picked up later that same afternoon by the canal steamer KEYPORT. Another name had been added to the long list of lost ships. The old steam barge had engaged in Great Lakes commerce for 37 years, a long life for a wooden ship!

The cities of Chicago, Detroit, Cleveland, Buffalo and Toronto, all large metropolitan areas today, were greatly enhanced in their growth by the cargoes of lumber hauled by these pioneer wooden steam barges. These cities were dependent on the lumber hookers and their cargoes all through the later 1800's and early 1900's. The boom of the lumber business and the insatiable appetite of the lumber barons for gold to line their pockets increased from the 1870's until it peaked in 1880. The cities were largely made of wood as were the vessels which transported it. The denuding of the mid-western forests continued unabated until there was no more supply and the wooden vessels which bore the brunt of lake storms passed into oblivion when the oak beams and planks could no longer be obtained to repair them and the giant steel vessels of today supplanted them.

Ready to load

BUILT:	Wolf and Davidson Shipbuilding Company, Milwaukee, Wisconsin	*REGISTRY NUMBER:*	US 81112
LENGTH:	122	*ENGINES:*	15″ and 28″ diameter × 26″ stroke Steeple compound
BREADTH:	28	*ENGINE BUILDER:*	Sheriffs Manufacturing Company, Milwaukee, Wisconsin
DEPTH:	9.6		
GROSS REGISTERED TONNAGE:	235.13		

In the St. Clair River

J. I. CASE

J. I. CASE at Pugh's dock in Racine

This full-rigged, three masted wooden schooner was built in 1874 for the J. I. Case Plow Works Company, of Racine, Wisconsin. F. M. Knapp of Racine acted as managing operator of the company's Great Lakes ships. The J. I. CASE was one of the largest three masters built on inland waters, and her main mast, towering nearly 200 feet above the waterline, was the loftiest on the Great Lakes. In her prime, the CASE had a white hull with green water line and white cabins. Because of her size, the CASE was a rare visitor to her home port of Racine where the narrow and often shallow Root River would not admit so large a vessel. Only in times of high water could the vessel dock there. (One such occasion is shown in the accompanying photograph, where the CASE is unloading a cargo of coal at the Pugh Brothers dock near the mouth of the Root River.)

This vessel sailed for Case and Knapp until 1892, when it was sold to John Corrigan of Cleveland, Ohio, and cut down to a tow barge. Subsequent owners were: C. E. Eastman of Saginaw, Michigan, in 1897; James Corrigan, again, in 1900; James O'Connor of Tonawanda, New York, in 1905; Frank Ronecker, also of Tonawanda, in 1908; Boland and Cornelius in 1909; Edward Hines Lumber Company of Chicago in 1912; and finally Sincennes-McNaughton Lines of Montreal, Canada, in 1920 (C. 141595). The vessel was abandoned because of its age and scuttled in deep water in the St. Lawrence River near Quebec City in the fall of 1933. Her official Canadian registry, however, was not closed until 1937.

This fine schooner had been named for Jerome I. Case, founder and first president of the Case Company. It is interesting to note that if the J. I. CASE were sailing today, fully rigged, she could not pass under a single bridge over any river, harbor or strait in the entire Great Lakes system, due to the maximum clearance over the water being about 120′, much less than the original masts could clear.

In the drydock

BUILT:	Rand and Burger, Manitowoc, Wisconsin	DEPTH:	14.5
LENGTH:	208	GROSS REGISTERED TONNAGE:	827
BREADTH:	34.5	REGISTRY NUMBER:	US 75720

CAYUGA

CAYUGA c. 1910

The Niagara Navigation Company Ltd., Toronto, decided in 1905 to order a steel, twin-screw passenger vessel to augment its service between Toronto and Niagara River ports. Designed by the well known naval architect Arendt Angstrom, who also was general manager of the shipyard, the new boat was christened CAYUGA by Miss Mary Osler, daughter of N.N.Co. president E. B. Osler. The launch took place in heavy rain on March 3, 1907.

Work on the upperworks proceeded quickly and CAYUGA ran her preliminary builder's trial trip on July 27, 1907, at which time her engines proved to be satisfactory. The official trial run took place on August 15th when she made an average speed of 21-1/2 m.p.h., and for two hours managed 22 m.p.h., over the 84-mile distance between Gibraltar Point Light at Toronto and Braddock's Light at Charlotte, New York. New blades were fitted on her propellors at Kingston in the autumn of 1907. She actually began regular service on June 10, 1908.

Niagara Navigation Company became a subsidiary of the Richelieu and Ontario Navigation Company Ltd., Montreal, in 1912 and in 1913, the R & O in turn was absorbed into Canada Steamship Lines Ltd. During the winter of 1946–47, CAYUGA was reboilered and converted to oil fuel at Kingston, Ontario. After a period of inactivity, she was sold by C.S.L. to the Cayuga Steamship Company Ltd., Toronto, in 1954 and she remained on the Niagara run through 1957. After lying idle at Toronto, she was scrapped there in 1961.

CAYUGA entered service when the Niagara River Line was at the height of its popularity, her running mates being CHICORA, CORONA and CHIPPEWA. One by one, these vessels were retired due to age, and after 1936, CAYUGA carried on alone.

Coming to the dock at Queenston

CAYUGA at Toronto

In Niagara River

Being scrapped 1961

BUILT:	Canadian Shipbuilding Co., Ltd., Toronto	*GROSS REGISTERED TONNAGE:*	2,196	
HULL NUMBER:	100	*REGISTRY NUMBER:*	C. 122219	
LENGTH:	306	*ENGINES:*	17½", 25", 36" & 52" diameter × 30" stroke	
BREADTH:	36.6 (inside guards)—51.8 overall		Twin Quadruple expansion	
DEPTH:	18	*ENGINE BUILDER:*	Shipyard	

CEDARVILLE

A. F. HARVEY (2) in the ice

Launched on the 9th of April, 1927 and christened by 15 year old Sarah Harvey, niece of Harvey, this was a bulk freighter in the Pittsburgh Steamship Company, part of United States Steel Corporation. Early in her career, on May 18, 1928, the HARVEY collided with the JOHN ERICSSON on Lake Huron in a dense fog. The ERICSSON was badly damaged but the HARVEY escaped serious injury. In her usual route the vessel carried iron ore cargoes from Duluth and Two Harbors, Minnesota, to lower lake ports. In 1956, she was transferred to the Bradley Transportation Company, a division of US Steel, and renamed CEDAR-VILLE. During the winter of 1956–57, she was converted to a self-unloader at the Defoe Shipbuilding Company, Bay City, Michigan, and entered the limestone and coal trade. The hull was painted in the customary grey color so familiar to the Bradley fleet over the years. In 1961, she was reboiled and a new streamlined stack was installed.

She served her owners well until the late morning hours of May 7, 1965. Groping her way through a dense fog just east of Mackinaw City in the Straits of Mackinac, the CEDARVILLE collided with the Norwegian motor vessel TOPDALSFJORD. The CEDARVILLE, loaded with limestone from Calcite, Michigan, sank within 21 minutes of the collision. Twenty-three survivors and two bodies were picked up from the icy waters by the German motorship WEISSENBURG. Ten other crewmen from the CEDAR-VILLE died in the tragedy but no one was lost from the TOPDALSFJORD. The latter ship proceeded to her destination after inspection by the Coast Guard, her hull battered but not in a sinking condition.

The CEDARVILLE's resting place on the bottom has become the grave for more men seeking to divest her of the few marine artifacts left on board. Skin divers have made her a frequent diving spot but the waters and the current have taken their toll so that the wreck has become known as a grave for unsuspecting and cautionless divers.

A. F. HARVEY (2) upbound at Mission Point

A. F. HARVEY (2) downbound with iron ore

CEDARVILLE downbound light

A. F. Harvey (2),
b) CEDARVILLE

BUILT:	Great Lakes Engineering Works, River Rouge, Michigan
HULL NUMBER:	255
LENGTH:	588.3
BREADTH:	60.2
DEPTH:	27.8
GROSS REGISTERED TONNAGE:	8,575
REGISTRY NUMBER:	US 226492
ENGINES:	24½″, 41″, 65″ diameter × 42″ stroke Triple expansion
ENGINE BUILDER:	Shipyard

CEDARVILLE in the St. Mary's River

CETUS

While it is not uncommon to find among Great Lakes ships two vessels having the same name, it is much more unusual to have one vessel bear the same name at two different times. Such was the case of the steel bulk freighter CETUS. Originally built in 1903 as the HENRY S. SILL for the Gilchrist Transportation Company, this vessel sailed for her first owners for an even decade. Interlake Steamship Company was organized in 1913 and bought many of the former Gilchrist fleet including the SILL which they renamed CETUS, for the first time.

In the fall of 1923 this ship sunk the HURONTON in Lake Superior off Caribou. Her bow was well stove in and Interlake put her in dry dock at Cleveland at the foot of West 54th street. Before repairs were made Forest City Steamship Co. bought her, as is, then made repairs and operated her the rest of that fall. In the spring of 1924 her name was changed to SAMUEL H. SQUIRE in honor of a banker friend of Mr. William Rap-

prich. Mr. Squire was from Elyria, Ohio and was a stockholder of Forest City Steamship Co. He was instrumental in getting other investors in that area, among them Mr. David S. Troxel, head of Troxel Mfg. Co., makers of bicycle and motorcycle seats. When Forest City Steamship Company ceased operations in 1928, the vessel was back in the Interlake fleet and carrying the name CETUS again.

In 1942, CETUS was one of several smaller freighters traded in to the US Maritime Commission in exchange for new tonnage. The ship was operated by Interlake management for the duration of World War II at the request of the Maritime Board. After the war ended in 1945, CETUS and 46 other war fleet vessels were laid up at Erie, Pennsylvania, in the same bay that once held Commodore Perry's fleet in 1813. Gradually each vessel was sent to the scrapper's torches at Hamilton, Ontario. CETUS was scrapped there in 1947.

HENRY S. SILL in 1912

CETUS in the St. Clair River

Henry S. Sill, b) Cetus, c) Samuel H. Squire, d) CETUS

BUILT:	Superior Shipbuilding Company, W. Superior, Wisconsin	*GROSS REGISTERED TONNAGE:*	4,720
		REGISTRY NUMBER:	US 200374
HULL NUMBER:	417	*ENGINES:*	22″, 35″, 58″ diameter × 40″ stroke
LENGTH:	416		Triple expansion
BREADTH:	50	*ENGINE BUILDER:*	Shipyard
DEPTH:	28		

SAMUEL H. SQUIRE in 1925

CETUS in the Detroit River

CHICAGO

CHICAGO in 1915

The steel package freighter CHICAGO was built for the Western Transit Company in 1901. The firm was the steamship division of the New York Central Railroad and served various ports on the Great Lakes with package freight and refrigerated service. The CHICAGO was a fast boat and served well throughout its brief career as a member of the Western Transit Company.

In 1915, when the United States government forced divestiture by the railroads of their steamship divisions because of anti-trust suits brought against them, the Western Transit Company sold its freighters to the newly organized Great Lakes Transit Corporation (GLTC) of Buffalo, New York. The CHICAGO operated in the package freight trade on the Lakes for this new owner. The GLTC also took over the Anchor Line in 1915. In 1925, all vessels of the fleet were painted white, adopting the former Anchor Line fleet markings.

The CHICAGO came to a sudden end just before the close of the 1929 season. A huge storm system enveloped the Great Lakes area towards the end of that year, and the ship was claimed as one of its victims. She was driven on the reef off Michipicoten Island in Lake Superior, on October 23, 1929, by the heavy seas. Because of the extreme heroism of some of the crew, all members of the ship's company were rescued. The icy waters of Lake Superior did not claim any human lives during this encounter but they did overcome the vessel. Salvage attempts were constantly thwarted after the storm in October, and November proved no calmer. The CHICAGO subsequently slid into deep water on December 19, 1929, and was declared a complete loss.

BUILT:	Buffalo Shipbuilding Company, Buffalo, New York	*GROSS REGISTERED TONNAGE:*	3,195
HULL NUMBER:	100	*REGISTRY NUMBER:*	US 127590
LENGTH:	324.2	*ENGINES:*	19″, 27½″, 48″, 58″ diameter × 42″ stroke Quadruple expansion
BREADTH:	44		
DEPTH:	14	*ENGINE BUILDER:*	Detroit Shipbuilding Company, Detroit, Mich.

CHICAGO in later years at Chicago

CHICORA

Originally built as a blockade runner in 1864, CHICORA's hull was paddle driven and divided into six watertight sections. She had a long turtle-backed forecastle. Owned initially by the Chicora Company of Charleston, South Carolina, she led a charmed life during her blockade running days and appears to have been the last runner to leave Charleston before its fall on February 7, 1865.

On February 1, 1866, she entered Canadian Registry at Halifax and in 1868 came to the Lakes, owned by a syndicate headed by Donald Milloy of Toronto. Cut in two at Quebec City in 1867, the sections were towed to Buffalo where she was rejoined and converted into an overnight lake-type passenger ship. She operated from Collingwood to Fort William. During the period 1868–1873, her cabins were enlarged several times. In 1870, she served as a troopship carrying Lord Wolseley's expedition to the Canadian Northwest. Laid up at Collingwood in 1873, she came out again in July and August 1874 as a private yacht for Lord Dufferin, Governor General of Canada.

Returned to lay-up at Collingwood, she remained inactive until 1877. She was then purchased by the Honorable Frank Smith and Barlow Cumberland, founders of the Niagara Navigation Co. Towed to Buffalo, she was again cut in two for passage through the Welland Canal. Rejoined at Port Dalhousie, she was rebuilt at Toronto in 1878 as a day steamer. She was placed in service on the Toronto-Niagara River run where she served without interruption until 1912. She then operated between Toronto and Olcott Beach, New York. She was withdrawn from service in 1914 by Canada Steamship Lines, and foundered at her dock in Toronto on October 27, 1919.

Raised later in the year, her hull was cut down to a barge in 1921 and sold to the Warren Transportation Co., Toronto. She was sold in 1923 to the Quinte Coal and Towage Co. By 1926, she was owned by the Pyke Salvage Co., Ltd., Kingston. She was rammed and sunk by SPRUCEBAY in Kingston Harbor in 1938. After being raised, her hull was found to be so badly damaged that she was broken up on Howe Island.

CHICORA early photo at the Soo

CHICORA at the dock

Let Her B.,
b) CHICORA,
c) Warrenko

BUILT:	William C. Miller & Son, Birkenhead, England
LENGTH:	221
BREADTH:	26
DEPTH:	10.9

GROSS REGISTERED TONNAGE:	740
REGISTRY NUMBER:	C. 53588
ENGINES:	52″ diameter × 48″ stroke Oscillating Condensing two cylinder
ENGINE BUILDER:	Fawcett & Preston, Liverpool, England

Leaving Toronto c. 1907

CHIPPEWA (2)

WILLIAM P. FESSENDEN

William P. Fessenden,
b) CHIPPEWA (2)

BUILT:	Union Dry Dock Co., Buffalo, New York
HULL NUMBER:	33
LENGTH:	191.8
BREADTH:	28
DEPTH:	12'6"
DISPLACEMENT TONNAGE:	545
ENGINES:	Beam Condensing 48" Diameter × 108" Stroke
ENGINE BUILDER:	Fletcher & Harrison, Hoboken, New Jersey—1866

With the ALEXANDER J. DALLAS on the outside

The iron sidewheel revenue cutter WILLIAM P. FES-SENDEN, the second revenue cutter to bear that name, was built in 1883. Her beam condensing engine with paddle wheels outside the hull came from her namesake predecessor. For twenty years the FESSENDEN was a familiar sight on the Great Lakes, especially at her headquarters, Detroit, at the famous government anchorage of "Chicken Bone Reef."

In 1903, she was taken to the Atlantic Coast, and for two years underwent repairs at Arundel Cove, Maryland. From 1905 through 1907, she was stationed at Key West, Florida.

In 1909, she was purchased by George Craig and rebuilt at Toledo, Ohio, as the attractive passenger steamer CHIPPEWA (US 206249; 198' × 28' × 10'; 452 gross tons, 285 net tons). She also received two new boilers (6'8" × 18') built by the Marine Boiler Works of Toledo. Craig, who had business connections with George Arnold, sold her to the Arnold Transit Company in 1913 for service between Cheboygan, Mackinac Island, and Sault Ste. Marie, Michigan.

She continued in the service until November 21, 1922, when the Sandusky and Islands Steamboat Company of Sandusky, Ohio, purchased her to replace the ARROW, which had recently burned. She served the western Lake Erie trade faithfully until 1938, carrying passengers, with an occasional excursion, and grapes on a seasonal basis. In 1938 the CHIPPEWA was supplanted by the smaller CITY OF HANCOCK. Her superstructure and engines were removed, and the hull was sold to the Peerless Cement Company for use as a barge.

She caused some consternation on June 1, 1942, when she broke away from the tug AMERICA while off Middle Sister Island, Lake Erie. The tug PROGRESSO ultimately picked her up and towed her into Amherstburg. Captain J. Earl McQueen, owner of the latter tug, sold her to the Steel Company of Canada, Ltd., and the old iron hull was scrapped at Hamilton, Ontario, in 1943, to aid the allied effort in World War II.

CHIPPEWA on Lake Erie

CHIPPEWA in the St. Mary's River

CHIPPEWA

When the directors of the Niagara Navigation Company Ltd., Toronto, decided in 1892 to add an additional steamer to their Lake Ontario operation between Toronto and Niagara River ports, they engaged the services of Frank E. Kirby to draw up the plans. The Hamilton Bridge and Shipbuilding Company was the successful tenderer for construction of the hull, boilers and upperworks. The work was done under the supervision of William Hendrie, president of the Hamilton firm and also a director of Niagara Navigation Co.

CHIPPEWA was launched at Hamilton on Tuesday, May 2, 1893 and was christened by Miss Mary Osler, daughter of Niagara Navigation director E. B. Osler, and by Miss Mildred Cumberland, daughter of Barlow Cumberland, General Manager of the company.

Her first trial trip was made July 26, 1893 but she did not officially join the Niagara Navigation fleet until May 1894, when her inaugural trip from Hamilton to Toronto was made with Capt. J. McGiffin on the bridge and William Fletcher at the controls of the engine his company had built.

The Niagara Navigation Company Ltd. was absorbed by the Richelieu and Ontario Navigation Company Ltd. in 1912. The R & O was swallowed up when Canada Steamship Lines Ltd. was formed in 1913.

CHIPPEWA continued in service on the Toronto-Niagara run until the close of the 1936 season. She was laid up at Toronto and remained idle until 1939 when her superstructure was stripped off. The hull was towed to Hamilton by the C.S.L. package freighter CITY OF MONTREAL on Sept. 19, 1939. Berthed at the scrapping yard of the Steel Company of Canada, she was soon cut up for scrap. Her registry was officially closed on Sept. 26, 1939.

CHIPPEWA in the Niagara River

BUILT:	Hamilton Bridge Company, Hamilton, Ontario	*GROSS REGISTERED TONNAGE:*	1514
HULL NUMBER:	2	*REGISTRY NUMBER:*	C. 100753
LENGTH:	308.5	*ENGINES:*	Beam Condensing
BREADTH:	36.3 (over guards 72)		75″ Diameter of Cylinder × 132″ Stroke
DEPTH:	12.5	*ENGINE BUILDER:*	W. & A. Fletcher Co., Hoboken, N.J.

CHIPPEWA
(1900)

CHIPPEWA at Mackinac Island

BUILT:	Craig Shipbuilding Company, Toledo, Ohio	*GROSS REGISTERED TONNAGE:*	996
HULL NUMBER:	78	*REGISTRY NUMBER:*	US 127440
LENGTH:	200	*ENGINES:*	Triple Expansion
BREADTH:	34.4		20″, 32½″, & 55″ Diameter ×
DEPTH:	19.8		30″ Stroke
		ENGINE BUILDER:	Shipyard

At Cheboygan with the IROQUOIS

S.S. "Chippewa" sailing between Victoria, B.C., and Seattle, Wash., U.S.A.

CHIPPEWA on the coast

In 1900, the Arnold Transit Company of Mackinac Island, Michigan, ordered a steel day-passenger propellor, the CHIPPEWA, the first of the many Arnold ships to carry that name, and she was launched at Toledo that same year. Her route was to be between Mackinac Island and Sault Ste. Marie. The following year, a new sister (IROQUOIS) was built for the same service. Two such ships, however, were more than Arnold needed for this route and, as a consequence, IROQUOIS spent most of her early years on charter while CHIPPEWA alone carried the Soo traffic.

In 1907, both ships were sold to the Black Ball Line

(Puget Sound Navigation Company) of Seattle. Since this was before the completion of the Panama Canal, both vessels made the long trip via the Magellan Straits around the horn of South America.

In 1932, CHIPPEWA was repowered with a Busch-Sulzer 8-cylinder diesel engine and rebuilt as a double-ended ferry. (200′ × 50.1′ × 17.1′; 887 gross tons.) As newer units were added to the State of Washington Ferry Service, CHIPPEWA was laid up in 1964 and listed as "Out of Documentation" in 1969. Unofficial reports indicate that the vessel burned and was scrapped.

As a double-ender

ALVAH S. CHISHOLM, JR.

ALVAH S. CHISHOLM, JR. in Lake Erie

The small twin engined wooden steamer ALVAH S. CHISHOLM, JR. was built in 1900 as a bulk freighter with separable compartments to facilitate the bulk carriage of sand. The original owner was the Kelley Island Lime and Transport Company, one of whose principals was Mr. James Corrigan and another, Mr. Chisholm, Sr. In 1906 the vessel received a new engine, a fore and aft compound of 16″ and 32″ diameter cylinders by a 24″ stroke built by the American Shipbuilding Company of Cleveland, Ohio. The CHISHOLM became a single screw steamer with this installment. The ship was converted to a sandsucker (dredge) in 1910 and served the line in that capacity until 1930.

On March 16, 1930 it was sold to the Lampe Construction and Trading Company who removed the engine to lighten the ship and increase carrying capacity as a barge. The scheme did not work and, shortly afterwards, the vessel was laid-up. It was sold in 1934 to the Lorain Washed Sand Company but was never moved. Following a fire on May 11, 1935 it was declared a total loss. When the City of Sandusky was renovating its waterfront, the CHISHOLM, JR. was ordered moved. It was towed into Lake Erie in July, 1937 and sunk. In 1940 the hull was taken to Plaster Bend, Ohio to be used as a dock. Her document was surrendered on December, 17, 1940.

At the dock at Kelley's Island

BUILT:	Alex Anderson, Marine City, Michigan	*GROSS REGISTERED TONNAGE:*	435
LENGTH:	152	*REGISTRY NUMBER:*	US 107557
BREADTH:	35	*ENGINES:*	Fore & Aft compound (2)
DEPTH:	8		12″ & 22″ diameter × 12″ stroke
			12″ & 20″ diameter × 10″ stroke

CITY OF ALPENA

CITY OF ALPENA passing the CITY OF DETROIT—painting by Sprague

The CITY OF ALPENA was launched on March 13, 1893 for the Detroit and Cleveland Steam Navigation Company. She was built expressly to serve the company's Lake Huron Division, "The Coast Line to Mackinac." She and her sister, the CITY OF MACKINAC, were the first of their type to receive bow rudders to enable them to back out unassisted from the small harbors along the Michigan shore of Lake Huron. During the summer months each vessel made two round trips per week between Toledo, Ohio and St. Ignace, Michigan. In 1912, the CITY OF ALPENA had the Roman numeral "II" added to her name.

With the beginning of World War I, business began to diminish. The "ALPENA II" lay idle at Detroit from 1919 to 1921. In 1921, she was sold to the Graham and Morton Transportation Company, Chicago, for service from Chicago to Holland and Saugatuck on Lake Michigan, and was renamed CITY OF SAUGATUCK. In 1924, Goodrich Tran-

sit Company acquired the G. & M. Line, and "SAUGATUCK" remained with Goodrich until that firm ceased operations in 1933. The Michigan Trust Company of Duluth, Minnesota, held the mortgage until 1938. In that year, the ship was acquired by Roen Steamship Company, Sturgeon Bay, Wisconsin, was renamed LEONA, and reduced to a pulpwood barge (241'7" × 38'5" × 13'3"; 999 gross tons and net tons).

In 1945 the Northern Paper Mills (Wisconsin) of Green Bay, Wisconsin, purchased the barge. The following year it was transferred to a Canadian subsidiary, Northern Paper Mills, Ltd., of Hansen, Ontario (241' × 39' × 13'3"; 987 gross and registered tons) and renamed NORMIL (C 176163). In 1955 Marathon Corporation of Canada, Ltd., Marathon, Ontario, became the owner, but operated the barge only slightly and finally scrapped the vessel in 1957.

CITY OF ALPENA at the dock at Alpena

CITY OF ALPENA, b) City of Alpena II c) City of Saugatuck, d) Leona, e) Normil

BUILT:	Detroit Dry Dock Company, Wyandotte, Michigan	*GROSS REGISTERED TONNAGE:*	1,735
HULL NUMBER:	114	*REGISTRY NUMBER:*	US 126974
LENGTH:	266.2	*ENGINES:*	Beam Condensing
BREADTH:	69.8		44″, 66″ & 90″ Diameter × 132″
DEPTH:	13.4		Stroke
		ENGINE BUILDER:	W. & A. Fletcher Company, Hoboken, New Jersey

CITY OF SAUGATUCK entering Holland harbor

LEONA in the St. Mary's River

NORMIL at Sturgeon Bay

CITY OF BANGOR

Mr. F. W. Wheeler had been a noted shipbuilder in West Bay City for many years. He had produced mostly wooden vessels which had served on the Lakes very well but in the 1890's turned his attention to steel ships. Such a vessel was the bulk freighter CITY OF BANGOR built in 1896 for the Eddy-Shaw firm of Bay City, Michigan. In 1905, the ship was lengthened to 445.5 feet to give her a greater capacity. The Lake Transit Company bought the vessel in 1906 to operate in the iron ore, coal and grain trades. For the next twenty years she operated with few unexpected incidences to marr her career.

Due to her relatively small capacity, even after lengthening, the steamer was sold in 1926 to the Nicholson Universal S.S. Company who specialized in the rather new concept of transporting new automobiles from Detroit to various ports on the Lakes. The new method of carrying these cars had not yet been perfected, but Nicholson was far ahead of any competitors in reaching this goal. Automobiles were loaded on the long steamers by means of a ramp, and elevators on their decks lowered the cars to the bottom of the cargo holds where they were driven to occupy every available spot on the tank-tops (that portion of the steel double bottom of every Lake ship). Some vessels had 'tween decks and these, too, were filled with the brand-new, sparkling autos. At the same time the upper deck was loaded with cars from the ramp constructed ashore. The spaces

between the hatches were planked over with wood inserts, making the former ore carrier similar in appearance to a "flat-top" aircraft carrier. Now the CITY OF BANGOR was ready to take aboard her complement of new cars.

Unfortunately, her career as an auto-carrier was short-lived. In a severe storm on Lake Superior, November 30, 1926 the BANGOR was driven ashore on the Keweenaw Peninsula of Michigan in Lake Superior. Her crew members were saved as the vessel did not sink from under them. The vessel went so hard on the rocky beach that they were able to walk ashore without much trouble. The U.S. Coast Guard took them to their station nearby where they thawed out. The cargo of 248 new Chrysler automobiles suffered no more than a thick coating of ice, and 230 of them were rescued from an icy grave in Lake Superior. The R. J. Kappahan Contracting Company was awarded a $35,000 contract to rescue the autos from the stranded ship which had a 20 foot hole in her bottom. Tractors were used to take the cars across the ice. The ones on deck were encased in 10 inches of ice and the men had to work in 15° weather to remove them. The cars were driven off the ship, much in the same manner as they had been loaded, by a roughly constructed ramp since the ship was broadside to the beach. The vessel was beyond repair and it was sold by the underwriters to T. L. Durocher of Detour, Michigan, who cut her up for scrap where the accident occurred.

CITY OF BANGOR—early view with three masts

CITY OF BANGOR in 1916

In 1924

With a load of automobiles at Chicago

BUILT:	F. W. Wheeler, West Bay City, Michigan
HULL NUMBER:	113
LENGTH:	327.5
BREADTH:	44.8
DEPTH:	23.5
GROSS REGISTERED TONNAGE:	3,690
REGISTRY NUMBER:	US 127131
ENGINES:	Triple expansion 22″, 35″, 59″ diameter × 44″ stroke
ENGINE BUILDER:	Shipyard

Aground at Keweenaw Point

Encased in ice

CITY OF BENTON HARBOR

CITY OF BENTON HARBOR when brand new

BUILT:	Craig Shipbuilding Company, Toledo, Ohio	*GROSS REGISTERED TONNAGE:*	1,286
HULL NUMBER:	100	*REGISTRY NUMBER:*	US 200919
LENGTH;	251.8	*ENGINES:*	Inclined Compound
BREADTH:	36.5		38″, 55″, 55″ Diameter × 78″
DEPTH:	14.4		Stroke
		ENGINE BUILDER:	Craig Shipbuilding Company

Outbound Chicago River

Built in 1904 for the Graham & Morton Transportation Company of Chicago, CITY OF BENTON HARBOR was a steel sidewheel passenger and freight steamer. She operated on the express passenger service and in the fresh fruit trade between Chicago and Benton Harbor-St. Joseph for two decades. She usually ran opposite the older CITY OF CHICAGO on this route, often referred to as the "Dustless Road to Happy Land." She was painted nearly all white initially, with a black smoke band at the top of her stack.

Later, about 1907, CITY OF BENTON HARBOR was painted green, but was briefly white again after 1922. Transferred to the Goodrich Transit Company in 1924, she took on their black hull and red stack, and continued to serve her regular cross-Lake Michigan route. A fine looking vessel with feathering paddles, fast, and always popular,

she was one of the finest of the later sidewheelers on the Great Lakes. Inactive after 1933 and repossessed by the Michigan Trust Company, she lay idle at her name city for several years.

Purchased at auction on Dec. 16, 1935 by Captain John Roen of Sturgeon Bay, CITY OF BENTON HARBOR served briefly as a recreation center at Green Bay, Wisconsin, and then was taken to Sturgeon Bay. Upon her arrival, Captain Roen concluded that the fine old lady was too good for the scrapper's torch, and converted her into a "show boat." The venture failed, however, and CITY OF BENTON HARBOR was laid up at the Roen yard. She was gutted by fire on Nov. 24, 1938, and scrapped completely in 1940, thus ending the career of one of Lake Michigan's most beautiful sidewheelers.

In Goodrich colors

CITY OF BUFFALO

CITY OF BUFFALO leaving Cleveland

The steel sidewheel passenger and freight steamer CITY OF BUFFALO was launched on December 25, 1895 for the Cleveland and Buffalo Transit Company for overnight service between those cities. Her greatest year was in 1901, when she made 306 trips delivering people to the Pan American Exposition which was being held at Buffalo.

Over the winter in 1903–1904, she was lengthened by the Detroit Ship Building Company at their Orleans Street yard in Detroit (340'3″ × 43'7″ × 17'; 2940 gross tons, 1604 net tons).

She maintained the Cleveland-Buffalo route during her entire career. In 1915 she began to take an occasional lake cruise, a day trip on her same route, and an infrequent trip to Cedar Point from Cleveland. Also in 1915, on June 6, CITY OF BUFFALO used the new East 9th Street Pier in Cleveland for the first time.

Most of her career was unexciting. However, at about midnight on June 23, 1923, her forward mast was shattered by a bolt of lightning off Erie, Pennsylvania. That and other storm damage amounted to $29,400. CITY OF BUFFALO commanded headlines in 1929 when, on May 2, she suffered a break in her high pressure steam chest. She was drifting helplessly in a seventy-five mile per hour gale until her

anchors finally took hold off Ashtabula, Ohio. She had on board about fifty passengers and a crew of eighty-five. Passengers danced, listened to the victrola, and played cards until a rescue took place. The situation was serious enough to fly her national flag upside down and plans were made to ground her off Fairport Harbor to ease rescue problems for the Coast Guard. Ultimately, the old girl was towed into Conneaut and passengers were transferred to the CITY OF ERIE. She had repairs estimated at $37,000 made by the American Ship Building Company in Lorain, where she was dry docked from May 6 through 21.

In 1921 she received six new Scotch boilers (13'2″ × 10'10″, built by American Ship Building Company, Cleveland, Ohio). Between 1934 and 1937, the CITY OF BUFFALO added other chores to her Cleveland-Buffalo trips; occasional trips from Cleveland were made to Port Stanley, Ontario.

Her end came on March 19, 1937, when she caught fire while moored at the East 9th Street Pier in Cleveland. Her burned out hulk was sold to Captain William Nicholson, but his plans to convert her to a cargo carrier fell through. She was scrapped at Detroit, in the River Rouge, in 1940.

BUILT:	Detroit Dry Dock Company, Wyandotte, Michigan	*GROSS REGISTERED TONNAGE:*	2,398
HULL NUMBER:	121	*REGISTRY NUMBER:*	US 127132
LENGTH:	298.3	*ENGINES:*	Beam Condensing 52″, 80″ & 96″ Diameter × 144″ Stroke
BREADTH:	75		
DEPTH:	17	*ENGINE BUILDER:*	W. & A. Fletcher Company, Hoboken, New Jersey

CITY OF BUFFALO with a good crowd aboard

CITY OF CHATHAM

This small wooden passenger steamer was built for the excursion trade in 1888. The first owners were the Chatham Navigation Company, and they placed her in service operating from Chatham, Ontario on the river Thames near Lake St. Clair to Detroit, Michigan. Licensed to carry 627 passengers, she remained in this service until 1908. A popular vessel, the CITY OF CHATHAM was a frequent visitor to all the small ports in the St. Clair River as well as in her regular trade.

Early in 1909 the vessel was sold to the St. Joseph Island and Soo Line, Ltd., of Sault Ste. Marie, Ontario. Even though her ports were changed, the little vessel still remained very popular. She ran down the St. Mary's River from the Soo to St. Joseph Island, Ontario, from 1909 until 1921.

After being partially stripped of her cabins at the Soo in 1921, the hull was towed down to Wiarton, Ontario on Georgian Bay. Although her owners had expected to rebuild the vessel, the old CITY OF CHATHAM lay at the dock for several years before her rotten old timbers were picked apart for firewood.

CITY OF CHATHAM on the Thames River

CITY OF CHATHAM at the Soo

BUILT:	Polson Iron Works, Toronto, Ontario	*GROSS REGISTERED TONNAGE:*	362
LENGTH:	125.6	*REGISTRY NUMBER:*	C 92734
BREADTH:	28.5	*ENGINES:*	Compound
DEPTH:	9		18″, 31″ Diameter × 24″ Stroke
		BUILDER:	Shipyard

CITY OF CHICAGO

CITY OF CHICAGO in winter quarters

Another vintage sidewheeler, CITY OF CHICAGO, was built in 1890 for Graham & Morton for Lake Michigan service. Equipped with side-by-side smoke stacks, she was a very graceful and handsome steamer of that era. In 1891, she went back to the shipyard and was lengthened (226 feet; 1,164 gross tons). In 1905, she was both lengthened and rebuilt (254′ × 34′ × 13.6′; 1,439 gross tons) with no expense spared to make her a truly luxurious steamer.

She was operated in the passenger and fruit transportation business between Chicago and Benton Harbor-St. Joseph, Michigan, along with CITY OF BENTON HARBOR until retired in 1929. On September 1, 1914, she caught fire in mid Lake Michigan, but raced to the pier at Chicago where she ran into the breakwater to save time. Fortunately there was no loss of life, a fact attributed largely to the calmness

and courage of her commander, the late Capt. Oscar Bjork. She was again rebuilt at South Chicago, having a single stack amidship, and renamed CITY OF ST. JOSEPH. Her boat deck was redesigned, additional lifeboat capacity was added and the original luxurious interior was fully restored. She bacame part of the Goodrich Fleet in 1925.

In 1935, after several years of inactivity, she was sold to Capt. John Roen, cut down to a barge and used in the pulpwood trade. Her end came on September 21, 1942 when she was cut away along with the barge TRANSPORT from her towing vessel, the tug JOHN ROEN and wrecked on the shore of Lake Superior. Fifty-two years of service, forty of them on the beloved "Dustless Road to Happy Land," attest to the excellence of this stately vessel.

CITY OF CHICAGO leaving St. Joseph

CITY OF CHICAGO at Chicago

CITY OF CHICAGO—stern view

CITY OF ST. JOSEPH awaiting her passengers

CITY OF CHICAGO,
b) City of St. Joseph

BUILT:	F. W. Wheeler & Co., West Bay City, Michigan
HULL NUMBER:	68
LENGTH:	211.6
BREADTH:	34
DEPTH:	13
GROSS REGISTERED TONNAGE:	1,073
REGISTRY NUMBER:	US 126627
ENGINES:	Compound Beam 36″, 54″ Diameter × 80″ stroke
ENGINE BUILDER:	W. & A. Fletcher Co., Hoboken, New Jersey

CITY OF ST. JOSEPH in Goodrich colors

CITY OF COLLINGWOOD

CITY OF COLLINGWOOD leaving her home port

The wooden passenger and freight propellor CITY OF COLLINGWOOD was launched at Owen Sound May 24, 1893. She made a trip to Collingwood in June 1893 for the completion of her upperworks, and entered service as the flagship of the North Shore Navigation Co., Ltd., familiarly known as the "Black Line." During the first season, she operated between Collingwood and Chicago carrying visitors to the World's Fair of 1893. She then operated on her owner's regular service between Georgian Bay Ports and Lake Superior.

In 1899, the "Black Line," after intense competition, was merged with the "White Line" (Great Northern Transit Co.) and the Beatty Line of Sarnia to form the Northern Navigation Co., Ltd. CITY OF COLLINGWOOD continued to operate for six years in the service of Northern Navigation Co., Ltd. On June 19, 1905 she was totally destroyed by fire at dock in Collingwood Harbor. Four lives were lost.

CITY OF COLLINGWOOD entering the locks at the Soo

BUILT:	James Simpson, Owen Sound	*REGISTRY NUMBER:*	C 94766
LENGTH:	213	*ENGINES:*	Triple Expansion
BREADTH:	34		18″, 36″, & 48″ Diameter × 30″
DEPTH:	12.6		Stroke
GROSS REGISTERED		*ENGINE BUILDER:*	John Inglis,
TONNAGE:	1,387		Toronto (1893)

CITY OF COLLINGWOOD on an early advertisement

CITY OF COLLINGWOOD with tug BALIZE aiding the grounded GERMANIC

CITY OF DETROIT

CITY OF DETROIT from an early woodcut

The composite sidewheel passenger and freight steamer CITY OF DETROIT was built for the Detroit and Cleveland Steam Navigation Company in 1878. Her engines, however, came from the D & C steamer R. N. RICE, which had burned and which she was built to replace. She ran on the overnight run between Detroit and Cleveland opposite the steamer NORTHWEST. On July 17, 1890, the ship made news when she collided with and sank the propeller KASOTA at the head of Fighting Island on the Detroit River. The CITY OF DETROIT made the Detroit Dry Dock Company ship yard before she too settled by her bow. When another CITY OF DETROIT was built by D & C in 1893, this vessel was renamed CITY OF THE STRAITS. For a short time she was transferred to Chicago, calling at Lake Michigan ports, then returned to Detroit and used to fill in on the Lake Huron Division.

In 1896, D & C jointly with the C & B inaugurated a Cleveland-Toledo service with CITY OF THE STRAITS and STATE OF NEW YORK. While on this run, she had the honor of receiving the first wireless installed on a lake vessel, this in 1901.

Her usefulness to D & C ended in 1914. She was sold to Baker and Leonard and converted to a barge (673 gross and net tons). She was passed on to the Reid Wrecking Company and, in 1917, was acquired by Charles S. Neff of Milwaukee. Neff changed her rig to a schooner, renamed her LIBERTY, and further rebuilt her (235′ × 36′ × 12′4″; 746 gross tons, 509 net tons).

In 1924, she was sold to G. W. Hayward (Hayward & Nicholson) of Detroit and her tonnage again was changed (746 gross tons and 709 net tons). She was towed to Detroit by the steamer THOMAS DAVIDSON from Lake Michigan.

In 1928, William Nicholson became her sole owner. He placed a six cylinder Bessemer diesel engine in the old hull at Great Lakes Engineering Works, Detroit, to use her in the packaged steel trade (757 gross tons, 462 net tons). Her first captain in this new dress was Walter Neal, sole survivor in the loss of the steamer MYRON on Lake Superior in 1919. In 1929 a corporate and final ownership change saw Nicholson Transit Company placed on her enrollment papers. The old hull was abandoned in 1940. Reportedly the engine was removed in 1948 and the hull was abandoned at the head of Bob-Lo Island in the Detroit River. Some time after this, the hull burned to the water's edge.

CITY OF DETROIT at the dock

CITY OF THE STRAITS leaving Cleveland

CITY OF DETROIT,
b) City of the Straits,
c) Liberty

BUILT:	Detroit Dry Dock Company, Wyandotte, Michigan
HULL NUMBER:	31
LENGTH:	234
BREADTH:	36
DEPTH:	13
GROSS REGISTERED TONNAGE:	1,094
REGISTRY NUMBER:	US 125662
ENGINES:	Beam Condensing 62″ Diameter × 132″ Stroke
ENGINE BUILDER:	Fletcher & Harrison, Hoboken, New Jersey (1866)

LIBERTY at Conneaut

CITY OF DETROIT III

In 1912, the Detroit & Cleveland Navigation Company commissioned a steel-hulled passenger sidewheeler, the largest one of its type on the Great Lakes. The CITY OF DETROIT III was designed by Frank E. Kirby. On October 7, 1911, the huge sidewheeler was christened by Miss Doris McMillan, daughter of Senator McMillan of Detroit, and slid into the murky waters of the Detroit River amid cheers from thousands. During the next few months, the superstructure was completed, with interior decorations designed by Louis O. Keil. Carpenters swarmed over the decks with a goal of completion for the sailing season of 1912. This vessel was the most beautiful of all the ships in the D & C fleet and large crowds of people came down to the river's edge to see the largest sidewheeler in the world. Her parlors, 21 in all, were exquisitely furnished and the 477 staterooms were fitted out with the latest equipment. This huge floating palace became the talk of the Lakes. When she made her first trip, people stared in awe at the giant passenger and freight vessel as she steamed majestically down the Detroit River.

For close to 40 years, this ship sailed between Detroit, Cleveland, and Buffalo. While her giant paddle wheels churned the waters, she was watched by sailors and shorebound people alike in fascination. Often the ship was chartered by various civic groups who enjoyed the fine cuisine and excellent service offered aboard. Honeymoon couples boarded the vessel at Detroit and Cleveland and travelled to Buffalo with connections to Niagara Falls. In her day, she was the ultimate in comfort and style. Many people around Detroit enjoyed the Sunday cruises up the St. Clair River in the last few years of her life. These were missed when the ship lay idle in 1950. The end of her career had come, not by accident or sinking, but by the economics of the times. The company had gone out of business.

The CITY OF DETROIT III lay at the dock for a few years until matters under litigation could be resolved. She looked so forlorn, waiting for her end to come. In 1956, the vessel was sold for scrap to Robert L. Rosen and Abraham Siegel. During the winter of 1956–57, she was dismantled by the Union Wrecking Company at Detroit. The upper works were stripped and the hull scrapped at Hamilton, Ontario, by the Steel Company of Canada. Some of her interior furnishings were saved for museum pieces by Frank Schmidt who bought them and shipped them to Cleveland. The woodwork and entire "Gothic Room" was preserved and subsequently returned to Detroit, where the room was restored and can be seen at the Dossin Marine Museum on Belle Isle in the Detroit River. Here her fond memory still lives, close to the waters she sailed. The room can be enjoyed by the thousands who once rode aboard her, and the countless others who can only imagine her opulence as she once was.

CITY OF DETROIT III downbound on the St. Clair River

CITY OF DETROIT III a good crowd on a Sunday excursion

BUILT:	Detroit Shipbuilding Company, Wyandotte, Michigan	*GROSS REGISTERED TONNAGE:*	6,061
HULL NUMBER:	187	*REGISTRY NUMBER:*	US 209571
LENGTH:	455.8	*ENGINES:*	63″, 92″, 92″ diameter × 102″ stroke
BREADTH:	55.5		Inclined compound
DEPTH:	22.5	*ENGINE BUILDER:*	Detroit Shipbuilding Company, Detroit, Michigan—1911

At the foot of Third St., Detroit, S.S. JAMES MACNAUGHTON at left. Tug B.H. BECKER at right

CITY OF DETROIT III with Tug IOWA in the locks at the Soo

CITY OF DOVER

This single screw wooden passenger and freight steamer was built in 1916 and registered at Port Dover on November 25, 1916 in the name of William Frederick Kolbe. Kolbe sold her in 1921 to N. K. Wagg of Midland, Ontario (Honey Harbour Navigation Co. Ltd. Midland—capitalized on formation in 1921 at $40,000—N. K. Wagg, H. R. Wagg and R. R. Wilson, Directors). The Waggs operated her to pick up and deliver laundry and supplies to the various islands adjacent to Honey Harbour.

In 1928, she was sold to the Georgian Bay Tourist and Steamships Ltd., Midland, and placed in daily service between Midland and Go Home Bay. On March 29, 1949, the Georgian Bay Tourist and Steamships, Ltd. was sold to R. A. McDonald, R. W. Emery, W. L. Smart and W. D. Hunter of Penetanguishene, Ontario. As a result, the CITY OF DOVER lay idle at Penetanguishene from 1952 until June 8, 1954 when she was towed to Midland and stripped of the furnishings and fittings. She was then sold at auction on April 20, 1955 to John and Larry Ballmore of Sault Ste. Marie, Onatrio. CITY OF DOVER left Midland on June 10, 1954 for drydock at Wiarton, Ontario. After reconditioning, she started her season running between Soo, Ontario and Michipicoten Harbor. This service did not last long and before the 1955 season was over, she was back on the daily service between Midland and Go Home Bay.

CITY OF DOVER did not fit out in 1960 and in October 1960 was sold to Andrew Light of Midland. He placed her in the lock at Port Severn at the close of the season, intending to have repairs made which would enable him to secure a license to operate. After the lock was drained for the winter, it was discovered that CITY OF DOVER required a costly new keel. Her owner decided repairs were too expensive and broke her up.

CITY OF DOVER nudged up to the bank in Georgian Bay

CITY OF DOVER in winter layup at Midland, Ontario

BUILT:	John E. Passch of Erie, Pennsylvania at Port Dover, Ontario	*GROSS REGISTERED TONNAGE:*	81
LENGTH:	74.8	*REGISTRY NUMBER:*	C 126647
BREADTH:	20	*ENGINES:*	Fore and Aft Compound
DEPTH:	7	*ENGINE BUILDER:*	Doty Engine Works Co., Ltd., Goderich, Ontario

CITY OF ERIE

CITY OF ERIE at her Madison Avenue dock, Toledo

The steel side-wheel steamer CITY OF ERIE was launched on February 26, 1898. She was built for the Cleveland and Buffalo Transit Company for overnight service between those ports, a route that earned her the title "the Honeymoon Special," for newlyweds bound for Niagara Falls. She replaced the CITY OF THE STRAITS on that route on June 19, 1898.

Her claim to enduring Great Lakes fame came on June 4, 1901, when she won the renowned race against the pride of the Detroit River region, the White Star Line steamer TASHMOO. In a one hundred mile race course between Cleveland and Erie, and with national attention and untold large sums of money wagered on the outcome, Captain Hugh McAlpine guided the CITY OF ERIE to victory by a scant forty-five seconds!

The popular vessel remained on the Cleveland-Buffalo route from 1898 to 1938, with only a two-year break, 1914–1915, when she ran from Cleveland to Cedar Point and Put-in-Bay. From 1916 through 1927, she reserved weekends for trips on the latter route. In 1921, she began running occasional moonlights and excursion lake rides. During a business slump in 1928, she lay tied to the dock during mid-season. From 1929 through 1938, she provided weekend cross-lake service between Cleveland and Port Stanley, Ontario. During most of the CITY OF ERIE's career, her running mate between Cleveland and Buffalo was the CITY OF BUFFALO.

After the completion of the 1938 season, she was laid up in Cleveland, never to turn her paddle wheels again. She was towed up the Cuyahoga River to the Otis Steel Company in 1941, where she was dismantled and scrapped.

116

CITY OF ERIE leaving Cleveland

BUILT:	Detroit Dry Dock Co., Wyandotte, Michigan	*REGISTRY NUMBER:*	US 127242
HULL NUMBER:	126	*ENGINES:*	Beam Condensing Triple Expansion
LENGTH:	316'		54", 96", & 80" Diameter × 144" Stroke
BREADTH:	44'		
DEPTH:	18'	*ENGINE BUILDER:*	W. & A. Fletcher Co., Hoboken, New Jersey—1898
GROSS REGISTERED TONNAGE:	2,498		

Sailing off into Lake Erie

CITY OF GRAND RAPIDS

CITY OF GRAND RAPIDS passing Marine City

The end of an era, CITY OF GRAND RAPIDS was the last steamer that the Graham & Morton line had built and was the flagship of the line. She was a single screw steel propellor, unlike her sidewheel fleet mates, with a single upright stack and two vertical pole masts. Her keel was laid during 1911, and the launching was held in the early Spring of 1912. She was completed and entered service in June of 1912, operating from Chicago to southern Michigan ports, including overnight service to Holland where railroad connections were made to Grand Rapids. Although CITY OF GRAND RAPIDS was a relatively large combination freight and passenger steamer, she had a shallow draft allowing her to enter the ports served by Graham & Morton.

After the 1925 merger with the Goodrich Transit Company, CITY OF GRAND RAPIDS was repainted in the traditional Goodrich standard colors. She was placed on the Chicago-Grand Haven-Muskegon run, running opposite ALABAMA in the cross-lake overnight service and giving this route two of Lake Michigan's finest steamers. She remained in this trade until Goodrich ceased operations.

In 1933, CITY OF GRAND RAPIDS was placed on the day excursion to Milwaukee and continued there until 1941 when she again was running across Lake Michigan to St. Joseph. She had changed ownership several times during this period, and the Cleveland & Buffalo Steamship Company became the last owner when they purchased the veteran in 1946. Extensive engine and boiler repairs stipulated in her Coast Guard inspection of 1951 were deemed too costly, and she was laid up at Benton Harbor. On May 24, 1951, she was sold to Hyman-Michaels, a Chicago scrap dealer, and in late 1952 resold to a Canadian scrap dealer. On October 27, 1952, the tug HELENA moved CITY OF GRAND RAPIDS to the lake pier, and on November 2, 1952, the tow left for Hamilton, truly the last trip of the "Grand Rapids Short Line."

BUILT:	American Shipbuilding Company, Cleveland, Ohio	*GROSS REGISTERED TONNAGE:*	3,061
HULL NUMBER:	455	*REGISTRY NUMBER:*	US 210065
LENGTH:	291	*ENGINES:*	4 cyl. Triple Expansion 26″, 42″, 51″, 51″ Diameter × 42″ stroke
BREADTH:	48		
DEPTH:	27	*ENGINE BUILDER:*	American Shipbuilding Company

CITY OF GRAND RAPIDS at the Soo

CITY OF GRAND RAPIDS leaving Milwaukee

CITY OF HANCOCK

OSSIAN BEDELL in the Niagara River

Ossian Bedell,
b) CITY OF HANCOCK

BUILT:	Buffalo Dry Dock Co., Buffalo, New York
HULL NUMBER:	99
LENGTH:	104'5"
BREADTH:	28'
DEPTH:	9'6"

GROSS REGISTERED TONNAGE:	296
REGISTRY NUMBER:	US 155414
ENGINES:	Compound 14"–30" Diameter × 20" Stroke
ENGINE BUILDER:	Whitman Mfg. Co. for American Shipbuilding Company—1901

OSSIAN BEDELL in drydock at Buffalo 1918

CITY OF HANCOCK in the upper Detroit River

This small steel-hulled vessel was launched on April 6, 1901 for her namesake, Ossian Bedell. She was built to run down the Niagara River from Buffalo to the Bedell House on Grand Island. By 1906, John Bedell was the registered owner. In 1909 Samuel S. Staley purchased the ship and placed her on the Buffalo to Erie Beach run. About 1918, the Niagara Ferry and Transportation Company took over her operation, this under the name of the Buffalo and Erie Beach Transportation Company. From 1926 through 1931, the New York-Ontario Ferries of Buffalo, maintained the BEDELL on this same route.

The following year she left Buffalo never to return. She was bought by James H. Gallagher of Boyne City, Michigan, to carry mail from Charlevoix to Beaver Island. After two years in this service, the Royale Line of Houghton, Michigan, acquired her, renamed her the CITY OF HANCOCK, and ran her from downtown Chicago to the Century of Progress Exposition.

With the closing of the Exposition, the small passenger ship maintained regular service from Houghton, Isle Royale, and Fort William, Ontario. She also had an occasional charter to carry Civilian Conservation Corp (CCC) boys to Isle Royale. In 1935, she passed into the hands of W. J. Petroskey of Chicago, and in 1936, to Harold L. Baldwin of Detroit (though still enrolled in Chicago). During this period she continued on the same run.

Finally in 1938, the Detroit and St. Clair Navigation Company of Detroit brought the vessel to Detroit for early season excursions and charters. In 1939, she spent the summer running from Sandusky to Lakeside and the islands in western Lake Erie. In 1940, CITY OF HANCOCK again returned to the CCC boys and Isle Royale. Plans for the same run in 1941 were scrapped when, in May of that year, the U.S. Coast Guard refused to renew her passenger license unless her upper works were completely rebuilt. She was taken off the dry dock at Great Lakes Engineering Works and tied to a dock. She never again turned a wheel. After eight years of "dock hopping," and after having been removed from documentation in 1945, she was scrapped in 1949 at the foot of Dubois Street in Detroit. Her last owner, from 1946 to 1949, was Troy Browning of Detroit.

CITY OF HOLLAND

The wooden passenger and freight propellor CITY OF HOLLAND was launched at Saugatuck, Michigan, on April 10, 1893 for the Holland and Chicago Transportation Company of Holland, Michigan, to run between those two ports. In 1900, ownership was transferred to William R. Owen of Chicago. In 1901, J. S. Thomson of St. Clair, Michigan, purchased her to replace the DOUGLAS. She became a familiar sight plying between Port Huron, way ports, and Alpena for the Thomson Line. In 1910, Charles Beyschlag, representing the Oscoda Transit Company, acquired her, and she became the MELBOURNE.

In 1915 the Point Lookout Navigation Company of Saginaw, Michigan, took ownership of her. They placed her on the run from Saginaw and Bay City to Point Lookout on a daily excursion basis. On August 6, 1918, she sank at

her dock in Saginaw. She was pumped out, but the following winter she rolled over at her dock in Battery Park.

In 1919, Clarence Lebeau, of Toledo, Ohio, purchased the wreck and rebuilt her as the freight and wrecking steamer CLARENCE E. LEBEAU (146'7" × 29'5" × 7'9"; 275 gross tons, 57 net tons). She was placed in the Lake Erie Island fruit trade and was to be used also as a wrecking tug. However, on July 11, 1922, she caught fire while laid up at the Pennsylvania Railroad dock near the Ash Street Bridge in along the Maumee River in Toledo. Lebeau's other vessel, the old former lumber carrier PHILETUS SAWYER, also burned at the same time. Both proved to be total losses with the sum of the former set at $27,000 and the latter at $38,000. Each was insured for $25,000.

CITY OF HOLLAND in the St. Clair River

MELBOURNE enroute to Point Lookout

CITY OF HOLLAND,
b) Melbourne,
c) Clarence E. Lebeau

BUILT:	R. T. Rogers, Saugatuck, Michigan
LENGTH:	141'5"
BREADTH:	29'3"
DEPTH:	10'
GROSS REGISTERED TONNAGE:	439
REGISTRY NUMBER:	US 126967
ENGINES:	Steeple Compound 18" & 36" Diameter × 28' Stroke
ENGINE BUILDER:	Wilson & Hendrie, Montague, Michigan

MELBOURNE at Au Gres, Michigan

CITY OF LONDON

CITY OF LONDON at St. Catharines in 1865.

The wooden passenger and freight propellor CITY OF LONDON was built in 1865 for the North Shore Transportation Co. which was incorporated under Dominion charter in 1869. She entered service when the lumbering business was expanding in the Georgian Bay area, and was used to transport bush workers, horses and camp supplies from Owen Sound, Meaford, Tobermory and Collingwood to lumbering centers on the North Shore of Georgian Bay. These included Collins Inlet, Little Current, John Island, Thessalon, Aird Island, Cutler, Macbeth Bay, Spragge, Algoma Mills, Blind River, Bruce Mines and Hilton. She remained in this service until totally destroyed by fire at Collins Inlet on August 20th, 1875.

BUILT:	Louis Shickluna, St. Catharines, Ontario
LENGTH:	145
BREADTH:	27
DEPTH:	11.6
GROSS REGISTERED TONNAGE:	450
ENGINES:	Single cylinder high pressure connected direct to the shaft —Fire Box boiler burning wood fuel
ENGINE BUILDER:	Unknown

CITY OF MACKINAC

The steel sidewheel steamer CITY OF MACKINAC was launched for the Detroit and Cleveland Steam Navigation Company on May 2, 1893. She was built, along with the CITY OF ALPENA, to replace two older vessels of the same names which had been sold out of the fleet. The D & C Line placed them on its Lake Huron Division, running between Toledo and St. Ignace, with stops at way ports on Michigan's Lake Huron shore. Stops were made at smaller ports as business warranted. During the summer months, each vessel made two round trips weekly, making ten regular stops upbound and nine downbound. With the northern Michigan and Mackinac Island area developing as a resort area the vessels proved very popular with the traveling public at the turn of the century. In 1912, the CITY OF MACKINAC received a Roman numeral "II" after her name, consistent with company policy.

However, as World War I set in, the passenger trade dwindled. The vessels were laid up at Detroit in 1919. In 1921 they were sold to the Graham and Morton Transportation Company of Chicago. The "MACKINAC" was renamed CITY OF HOLLAND and was placed on the Chicago, Holland, Saugatuck route. The Goodrich Transit Company of Chicago acquired the G & M properties in 1924. When the Depression struck the nation, the Goodrich firm went out of business. In 1933, the CITY OF HOLLAND was laid up and ownership was transferred to the Michigan Trust Company (Michigan) of Duluth, Minnesota. On Dec. 16, 1935, the vessel was purchased by Captain John Roen and towed to the bone yard at Sturgeon Bay, Wisconsin, in 1936. There she was scrapped in 1940.

CITY OF MACKINAC at the Soo

CITY OF MACKINAC, **b) City of Mackinac II** **c) City of Holland**		*DEPTH:* *GROSS REGISTERED* *TONNAGE:* *REGISTRY NUMBER:*	13.4 1,749 US 126988
BUILT:	Detroit Dry Dock Company, Wyandotte, Michigan	*ENGINES:*	Beam Condensing 44″, 66″ & 88″ Diameter × 132″
HULL NUMBER:	116		Stroke
LENGTH:	266	*ENGINE BUILDER:*	W. & A. Fletcher Company,
BREADTH:	69.2		Hoboken, New Jersey

CITY OF MACKINAC II in the lake at speed

In the St. Clair River

CITY OF HOLLAND in Holland harbor

CITY OF MILWAUKEE

CITY OF MILWAUKEE heading across the lake

CITY OF MILWAUKEE,
  b) Holland,
  c) Muskegon

BUILT:	Detroit Dry Dock Co., Wyandotte, Michigan
HULL NUMBER:	44
LENGTH:	230.7
BREADTH:	33.5

DEPTH:	12.3
GROSS REGISTERED TONNAGE:	1,148
REGISTRY NUMBER:	US 125906
ENGINES:	Condensing Beam 53″ Diameter × 144″ Stroke
ENGINE BUILDER:	W. & A. Fletcher Co., New York, N.Y.

CITY OF MILWAUKEE in a contemporary artists conception

The iron sidewheel passenger liner CITY OF MILWAU-KEE was launched on February 11, 1881. This vessel, MICHIGAN and WISCONSIN were the first metal ships owned by the Goodrich Transportation Company. Built at a cost of $179,000, staggering for those times, the palatial ship had the most elegant interior of any ship on the Lakes and was quickly dubbed "Queen of the Lakes" by the press. All three ships were intended for cross Lake Michigan service in connection with the Detroit, Grand Haven, and Milwaukee railroad.

The railroad entered the service with other ships in 1882, however, and in order to recover its investment and avoid a serious financial crisis, Goodrich sold all three ships to the railroad on May 1, 1883. CITY OF MILWAUKEE continued on this route until 1892 when the railroad withdrew

from shipping operations. She was then sold to Graham & Morton Transportation Company and used on the passenger and fruit shuttle between Benton Harbor-St. Joseph and Chicago. In 1905, when the new CITY OF BENTON HARBOR came out, CITY OF MILWAUKEE was placed on G & M's Chicago to Holland line and renamed b) HOLLAND. She was sold to the Crosby Transportation Company in 1916 and was renamed c) MUSKEGON in 1919.

Beautiful and luxurious as she was, this ship was beset with accidents and eventually came to be looked upon with fear. Her ill luck plagued her to the last. She piled up on the pierheads of Muskegon in a heavy sea on the night of October 28, 1919 and foundered with a loss of 29 lives.

HOLLAND

MUSKEGON at Muskegon

CITY OF RACINE

The wooden passenger and freight propellor CITY OF RACINE was built in 1889 for Goodrich Transportation Company at a cost of $125,000. She was launched on April 18, 1889 and named in honor of Wisconsin's second city, an important port of call on the Goodrich itinerary. She served reliably on all her owner's routes from Chicago all the way to the Soo and Georgian Bay ports, although she initially was placed on the Chicago-Milwaukee route in night service with a stop at Racine in both directions.

Completely rebuilt at Manitowoc in 1912, CITY OF RACINE received new cabins with increased overnight capacity and was renamed ARIZONA. She was retired from the line in 1925 and, after being chartered out for a few seasons, was permanently laid up at Manitowoc.

In the early thirties, ARIZONA was purchased by a contracting firm and utilized as a power plant in the construction of the Livingstone Channel in the lower Detroit River. Her sistership INDIANA also was used in that project. She was then taken to Toledo where she lay for some years, eventually being stripped to the water line. Her bones still lie in the Maumee River and may be seen at low water.

CITY OF RACINE at Racine, Wisconsin

CITY OF RACINE,
b) Arizona

BUILT: Burger & Burger,
Manitowoc, Wisconsin
LENGTH: 203.5
BREADTH: 40
DEPTH: 13.5

GROSS REGISTERED
TONNAGE: 1,041
REGISTRY NUMBER: US 126551
ENGINES: Fore & Aft Compound
28″ & 50″ Diameter × 36″ Stroke
ENGINE BUILDER: C. F. Elnes,
Chicago, Illinois

ARIZONA at Muskegon

ARIZONA at Toledo, abandoned

CITY OF SOUTH HAVEN

CITY OF SOUTH HAVEN entering South Haven

The steel single screw excursion steamer CITY OF SOUTH HAVEN was built in 1903 for the Dunkley-Williams Company, Chicago. Very fast and a good sea boat, she was called "The White Flyer of Lake Michigan." Her route was between the city of her name and Chicago, carrying excursionists and large cargoes of fruit. She continued in this service for her new owners of 1907, the Chicago-South Haven Line.

CITY OF SOUTH HAVEN was requisitioned by the U.S. Shipping Board in 1918 for World War I service on the Atlantic, but two years later was resold to the Miami-Havana Navigation Company, who renamed her b) CITY OF MIAMI. She operated for two years between Miami and Havana, and then was sold back onto the Great Lakes.

Purchased by the Crosby Transportation Company and renamed c) E. G. CROSBY (2), she returned to Lake Michigan in 1923 and commenced sailings out of Milwaukee. Although sold again in 1927 to the Wisconsin & Michigan Company, she continued in this service until the early thirties.

She then lay idle at Sturgeon Bay, where she was all but destroyed by fire on December 3, 1935. Plans were afoot to rebuild her during World War II but did not materialize and she was broken up in the early forties. Throughout her long career, her appearance was little changed.

CITY OF MIAMI on salt water

E. G. CROSBY entering Muskegon harbor

CITY OF SOUTH HAVEN,
b) City of Miami,
c) E. G. Crosby (2)

BUILT:	Craig Shipbuilding Co., Toledo, Ohio
HULL NUMBER:	93
LENGTH:	247.7
BREADTH:	40.3
DEPTH:	21.7
GROSS REGISTERED TONNAGE:	1,719
REGISTRY NUMBER:	US 127731
ENGINES:	Triple Expansion 23″, 37½″, & 63″ Diameter × 40″ Stroke
ENGINE BUILDER:	Shipyard

E. G. CROSBY at the dock at Muskegon

CITY OF TOLEDO

CITY OF TOLEDO in the St. Clair River

BUILT:	Craig Shipbuilding Co., Toledo, Ohio	*GROSS REGISTERED TONNAGE:*	1,003
HULL NUMBER:	45	*REGISTRY NUMBER:*	US 126738
LENGTH:	212'	*ENGINES:*	Inclined Triple Expansion
BREADTH:	31'7"		26"-42"-66" Diameter × 72"
DEPTH:	12'8"		Stroke
		ENGINE BUILDER:	Cleveland Shipbuilding Co., Cleveland, Ohio (1891)

At speed

The steel sidewheel excursion steamer CITY OF TOLEDO was launched on January 24, 1891. Her inclined compound engine was the first of its type on the Great Lakes. She was built for the Toledo and Islands Steamship Company of Toledo to run from that city to the Lake Erie Islands. In 1893, she was one of many excursion vessels chartered for use in transporting the crowds from downtown Chicago to the Columbian Exposition grounds. In 1894, she returned to her original route, which lasted for only one more year.

In 1895, she was sold to Detroit's White Star Line to run from there to Port Huron. She would remain under this ownership until 1926, and on this run until 1916. She experienced a tonnage change in 1911 (698 gross tons). From 1917 through 1930 she ran from Detroit to Toledo. Prior to being placed on the latter route, she was lengthened and, to provide more symmetry, another stack was added (252' × 33'2" × 12'8"; 796 gross tons). A corporate change occurred in 1926, and CITY OF TOLEDO was acquired by the Anchor Line (Michigan), of Detroit.

As automobiles increased and dark financial clouds spread across the region and country, patronage dropped. The ship was laid up in 1930 and, within the next two years, passed into the ownership of Dewey G. Gebo of River Rouge, Michigan, then to I. M. Massey of Superior, Wisconsin.

In 1932, Charles V. Fix, of Grand Island, New York, purchased the CITY OF TOLEDO. He towed her to his small shipyard at Buffalo, and converted her to an auto and passenger ferry for crossing the Niagara River (250'6" × 33'7" × 12'2"; 670 gross tons, 422 net tons). After nine undramatic years, she again was laid up in 1941. Finally, in 1948, the CITY OF TOLEDO was towed to Hamilton, Ontario, where she was fed to the furnaces of the Steel Company of Canada.

CITY OF TOLEDO with two stacks

D. M. CLEMSON (I)

The bulk freight steamer D. M. CLEMSON was launched on May 20, 1903 for the Provident Steamship Company, operated by A. B. Wolvin of Duluth, Minnesota. In her day, she and her sister ships, the D. G. KERR (later the HARRY R. JONES) and JAMES H. REED, were second in size on the Lakes only to the larger Wolvin ships of 1900. The shortest lived of the three sisters was the D. M. CLEMSON. She disappeared with her crew of 24 on a cold, stormy day on Lake Superior in 1908. The five-year-old vessel had grounded twice in the last few months of her career, perhaps having an influence on her final end.

Bound from Lorain, Ohio, to Superior, Wisconsin, with coal, the CLEMSON left the Soo Locks on the morning of November 30, 1908 and entered Whitefish Bay along with the steamer J. J. H. BROWN. She was never seen again. A gale of devastating proportions with a great deal of snow descended on the eastern end of Lake Superior during the first few days of December that year. It was the final storm that this fine vessel would encounter. Immediate concern for overdue ore and coal carriers was not forthcoming in those days of scant communication, but when the CLEMSON did not report at Superior by December 4, search parties were sent out in an attempt to locate the vessel. Much wreckage was found. Convincing evidence, however, was not forthcoming until ten days later when an unidentified body was washed up on the beach near Vermilion Station of the Life Saving Crew. The body wore a life preserver with the letters "D. M. CLEMSON" stenciled on it. "Overdue, presumed lost," became "Disappeared with all hands" in the newspaper headlines of the day. Only one other body from that crew was ever recovered. Lake Superior had claimed another victim. To this day, only the cold depths hold the answer to the cause of her disappearance.

D. M. CLEMSON at the Soo

BUILT:	Superior Shipbuilding Company, West Superior, Wisconsin	GROSS REGISTERED TONNAGE:	5,531
HULL NUMBER:	510	REGISTRY NUMBER:	US 157703
LENGTH:	468	ENGINES:	Quadruple expansion
BREADTH:	52		15″, 22¾″, 36½″, 56″ diameter × 40″ stroke
DEPTH:	28	ENGINE BUILDER:	Shipyard

CLEVECO

Steel tank barges were a rather new concept when this one was built in 1913. At the turn of the century, the first one was built by McDougall, at Superior, Wisconsin. The idea of tanker ships to carry oil and liquid cargoes was not new on the oceans, but the use of this type of ship on the Great Lakes was novel. The Standard Oil Company had ordered a few of these ships previous to the S. O. CO. NO. 85, and built more of them for ocean service than for lake use. The Canadian Imperial Oil Company built self-propelled steamers for lake use in the early 1900's.

This tank barge was owned by the following companies during her career, both on the high seas and on the Great Lakes: Standard Oil Company, 1913–1921; Standard Transportation Company, 1921–1929; Gotham Marine Corporation, 1929–1940; and the Cleveland Tankers Incorporated, 1940. She also had various names. S. O. CO. NO. 85; S. T. CO. NO. 85, 1916; SOCONY 85, 1921; GOTHAM 85, 1929; and CLEVECO, 1940.

She had seen service on the Lakes under her Gotham Marine name, but her time as the CLEVECO was to be limited to three years of service. She was usually towed by the tug ADMIRAL of the Cleveland Tankers fleet, and she went down with the tug during early December of 1942. The two of them had left Toledo for Cleveland when a severe storm struck the area. The details of those last frightful nights are not clear to us because no one was saved. During either the night of December 2, 1942 or the early morning of the following day, they both disappeared. Eleven crewmen of the barge were lost, and the seven from the tug never saw the light of day again.

For quite some time, the location of the sunken barge was unknown. In 1967, however, through the efforts of some enthusiastic young skin divers, the hull of the barge was found just off Cleveland harbor. Because of the shallowness of the water and the proximity of the wreck to the shipping lanes, the barge was raised and towed to deeper water where she was allowed to sink once more. The value of scrapping the old tanker was minimal, so the decision to sink her once again was deemed the most practical.

GOTHAM 85 at Detroit

S. O. Co. No. 85, b) S. T. Co. No. 85, c) Socony 85, d) Gotham 85, e) CLEVECO

BUILT: American Shipbuilding
Company,
Lorain, Ohio
HULL NUMBER: 702
LENGTH: 250

BREADTH: 43
DEPTH: 26
GROSS REGISTERED
TONNAGE: 2,441
REGISTRY NUMBER: US 211035

CLEVECO at the dock

In Lake St. Clair

COLONEL

COLONEL was a steel bulk freighter built in 1901 for A. McVittie of Detroit. In 1910, her ownership was listed as Michigan Steamship Company of which Mr. Maurice McMillan of Detroit was manager.

In 1916, she was sold to the Bristol Transportation Company (Richardson Fleet) of Cleveland, and in due time passed to its successor, the Columbia Steamship Company, in whose colors she sailed until 1925. In that year, COLONEL became part of the Fontana Steamship Company, managed by Cleveland-Cliffs. In 1942, COLONEL and four other of the older Cliffs vessels, CHACORNAC, MUNISING, NEGAUNEE and YOSEMITE, were handed over to the U.S. Maritime Commission in exchange for new tonnage (CADILLAC and CHAMPLAIN).

She was operated by Cliffs for the duration of World War II and for several years thereafter, although many of the other "trade-ins" except the five Cliffs vessels were scrapped immediately afterward. COLONEL finally ran out of reprieves after the Korean War and was scrapped at Buffalo in 1953.

COLONEL in Richardson colors

COLONEL in 1928

COLONEL in her last year of operation

BUILT:	Detroit Shipbuilding Company, Wyandotte, Michigan	*GROSS REGISTERED TONNAGE:*	3,879
HULL NUMBER:	142	*REGISTRY NUMBER:*	US 127553
LENGTH:	356	*ENGINES:*	Triple Expansion
BREADTH:	50		18″, 29″ & 48″ Diameter × 40″ Stroke
DEPTH:	28	*ENGINE BUILDER:*	Detroit S.B. Co. (Engine Div.), Detroit, Michigan

CHRISTOPHER COLUMBUS

CHRISTOPHER COLUMBUS new

This one-of-a-kind passenger ship was built by Alexander McDougall for the World's Fair Steamship Company of Chicago. Although forty-three whalebacks were built (thirty-nine by the American Steel Barge Company at Superior, Wisconsin), CHRISTOPHER COLUMBUS was the only passenger excursion vessel ever built. Her keel was laid in September of 1892 and she was launched on December 3, 1892 (Whaleback #128). Designed primarily as a day boat, she entered service in the Spring of 1893 as a ferry between the foot of Randolph Street, in downtown Chicago, and the grounds of the World's Fair Columbian Exposition at Jackson Park. She originally had two decks and her hull and cabins were painted white while the stack was cream-colored. She quickly became a secondary highlight of the World's Fair, and carried over two million passengers in her first year of existence.

After the close of the fair, CHRISTOPHER COLUMBUS was purchased by the Hurson Line of Chicago, a company founded by a former Goodrich employee. From 1894 to 1898, COLUMBUS ran day excursions to Milwaukee in opposition to the fast Goodrich liner VIRGINIA. The two ships often raced, and the COLUMBUS, with her 4,000 horsepower and 18 foot wheel providing a speed of 20 mph,

usually won as long as the weather was moderate. VIRGINIA, however, was an excellent sea boat and usually won in heavy weather. During this period, Hurson's finances caused control of CHRISTOPHER COLUMBUS to be taken over by a group known as the Columbian Whaleback Steamship Company.

In 1898, CHRISTOPHER COLUMBUS was sold to the Chicago & Milwaukee Transportation Company, an organization put together by Mr. A. W. Goodrich. This company in turn chartered the COLUMBUS to the Goodrich Transportation Company. During the Winter of 1899–1900, COLUMBUS was sent to the shipyard at Manitowoc for a complete overhaul and rebuilding. A third deck was added to increase passenger capacity, and the traditional Goodrich colors of black hull and red stack were adopted. She later was actually sold to Goodrich in 1909.

The vessel ran on the Milwaukee excursion service until retired in 1931. "Old CHRISTOPHER" probably carried more people than any other Great Lakes ship. Scrapped at Manitowoc in 1936, her deep throated whistle later served as that city's air raid siren during World War II. This ship lives on in the hallowed memory of the thousands who rode her broad decks.

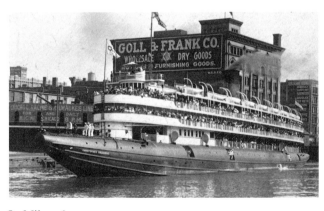

In Milwaukee

BUILT:	American Steel Barge Company, Superior, Wisconsin
HULL NUMBER:	128
LENGTH:	362
BREADTH:	42
DEPTH:	24
GROSS REGISTERED TONNAGE:	1,511
REGISTRY NUMBER:	US 126592
ENGINES:	Triple Expansion 28″, 42″ & 70″ Diameter × 42″ Stroke
ENGINE BUILDER:	S. F. Hodge Company, Detroit, Michigan

J. B. COMSTOCK

J. B. COMSTOCK at a lumber yard

This two-masted wooden schooner was built in 1891 for Smith and Comstock, lumber dealers, by Abram Smith who was also a prominent Algonac businessman. Mr. A. W. Comstock of Alpena, Michigan, originally intended that the ship be named JOSEPH B. COMSTOCK, for a relative, but the use of just initials was decided upon before the launch.

In 1898, the COMSTOCK was sold to Charles Bradley of Bay City, Michigan, also a lumber dealer, and in 1902, she went to J. W. Ritchie of the same city. In 1904, the vessel was again sold, this time to Charles A. Eddy, another lumber dealer in Bay City.

While the COMSTOCK was bound from Collingwood, Ontario, to Bay City with rough pine lumber in tow of the steam barge LANGELL BOYS, with the ABRAM SMITH as the other consort, a gale forced the steamer and her barges to shelter behind Duck Island in upper Lake Huron. The wind shifted and the tow line parted. The two barges stranded on the south side of Outer Duck Island on Friday, October 8, 1906 and were dashed to pieces by the towering seas, littering the shore with their cargoes. No one was lost in the violent winds, but the 60 mph gale demolished both vessels.

BUILT:	Abram Smith, Algonac, Michigan
LENGTH:	139.4
BREADTH:	30.1
DEPTH:	10.9
GROSS REGISTERED TONNAGE:	325
REGISTRY NUMBER:	US 76941

CORALIA

CORALIA at Escanaba

CORALIA,
b) T. H. Browning,
c) L. D. Browning

BUILT:	Globe Iron Works, Cleveland, Ohio
HULL NUMBER:	64
LENGTH:	413.2
BREADTH:	48
DEPTH:	24
GROSS REGISTERED TONNAGE:	4,330
REGISTRY NUMBER:	US 127129
ENGINES:	Triple Expansion 24″, 39″, 63″ Diameter × 42″ Stroke
ENGINE BUILDER:	Shipyard

CORALIA being towed up the Black River at Lorain

CORALIA downbound in Lake St. Clair

The steel bulk freighter CORALIA was built for the Mutual Transportation Company of Escanaba. She had 13 hatches and an extra stiff and strong hull with two masts and one tall stack. Her forward cabin and pilot house were originally behind the second hatch. Her original colors were a black hull with white stripe, dark brown cabins with white trim and a black stack with a white globe on the sides. Her name, honoring the wife of L. C. Hanna, manager of the fleet, was decided upon five minutes before she was launched, and was not painted upon the ship until after she was in the water. She was the largest ship on the Great Lakes at the time of her completion. Her first cargo, 4869 net tons of ore loaded at Escanaba, was the largest of its kind ever carried up to that time. In hull and machinery she was a duplicate of the SIR WILLIAM SIEMENS and SIR HENRY BESSEMER.

In 1901, the vessels of the Mutual fleet became part of the Pittsburgh Steamship Company and thus the CORALIA became a "tin stacker." Around 1920, she was rebuilt with a new pilot house on the forecastle and her deckhouse placed atop the after cabin, immediately behind the stack (4349 gross tons). This may have been the first example of the present day practice of placing the proverbial "dog house" in this position.

In 1927, CORALIA was sold to Nicholson-Universal S.S. Co. and rebuilt as an auto carrier. She was converted back to the bulk trade during World War II, and in 1949 became part of the T. H. Browning S.S. Company. She was renamed T. H. BROWNING in 1950, and L. D. BROWNING in 1952. In the Winter of 1953–54, she was equipped with an oil burner, receiving the equipment which had previously served in the PUT-IN-BAY and THEODORE ROOSEVELT. She was sold in 1955 to the Continental Grain Company (Beta Lake S.S. Company) and used as a storage barge at Buffalo for several years. The L. D. BROWNING was scrapped in 1964 at Hamilton.

T. H. BROWNING in the Detroit River

L. D. BROWNING downbound at Mission Point

HENRY CORT

PILLSBURY brand new with tugs BUFFALO and JOHN MARTIN

This steel whaleback steamer was built for the Minneapolis, St. Paul & Buffalo Steamship Co. (Soo Line Railroad) as a package freighter. She was launched on June 25, 1892 and left the yards on her first trip in August of that year.

On April 18, 1896, the Bessemer Steamship Co. purchased the PILLSBURY and on June 16, 1896 renamed her HENRY CORT, the name she retained the rest of her life. In 1901, when the United States Steel Corporation was formed, Rockefeller's Bessemer S.S. Co. was included and thus the HENRY CORT passed into the Pittsburgh Steamship Co., the marine division of U.S. Steel. From 1901 till 1917, she operated at her usual work-a-day life carrying the same raw materials needed by her owners to the steel mills, or coal for the railroads in the Iron Range. Usually the ship was out early in the season as she was a good ice breaker.

In 1917, with a war going on in Europe and the United States fully committed to it, the navigation season was extended somewhat. With an early heavy freeze, the HENRY CORT was called on to break ice in Western Lake Erie, and here fate started to haunt her. She was involved in a collision with the Hanna ore carrier MIDVALE, and was sunk.

The whaleback was salvaged in 1918 and towed to Toledo, Ohio, for drydocking and heavy repairs which, because of a lack of shipyard space, were delayed until late Fall. After drydocking, she was towed to Conneaut, Ohio, where Pittsburgh Steamship Co. had a repair yard, and her deck was raised 4 feet and her cabins fully rebuilt.

In the Spring of 1927, while again engaged in ice breaking operations the CORT was stranded on Colchester Reef in Lake Erie, near her last point of grief. She was abandoned to the underwriters, and afterwards sold to the Lake Ports Shipping and Navigation Co. of Detroit, Michigan, owned by Mr. Andrew Green Jr., who recovered her. The ship was then given two whirly cranes on deck and had her hatches enlarged for carrying finished steel, scrap, and any other cargo that could be handled by cranes.

Early in the season of 1933, she left Detroit with a load of steel, but was holed by the ice and had to return to the Nicholson Dock. She didn't quite make it as she settled to the bottom before arriving. Although raised and repaired, her days were now numbered.

In late 1934, she was engaged in the steel trade on Lake Michigan when she met her end. While trying to negotiate the pierheads at Muskegon during a heavy gale on December 1, 1934, she struck the north breakwall and again sank. All on board were rescued, but the veteran "pig" was considered beyond repair when, a few weeks later, her bow broke off and sank. At the time of her final misfortune, she had on board 600 tons scrap steel destined for Cannon's, Wynant and Campbell's South Haven Foundry. Most of the attempts to salvage her failed but much scrap steel was recovered in the severe days of World War II. Thus ended one more of the unique whaleback vessels. Only one now remains, the METEOR, a museum near their birthplace at Superior, Wisconsin.

HENRY CORT in 1916

	Pillsbury			
	b) HENRY CORT			
BUILT:	American Steel Barge Company, West Superior, Wisconsin	*DEPTH:*	25
		GROSS REGISTERED TONNAGE:	2,234
HULL NUMBER:	125	*REGISTRY NUMBER:*	US 150587
LENGTH:	320	*ENGINES:*	23″, 37″, 62″ Diameter × 42″ Stroke Triple Expansion
BREADTH:	42	*ENGINE BUILDER:*	Samuel F. Hodge & Co., Detroit, Michigan

As a crane boat

THOMAS CRANAGE

The THOMAS CRANAGE was launched on July 29, 1893, and an estimated ten thousand people gathered to watch what was then the largest wooden steamship in the world hit the water. She was built largely with Bay City money for the McGraw Steamship Company. Principal investors were J. Will McGraw, Thomas and S. P. Cranage, H. H. Norrington, Captain J. S. Neil, all of Bay City, and Edward Smith, of Buffalo. Captain Neil would sail the large vessel.

Ownership later was transferred to the Cranage Steamship Company, but the same individuals basically retained their financial interest in her. Edward Smith managed her for quite some time, but later S. P. Cranage assumed those duties. The CRANAGE remained a "Bay City" boat for her entire career and was always enrolled at Port Huron.

On September 25, 1911, while carrying a cargo of wheat from Duluth for Tiffin Harbor, Ontario, on Georgian Bay, the CRANAGE stranded on Watchers Reef, five miles northeast of Hope Island, not far from her intended destination. Captain L. H. Powell notified his Bay City office and S. P. Cranage personally came to the wreck site to supervise salvage operations. He brought with him a salvage crew from Midland, Ontario. They found the hapless vessel's bow six feet out of the water. Less than a week after their arrival, a bad storm centered around the Soo area and dashed any hopes of retrieving the vessel. Cranage abandoned the vessel after ten days of work and released the Midland salvors. The CRANAGE's bones still are there.

THOMAS CRANAGE in 1906

BUILT:	James Davidson, West Bay City, Michigan	GROSS REGISTERED TONNAGE:	2,218
HULL NUMBER:	57	REGISTRY NUMBER:	US 145648
LENGTH:	305'	ENGINES:	Triple Expansion 20", 33" & 54" Diameter × 42" Stroke
BREADTH:	43'		
DEPTH:	20'7"	ENGINE BUILDER:	Dry Dock Engine Works, Detroit, Michigan

CRETE

CRETE downbound in Lake St. Clair

BUILT:	American Shipbuilding Company, Lorain, Ohio
HULL NUMBER:	352
LENGTH:	480
BREADTH:	52
DEPTH:	30
GROSS REGISTERED TONNAGE:	6,189
REGISTRY NUMBER:	US 204587
ENGINES:	22½", 36", 60" Diameter × 42" Stroke Triple Expansion
ENGINE BUILDER:	Shipyard

If you had been in a Lorain, Ohio, shipyard on Saturday afternoon, September 7, 1907, you might have wondered why the steamship being launched was named for the far-away Mediterranean island of Crete. The steamer took the Crete Mining Company and the Island of Crete as its dual namesakes. The mining company was active on the Mesabi Range of Minnesota and was a property managed by Pickands Mather & Company. Had you been brash enough to suggest to petite Miss Bessie Whitmore, the sponsor of the boat, that the CRETE was designed to sail the waters of the romantic Mediterranean, she probably would have given you a disbelieving glance. If you had asked Captain F. B. Huyck, the proud master of the new ship, why the name CRETE was selected, he may have reminded you that he was not in on the decision making. Mr. Jay C. Morse, a PM partner who was particularly partial to locations in the Mediterranean area, could have given you the correct answer to your question.

The CRETE, originally built for the Lackawanna Steamship Company, was sold in 1913 to the Interlake Steamship Company. She was always operated by Pickands Mather and lasted longer than many of the ships built in the same year. Before 1948, when she and the J. P. MORGAN, Jr. of the Pittsburgh Fleet, collided head-on in a dense fog off Devil's Island, Lake Superior, this vessel had been relatively free from serious accidents. The staunch vessel had ridden out the terrific storms of 1913 and 1940 without serious damage and had seen many similar vessels struck down in the prime of their lives. But age and small carrying capacity caught up with the ship and on June 27, 1962 she sailed through the Welland Canal flying the Italian flag, bound for a scrap pile in Genoa, Italy. After many years of service to Pickands Mather, this vessel was to see the Mediterranean after all!

CRETE off Harsens Island

CUMBERLAND

CUMBERLAND at the Soo

This wooden bulk carrier was built in 1881 for the Winslow Interests of Buffalo and Cleveland. The Winslows went out of business in 1887 and soon after this, she was acquired by the Gilchrist Transportation Co., Cleveland. In 1901 her engines were rebuilt to 21", 44" Diameter × 48" Stroke. When the Gilchrist Fleet was being liquidated in 1913, CUMBERLAND was sold on January 13 to Capt. Frank Peterson and J. B. McMillan and was renamed COLLINGE.

She did not remain under Capt. Peterson's management for long, as she was sold in February 1916 to the Canada Import Company and transferred to Canadian registry as STUART W. (C. 138096), being owned by the subsidiary company, Stuart W. Ltd., Quebec.

When the Bay Line Ltd., Montreal, was formed in 1923 by Ogilvie Flour Mills and others, STUART W. was transferred to the new fleet and renamed YEWBAY. The name of the new company was soon changed to Tree Line Navigation Co., Ltd. YEWBAY was already in poor condition when taken over in 1923. She was retired from service at the end of the 1924 season and laid up in Portsmouth Bay at Kingston, Ontario. The hull was finally towed out and scuttled in deep water off Kingston.

CUMBERLAND, b) Collinge, c) Stuart W, d) Yewbay

BUILT:	Quayle & Sons, Cleveland, Ohio
LENGTH:	251
BREADTH:	38.4
DEPTH:	19.6
GROSS REGISTERED TONNAGE:	1601
REGISTRY NUMBER:	US 125918
ENGINES:	Fore and Aft Compound 30", 54" Diameter and 48" Stroke
ENGINE BUILDER:	Samuel F. Hodge & Co., Detroit, Engine #160

COLLINGE in 1915

LOU A. CUMMINGS

The wooden passenger and freight propellor LOU A. CUMMINGS was built in 1883 for George Robinson of Grand Haven, Michigan. She was one of several small steamers that served the many small resort areas along the Lake Michigan coastline. In 1887, she was transferred to the ownership of C. W. Casky of Cheboygan, Michigan. After only two years, ownership again was changed, this time to J. U. Emory of Northport, Michigan. In 1897, H. J. Webb of Cassopolis, Michigan, acquired the CUMMINGS. During the period 1895–1907, the vessel became popular on the Charlevoix-East Jordan-Petoskey run. Webb also operated the CRESCENT between Northport and Traverse City, Michigan, along with COLUMBIA. In 1907, Oliver E. Wilbur, of Charlevoix, purchased the CUMMINGS, and in 1910 renamed her CITY OF BOYNE. That same year, she was rebuilt (87'8" × 19'7" × 7'8"; 99 gross tons). In 1913, she again had a tonnage change (121 gross tons). During this time, the boat ran from Charlevoix to Boyne City. Charles Roe of Harbor Springs, Michigan, acquired the vessel in 1915 to run on Little Traverse Bay and, in 1917, renamed her AMERICA. That same year, she was rebuilt (93'5" × 19'6" × 6'3"; 75 gross tons).

In 1931, the AMERICA was sold to Bay Port Transportation Company of Bay Port, Michigan, and received her fourth and last name, BAY PORT. She again was readmeasured (90 gross tons). Finally, in 1937, the trim craft was sold to Waterways Construction Company of Maryland and registered out of Baltimore. The company, with an office in Cleveland, Ohio, intended to use her as a tug, but shortly thereafter she was partially burned while lying in the Plowdry slip at Bay City, Michigan. Although she did not drop from enrollment until 1944, the vessel remained where she burned. In about 1958, what remained of the bones of this much-traveled little steamer were removed to make way for a new marina.

LOU A. CUMMINGS at the dock

CITY OF BOYNE on the lake

AMERICA at the dock

LOU A. CUMMINGS,
b) City of Boyne, c) America,
d) Bay Port

BUILT:	Duncan Robertson, Grand Haven, Michigan
LENGTH:	83.3
BREADTH:	16.3
DEPTH:	7.6
GROSS REGISTERED TONNAGE:	62
REGISTRY NUMBER:	US 140644
ENGINES:	16″ × 16″ Non-condensing
ENGINE BUILDER:	Grand Haven Iron Works, Grand Haven, Michigan

BAY PORT on the beach

CYPRUS

One of five identical steamers built during the steel shipbuilding boom of the early 1900's, the steel bulk freighter CYPRUS was launched on September 17, 1907 for the Lackawanna Steamship Company. Quite extraordinary only in the shortness of her career, the CYPRUS was no different from her sisters, the ADRIATIC, HEMLOCK, ODANAH, and CALUMET. On her first trip up the Lakes she was photographed by the Marine City photographer, Pesha, the only one known to have taken her picture, as she steamed proudly by the small town on the St. Clair River. Her first voyage was quite uneventful and she loaded iron ore for the lower Lake ports. She began her second voyage, again uneventfully, but never finished it.

At 9 A.M. on October 9, 1907, the CYPRUS cleared Superior, Wisconsin with a load of iron ore, destined for the Lackawanna, New York, steel mills. The fall storms on Lake Superior are vicious and the CYPRUS met one head on. So severe were the seas that she made little headway the first day out. By October 11, she was no further in her voyage than near Deer Park, Michigan, on the South shore of Lake Superior. Sometime during that night, the ship was wiped off the face of the Lake and never seen again. Four of her crew did manage to get on a life raft and head for shore through the giant breakers. The raft hit the shore and tumbled the men out into the freezing lake waters. Only one man survived but was barely alive when found by U.S. Life Savers from the Deer Park and Two Heart River stations. He was fed and cared for by these dedicated men and later returned home where he was confronted by the press and the vessel's owners in order to learn the horrifying details of the sinking of the CYPRUS. According to the survivor, the ship had been so battered that the waves tore off some of the hatch covers, allowing the heavy seas to enter her hold and swamp the ship.

CYPRUS on her first trip past Marine City

CYPRUS (Father Dowling painting) leaving Superior harbor on last trip

BUILT:	American Shipbuilding Company, Lorain, Ohio	*GROSS REGISTERED TONNAGE:*	4,900
		REGISTRY NUMBER:	US 204527
HULL NUMBER:	353	*ENGINES:*	22″, 35″, 58″ diameter × 42″ stroke
LENGTH:	420		Triple expansion
BREADTH:	52	*ENGINE BUILDER:*	American Shipbuilding Company, Lorain, Ohio
DEPTH:	28		

DALHOUSIE CITY

DALHOUSIE CITY,
b) Island King II,
c) Bucknor

BUILT:	Collingwood Ship Building Co., Ltd., Collingwood, Ontario
HULL NUMBER:	30
LENGTH:	199.8

BREADTH:	37
DEPTH:	20.9
GROSS REGISTERED TONNAGE:	1,256
REGISTRY NUMBER:	C. 130312
ENGINES:	Triple Expansion 18″, 29″ & 48″ Diameter × 30″ Stroke
ENGINE BUILDER:	Shipyard

DALHOUSIE CITY C. 1946

ISLAND KING II at Montreal

The day passenger steamer DALHOUSIE CITY was built in 1911 for the Dalhousie Navigation Co., Ltd., Toronto, a subsidiary of the Canadian Northern Railway (later Canadian National Railway Co.). She was designed by the famous yacht designer, George Owen. Laid down as DALHOUSIE, her name was changed before she was launched. She was christened by Miss Mary Hanna at Collingwood on June 24, 1911.

When DALHOUSIE CITY entered service, she carried her anchors quite close to the waterline. This caused her to be extremely wet forward in even a moderate sea. After her first season of operation, her anchors were repositioned farther above the water line and bilge keels were added to correct excessive rolling. She was designed to attain a speed of 15 MPH but in actual service her speed was 12 MPH. A new wheel, fitted in the early 1920's, made a

slight improvement. A dance deck was added about 1927. DALHOUSIE CITY operated in the Toronto-Port Dalhousie service until the close of the 1949 season. Owing to the destruction of her running mate NORTHUMBERLAND at Port Dalhousie on June 2, 1949, she operated alone during 1949.

Early in 1950 she was sold to Lakeshore Lines Ltd., Lachine, Quebec, and she left Port Dalhousie for the last time on April 21, 1950. Renamed b) ISLAND KING II, she entered service in 1950 from Victoria Pier, Montreal, on various excursion runs. While in winter quarters at Lachine, she was destroyed by a fire of suspicious origin on the night of November 13–14, 1960. The burned-out hull sank in the Lachine Canal and was sold to Buckport Shipping Ltd. She was salvaged and renamed c) BUCKNOR. It was planned to rebuild her as a barge but the plan was abandoned and she was dismantled at Montreal in 1961.

JAMES E. DAVIDSON

JAMES E. DAVIDSON in 1915

BUILT:	Great Lakes Engineering Works, Ecorse, Michigan
HULL NUMBER:	5
LENGTH:	504
BREADTH:	54.2
DEPTH:	31
GROSS REGISTERED TONNAGE:	6,206
REGISTRY NUMBER:	US 201961
ENGINES:	18″, 27″, 40″, 62″ diameter × 42″ stroke Quadruple expansion
ENGINE BUILDER:	Great Lakes Engineering Works, Ecorse, Michigan

The JAMES E. DAVIDSON was a steel bulk freighter owned by the Inter-Ocean Steamship Company and managed by the Tomlinson Fleet. Captain James E. Davidson was a famous builder of wooden ships on the Great Lakes. When everyone else had quit building wooden freighters at the turn of the century, he still maintained that these vessels were invaluable for the times. He continued to build this type of vessel until no one would buy them. Only then did he cease his operations and leave the vessel building business to the steel shipbuilding companies. His base of operations was Bay City, Michigan, and he continued his work there until the first decade of the 20th century. No other builder of wooden vessels lasted as long, or did such a competent job.

The JAMES E. DAVIDSON, like her namesake, had a long and useful life. She escaped disaster at least one time before her end. On Monday, October 21, 1929, the vessel cleared Duluth, Minnesota, with iron ore for Cleveland. The weather was heavy and by Tuesday evening the DAVIDSON had reached only the Keweenaw Peninsula area and was taking a severe pounding. Her master decided to run for the cover of the North shore of Lake Superior. In the process, her anchor was torn from its hawse pipe and water completely wrecked her forward cabins. Seven of the hatch covers gave way and she was deeply down at the bow when she finally tied up at the Murphy-Meade Coal Dock at Fort William, Ontario, on Thursday, October 24th. Except for this incident the JAMES E. DAVIDSON had only minor scrapes in the course of her service and performed successfully until being sold for scrap in 1963. The DAVIDSON was towed overseas to Genoa, Italy, the same year, thus ending her days on the Lakes. Maybe that Ferrari you're driving is part of the remains of this ship.

Downbound past Belle Isle

WILLIAM B. DAVOCK

The steel bulk carrier WILLIAM B. DAVOCK was built for the Vulcan Steamship Company and was launched April 25, 1907. William B. Davock, a Great Lakes vessel manager, owned the firm. The vessel was designed to carry iron ore, grain and coal.

The Great Lakes Engineering Works had established a plant at St. Clair, taking over the defunct Columbia Iron Works in 1903. For several years, they built freighters and sections of the Detroit-Windsor railroad tunnel at this site until 1911, when the plant was moved to Ashtabula, Ohio. The ships built at St. Clair had a variety of careers, but perhaps the DAVOCK had one of the most interesting and yet tragic lives.

In 1915 the Interlake Steamship Company, Pickands Mather & Co. managers, took over many vessels including the WILLIAM B. DAVOCK. This fleet was engaged in a variety of trade movements, dealing mainly in the iron ore, coal and grain trades. For the next quarter century, the DAVOCK labored hard with a variety of commands.

It was a trip to Lake Michigan that was her last. The waves and gale-force winds that buffeted the Lakes, especially Lake Michigan, on November 11, 1940, have become known to all Lakes' sailors as the Armistice Day Storm of 1940. Within a few hours the seas were so vicious that many ships were caught in the open lake with no shelter. Three ships were lost within a matter of hours, two of them under mysterious circumstances. The NOVADOC was wrecked off Pentwater, Michigan, but most of her complement were saved. The WILLIAM B. DAVOCK and the ANNA C. MINCH were not so fortunate. Both these vessels disappeared with all hands somewhere in the general vicinity of Pentwater. Thirty-two men lost their lives from the DAVOCK, and only wreckage floated ashore. The question was whether there was a collision between the MINCH and the DAVOCK as they were struggling to outlast the giant waves. Skin divers recently have probed the site of the tragedy and have confirmed, by the condition of the hull of the MINCH, that collision was a distinct possibility. Additionally, bodies from both vessels came ashore in the same vicinity. Whatever the cause, the DAVOCK sailed no longer and her men perished in that violent combination of wind and seas. No one knows of her last desperate struggle to remain afloat, and the terrible ordeal her men suffered as they finally realized that their ship was heading to the bottom.

WILLIAM B. DAVOCK passes Marine City

BUILT:	Great Lakes Engineering Works, St. Clair, Michigan	*REGISTRY NUMBER:*	US 204121
HULL NUMBER:	26	*ENGINES:*	21″, 34½″, 57″ diameter × 42″ stroke Triple expansion
LENGTH:	420		
BREADTH:	52		
DEPTH:	23	*ENGINE BUILDER:*	Great Lakes Engineering Works, St. Clair, Michigan
GROSS REGISTERED TONNAGE:	4,468		

DENMARK

DENMARK in the St. Clair River

BUILT:	Toledo Shipbuilding Company, Toledo, Ohio	*GROSS REGISTERED TONNAGE:*	5,448
HULL NUMBER:	114	*REGISTRY NUMBER:*	US 206152
LENGTH:	440	*ENGINES:*	22½″, 36″, 60″ diameter × 42″
BREADTH:	56		stroke
DEPTH:	28		Triple expansion
		ENGINE BUILDER:	Shipyard—1909

In the Detroit River

Full steam in Lake Huron

The steel bulk carrier DENMARK was built in 1908 for the Maumee Steamship Company. She was launched on Saturday, March 27, 1908, when christened by Miss Florence Calder at the Toledo yard on the Maumee River. DENMARK was always a fine looking ship. She was especially wide for her length and this lent her an impression of strength.

For the first few years, the DENMARK was the only ship of the Maumee Steamship Company. The manager of this Cleveland-based company was a man whose name was carried on another well-known vessel, Mr. Rufus P. Ranney. In 1911, the DENMARK passed into the fleet of the United States Transportation Company which became part of Great Lakes Steamship Company in 1912. She remained with this fleet through the 1956 season. The ship's colors were black hull, white cabins, and black stack with a wide gold band below the black smoke band on top.

In the spring of 1957, Wilson Marine Transit Company purchased the Great Lakes Steamship Company. The DEN-MARK, however, was immediately resold to T. J. McCarthy

Steamship Co. of Detroit. The DENMARK then received the stack colors of this fleet, the wide red band with a white "M" and small green "C" imposed upon it, but maintained the black Great Lakes Steamship hull. She sailed for McCarthy her last four years. On June 22, 1961, after loading a cargo of scrap at Lorain, Ohio, she transited the Welland Canal bound for Quebec for scrapping overseas. From Quebec, where she was "buttoned-up," the DEN-MARK was towed across the Atlantic by the tug ELBE, in tandem with the steamer MICHAEL GALLAGHER of the Midland fleet. DENMARK arrived at her final port, LaSpezia, Italy, on August 6, 1961.

On June 24, 1961, a St. Catharines, Ontario newspaper carried a large picture of the DENMARK passing under two bridges in the Welland Canal. But, as newspapermen occasionally do, the reporter wrote about the two bridges instead of the final voyage of this ship. He, too, must have felt that the DENMARK looked too nice for the scrapyard.

DUCHESS OF YORK

DUCHESS OF YORK running the rapids of the St. Lawrence

DUCHESS OF YORK, b) Sorel, c) Pelerin, d) Beloeil

BUILT:	Tate's Dock (William C. White), Montreal	*GROSS REGISTERED TONNAGE:*	490
LENGTH:	156.8	*REGISTRY NUMBER:*	C. 103342
BREADTH:	25.3	*ENGINES:*	Beam Condensing 34″ Diameter × 108″ Stroke
DEPTH:	9.4	*ENGINE BUILDER:*	George Brush, Montreal, P.Q.

PELERIN in the St. Lawrence Canals

This steel passenger steamer was built in 1895 for the Ottawa River Navigation Company and was designed for the picnic and moonlight excursion trade out of Montreal. Her engine, with solid walking beam, came from the steamer PRINCE OF WALES (1860–94) and part of her superstructure, including the dome on her upper deck, was also transferred from the same vessel. She had one boiler and the paddle wheels were of the large radial type. During spring and fall DUCHESS OF YORK operated in her owner's market line between Montreal, Carillon and Point Fortune. She took SOVEREIGN's place on the Montreal-Carillon run in 1906 and was sent to the Upper Ottawa River run to replace the EMPRESS in 1907.

In 1909 the Ottawa River Navigation Company was sold to a syndicate operating under the name of the Central Railway of Canada. The through line of steamers from Montreal to Ottawa continued to operate for one more season. Beginning in 1911 the steamers ran excursions out of Montreal and Ottawa. DUCHESS OF YORK now began

a varied career under numerous owners and names. From 1914–1918, she was owned by the King Edward Park Co., Ltd., and operated to that resort from Montreal. During 1921–1922 she operated at Montreal as a ferry to St. Helen's Island. By this time, her old radial paddlewheels had been replaced by the smaller feathering wheels which came out of C.S.L.'s CASPIAN which was being dismantled at Sorel.

For a number of years she ran excursions down river from Montreal and in 1925 was renamed b) SOREL. Again the name was changed in 1927 to c) PELERIN and it was under this name she was chartered to run weekly cruises in 1933 between Montreal, Toronto and Hamilton. This service proved to be unprofitable. Her owners at this time were Quebec and St. Lawrence Navigation Co., Ltd. In 1935 the name was changed again to d) BELOEIL. Her upperworks were removed in 1938 and the steel hull was sold to Sauvageau Bros., of Three Rivers, Quebec and used as a pulpwood barge. The vessel was finally broken up in 1943–44.

BELOEIL

DULUTH

DULUTH in Western Transit Co. colors

BUILT:	Chicago Shipbuilding Company, Chicago, Illinois	*GROSS REGISTERED TONNAGE:*	4,623
HULL NUMBER:	64	*REGISTRY NUMBER:*	US 200593
LENGTH:	381.6	*ENGINES:*	20¾″, 30″, 43½″, 63″ diameter
BREADTH:	50.2		× 42″ stroke
DEPTH:	26		Quadruple expansion
		ENGINE BUILDER:	Detroit Shipbuilding Company

Downbound in Lake St. Clair

DULUTH in the St. Mary's River

The DULUTH was built in 1903 for the Western Transit Company, a subsidiary of the New York Central Railroad. This steel, single screw package freighter had 11 hatches in total and 6 gangways on each side. Her pilot house was behind number one hatch and she had two tall raked masts, one forward and one amidships. All of the Western Transit ships had light brown hulls, white cabins, tall yellow spars, and black stacks with a wide orange band.

In 1915 the ships of this fleet, as well as those of most of the other railway lake lines, passed into the ownership of the Great Lakes Transit Corporation (GLTC) of Buffalo. Until 1925, all the GLTC ships were painted in the old Western Transit colors, while after that year they carried the colors of the former Pennsylvania Railroad freighters, with white and green hulls, white cabins and crimson funnels. The majority of vessels had previously served this fleet and the colors were more distinctive.

The DULUTH was one of the few package freighters that was never renamed. Requisitioned by the War Shipping Administration in 1942, the DULUTH and several other package freighters were taken to salt water via Chicago and the Mississippi River and were rebuilt for war duty. She was completely revamped topsides and was almost unrecognizable from her former lines as a laker.

Soon after the end of World War II, DULUTH and many of her sister lakers were laid up at Seattle, their jobs done. Some were sold foreign and saw additional service, but the DULUTH's days had ended. In 1955, she was removed from documentation and sold to Japanese buyers for scrap. She left Portland, Oregon on June 23, 1955 and sailed for the last time into the setting sun and was cut up in Japan later that year.

MAGGIE DUNCAN

MAGGIE DUNCAN at the Soo

MAGGIE DUNCAN,
b) Mohawk

BUILT:	Andrew R. Johnson, Fort Howard, Wisconsin
LENGTH:	164'5"
BREADTH:	31'8"
DEPTH:	11'7"
GROSS REGISTERED TONNAGE:	535
REGISTRY NUMBER:	US 92168
ENGINES:	Steeple Compound 12" & 36" Diameter × 30" Stroke
ENGINE BUILDER:	Manistee Iron Works, Manistee, Michigan

MOHAWK entering Boston harbor

The three-masted wooden lumber steamer MAGGIE DUNCAN was built in 1890 near Green Bay for John Duncan, and was enrolled at the Milwaukee customs house on April 18 of that year. In June, 1891, ownership and enrollment was transferred to Frank Clark at Detroit, Michigan. However, by October 1892, the DUNCAN reverted back to John Duncan, first at Chicago, then at Milwaukee. In the spring of 1893 Sidney Neff of Milwaukee, purchased the small vessel. In March 1896, the DUNCAN passed on to Runnels, Sinclair, and others of Port Huron, Michigan.

As the ice cleared on the upper lakes, the MAGGIE DUNCAN, along with the schooner O. O. CARPENTER, arrived at Buffalo, New York, on May 3, 1905. After extensive repairs, the vessels, now owned by W. H. Brigham, of Boston, Massachusetts, headed for new careers in the Atlantic Coast coal trade. The following year, MAGGIE was renamed MOHAWK. Over the years, she changed ownership frequently and called, successively, Boston, Portland, Boston, and Belfast home, and finally, Boston, again. On August 9, 1922, the MOHAWK stranded at Castle Hook, New Jersey, a long way from the waters of Green Bay, Lake Michigan.

JAMES B. EADS

The winter of 1893–94 had been a poor one for the shipbuilding industry and, for this reason, the GLOBE was built on speculation to the builders' own account, mainly as a means of keeping the yard force employed. She was a steel, double-decked package freighter.

During her early years, GLOBE operated in the general freight trade under charter to a Buffalo concern then known as Great Lakes Steamship Co., managed by Messrs. Gordon and Aitken. As of 1897 her home port was listed as Buffalo, which suggests that Gordon and Aitken may have bought the vessel.

However, in 1899 the ship was purchased by the fast-growing Bessemer Steamship Co., converted into a bulk freighter, lengthened to 400 feet (with 3746 gross tons) and renamed b) JAMES B. EADS in honor of the well-known structural engineer.

The Bessemer fleet became part of Pittsburgh Steamship Co. in 1901, and for 26 years thereafter, the EADS sailed as a "Tin Stacker." She was rebuilt extensively in 1920, getting a raised forecastle with a new pilothouse positioned on it (2704 gross tons). The late Capt. Arthur C. Johnson was assigned his first command in 1921 as captain of the JAMES B. EADS.

The EADS was owned briefly by Nassau Ship and Dredge Company in 1926, and in 1927 she was resold to James Playfair of Midland, Ontario (C. 153126). In the middle Thirties, Playfair's ships joined the fleet of Upper Lakes & St. Lawrence Transportation Co., Ltd.

In the early 1960's, she was equipped with deck cranes and used briefly as a package freighter for the second time in her long life. The vessel was broken up at Port Weller, Ontario in 1967.

GLOBE with an Inman tug entering Superior Entry

JAMES B. EADS in 1919

Globe,
b) JAMES B. EADS

BUILT:	Globe Iron Works, Cleveland, Ohio
HULL NUMBER:	53
LENGTH:	330.4
BREADTH:	42

DEPTH:	24.3
GROSS REGISTERED TONNAGE:	2,995
REGISTRY NUMBER:	US 86307
ENGINES:	Triple Expansion 24″, 39″ & 63″ Diameter × 42″ Stroke
ENGINE BUILDER:	Shipyard—1896

Opposite Sarnia, Ontario

EASTLAND

EASTLAND was a palatial steel, twin screw vessel built in 1903 for day passenger and fruit transportation across Lake Michigan to Chicago. Her original owners were the Michigan Steamship Company, operating between Chicago and South Haven. Later she operated out of Cleveland to Cedar Point and it was while she steamed on Lake Erie that a post card was issued extolling her virtues and the desirability of a cruise on her decks. Three pennants on the card emphasized "Past-Golden Memories: Present-Happy Days: Future-That you'll remember me." She was back on Lake Michigan for the season of 1915, however operating for the St. Joseph-Chicago Line. Although fast and with fine lines, this ship had gained a bad reputation early in her life because of her tendency to roll, and was generally looked upon with fear.

"The most ill-fated vessel on the Great Lakes." Such words have described the stately passenger steamer because of the monstrous tragedy that befell this ship on Saturday, July 24, 1915. The EASTLAND and three other Chicago passenger vessels, MISSOURI, CITY OF SOUTH HAVEN, and THEODORE ROOSEVELT, were chartered for the annual employees' picnic of the Western Electric Company. At 7:30 that morning, the EASTLAND was loaded with 2,500 persons and ready to depart from her Clark Street dock, with the tug KENOSHA of Great Lakes Towing Company assisting.

Scarcely had the hawser pulled tight when the big liner rolled over pinning 812 passengers on the underside. No chance whatever was given to so many men, women and children who were hopelessly trapped inside the vessel as it turned over on its port side. This was the greatest single casualty loss of any Great Lakes vessel accident, and made one of Chicago's saddest days. For days afterwards, she

rested on her side on the bottom of the muddy Chicago River less than 20 feet from the dock, with a great part of her starboard side still above the water. The rescuers worked tirelessly, first to aid those still alive or trapped between decks, then to retrieve the bodies of those drowned. This grisly task was theirs for many days after the accident. Three weeks later, the undamaged hull was pumped out and righted by the powerful pumps and crane of the wrecking tug FAVORITE (2) and was towed up the Chicago River to North Halstead Street bridge.

No one wanted her. She was a pariah with ghosts of screaming, drowned humanity in her bosom. The disaster so infuriated the people of Chicago that some of the lawsuits resulting from the horror have been settled in the courts just in very recent years. In 1917 the U.S. Navy purchased the hull, had it cut down and rebuilt as a training vessel and renamed it WILMETTE. For 31 years she was a successful unit of the Navy and saw duty in two wars. Early in World War II she was rebuilt topsides and had only one stack and a tripod military mast forward instead of her two original spars. The war ended before she saw service on the high seas but WILMETTE trained many recruits to sink the dreaded U Boats. One of the latter, a World War I submarine, the U-97, on display at Chicago since the 1920's, was sunk in gunery practice on Lake Michigan while training the sailors of World War II.

The former EASTLAND's career finally came to an end under the scrappers' torch at Chicago in 1948, and even then, she made the front pages of the Chicago papers. Her name had been changed way back in 1917 but even this disguise failed to stem the hatred of Chicagoans, especially those who were in any way connected with the tragedy.

EASTLAND ready to launch at Port Huron

EASTLAND at South Haven

EASTLAND,
b) USS Wilmette

BUILT:	Jenks Shipbuilding Co., Port Huron, Michigan
HULL NUMBER:	25
LENGTH:	265
BREADTH:	38.2
DEPTH:	19.5
GROSS REGISTERED TONNAGE:	1,961
REGISTRY NUMBER:	US 200031
ENGINES:	Triple Expansion (2) 21″, 39″, 56″ Diameter × 30″ Stroke
ENGINE BUILDER:	Shipyard

Chicago-South Haven Line

171

EASTLAND, the disaster

Rescue operations

Towing the wreck away—tug Kenosha

Last of the ill-fated ship EASTLAND

U.S.S. WILMETTE on patrol

EMBURY

The wooden freight steamer COLIN CAMPBELL was launched on April 10, 1869. She was built for the Northwestern Transportation Company, Robert J. Hackett, secretary, of Detroit, Michigan. The hull was towed to Cleveland to receive her machinery. In April 1873, in a business reorganization, the firm name was changed to the Western Transportation and Coal Company, also of Detroit.

One year later, the CAMPBELL was sold to William H. Ingram and Joseph W. Dennis, both of Buffalo. In 1875, Ingram bought his partner's interest in the vessel. However, the general downward economic trend of the 1870's apparently caught up with Ingram because, on March 30, 1876, the CAMPBELL was sold at a sheriff's sale in Chicago for $16,000. She was enrolled at Milwaukee with Matthew

Englemann, of the well-known Lake Michigan Englemann Line, as owner. In 1878 Otto Kitzinger, also of Milwaukee, purchased the ship. Subsequent Milwaukee owners were John Cochran (1879) and Olaf N. Anderson (1889).

In March, 1900, the little vessel was sold to W. L. Martin, a prominent Cheboygan, Michigan, lumberman. While in winter lay-up at Cheboygan she partially burned on January 25, 1901. Martin rebuilt her and renamed her EMBURY. She served in the lumber trade for only a few years. On December 4, 1903, she again caught fire, this time near Tonawanda, New York, on the Niagara River. Her hulk was beached on Grand Island to end nearly forty years of freshwater service.

EMBURY with a load of lumber

Colin Campbell, b) EMBURY		GROSS REGISTERED TONNAGE:	373
BUILT:	Linn & Craig, Gibraltar, Michigan	REGISTRY NUMBER: ENGINES:	US 5719 High pressure non-condensing
HULL NUMBER:	6		24½" Diameter × 30" Stroke
LENGTH:	158'7"	ENGINE BUILDER:	Cuyahoga Iron Works,
BREADTH:	30'2"		Cleveland, Ohio
DEPTH:	11'4"		

TEMPLE EMERY

TEMPLE EMERY heading for a tow

In 1886, James Davidson built a fine wooden tug for his account and named it TEMPLE EMERY. Shortly, H. Mann of Milwaukee, Wisconsin, purchased the vessel and ran her in the towing trade out of that port until 1907, when she was purchased by W. L. Martin of Cheboygan, Michigan. This tug was a popular sight in the Straits of Mackinac area, where it was engaged in towing as well as in the salvaging of stranded vessels. In 1911 the Buffalo Dredging Company bought the tug and took the EMERY to lower Lake Erie to be used in river and harbor dredging projects. As originally built, she was a high-sided tug used in cross-lake business, but in 1913 she was cut down to a harbor tug and her gross tonnage reduced to 88.

This was the same year the EMERY was purchased by the Great Lakes Dredge Company of Buffalo, New York.

This firm became known as Great Lakes Dredge and Dock Company in the latter half of 1921 with the TEMPLE EMERY becoming a unit of this company.

Because of her age, the EMERY was not used much and she was abandoned in 1923 after 43 years of service. Thus ended the career of one staunch wooden tug, of which there were hundreds in the late 1800's and the early 1900's. Many times these workhorses of the Lakes could be seen towing as many as eight schooners behind them through the St. Mary's, St. Clair and Detroit Rivers. At the turn of the century, they usually towed only two or three tow-barges or cut-down schooners. They were employed in various trades, and many of them were cut down to harbor or dredge tugs after the schooner towing business ceased.

At Cheboygan with the JOHN R. STERLING & CITY OF ALPENA

BUILT:	West Bay City Shipbuilding Company, West Bay City, Michigan
LENGTH:	83.2
BREADTH:	20.6
DEPTH:	10.1
GROSS REGISTERED TONNAGE:	155
REGISTRY NUMBER:	US 145421
ENGINES:	19″, 32″ diameter × 26″ stroke Steeple compound
ENGINE BUILDER:	Filer & Stowell Company, Milwaukee, Wisconsin

RHODA EMILY

RHODA EMILY in 1910

In 1884 the wooden steam barge RHODA EMILY was built for W. R. Owen of Chicago, Illinois and ran for the Eastern Transit Company on Lake Michigan until sold to C. R. Jones of Cleveland, Ohio in 1896. In 1900, the EMILY was sold to the Saginaw Bay Transit Company of Cleveland. She was used mostly in the lumber and coal trade and often towed a consort schooner barge. Sold to Winnefred Schlosser of Milwaukee, Wisconsin, in 1910, she was renamed CREAM CITY in 1913.

Again sold in 1917, she went to the James R. Andrews Transit Company of Escanaba, Michigan. By this time the ship was getting tired, but continued in use in the lumber trade on northern Lake Huron.

On July 1, 1918, while towing the barge GRACE HOLLAND, she was headed for False Detour Passage in northern Lake Huron in a dense fog. Not having the advantage of modern day navigation safety devices, the CREAM CITY stranded on Wheeler Reef, one-half mile south of False Detour passage, near Kitchener Island. Both the CREAM CITY and the GRACE HOLLAND went fast on the Reef. No one was injured from either vessel but the ships were high and dry. Attempts to save both the CREAM CITY and the GRACE HOLLAND failed, and they ended their days on this spot. After a long life, this lumber hooker was no more.

CREAM CITY in 1915

RHODA EMILY
b) Cream City

BUILT:	Linn and Craig, Trenton, Michigan
HULL NUMBER:	27
LENGTH:	166.1
BREADTH:	32

DEPTH:	12.6
GROSS REGISTERED TONNAGE:	570.33
REGISTRY NUMBER:	US 110641
ENGINES:	21″, 32″ diameter × 36″ stroke Steeple compound
ENGINE BUILDER:	S. F. Hodge & Company, Detroit, Michigan

EMPEROR

Inland Lines, Limited, Mr. James Playfair, Manager, had a steel bulk carrier built in 1910. In 1913, when Canada Steamship Lines (CSL) was organized and a giant fleet emerged, Inland Lines were absorbed and the EMPEROR became a member of the fleet. Her first year of sailing for this new fleet was 1914 and she continued in this same fleet the rest of her life. Through two World Wars she worked on the Great Lakes, carrying cargoes of grain and iron ore.

Under mysterious circumstances, EMPEROR met her end on a calm day, June 4, 1947. After loading a cargo of ore, she proceded downbound on Lake Superior when suddenly the ship hit hard on the Canoe Rocks, a pinacle jutting out of the depths near Isle Royale. She hit with such force that her after-end broke off almost immediately and sank into deep water. The forward end remained pinned to the rocks and water covered the pilot house. The mast remained above water and many of the crew were able to scramble into life boats. Even though the US Coast Guard cutter KIMBAL came to her rescue, 12 men perished in the cold waters of Lake Superior. After a short while, the forward end also plunged to the bottom, taking the master along.

Disaster befalls the Lakes at odd intervals in these days of modern safety equipment and electronic devices. Human error still cannot be avoided in spite of these wonderful inventions, and men still lose their lives because of it. The EMPEROR will be remembered as a staunch vessel which served its owners well over 37 years.

EMPEROR on Lake St. Clair

BUILT:	Collingwood Shipbuilding Company, Collingwood, Ontario	*GROSS REGISTERED TONNAGE:*	7,031
HULL NUMBER:	28	*REGISTRY NUMBER:*	C 126654
LENGTH:	525	*ENGINES:*	23″, 38½″, 63″ diameter × 42″ stroke
BREADTH:	56.1		Triple Expansion
DEPTH:	27	*ENGINE BUILDER:*	Shipyard

EMPRESS

Peerless,
b) EMPRESS

BUILT: Peter Kilduff,
    Ottawa, Ontario
LENGTH: 202'
BREADTH: 28'5"
DEPTH: 8'4"

GROSS REGISTERED
TONNAGE: 1,039
REGISTRY NUMBER: C. 73086
ENGINES: Beam Condensing
    38" Diameter × 120" Stroke
ENGINE BUILDER: G. Brush,
    Montreal

EMPRESS in the Lachine Rapids

The iron hull of the steamer PEERLESS was fabricated at Newcastle-on-Tyne, Great Britain, and shipped in sections to Canada in 1872. The vessel was built at Ottawa, Ontario, in 1873 under the supervision of Peter Kilduff, an Ottawa blacksmith and iron worker. Superstructure was done by Curry of Montreal. The PEERLESS was the first iron-hulled steamer built for the Ottawa River Navigation Company and the largest passenger steamer ever to operate on the Ottawa River. She also was the first steamer on the Ottawa to be lighted by electricity.

She ran between Ottawa and Grenville, with through passengers for Montreal being conveyed from Grenville to Carillon by the Carillon and Grenville Railway, also owned by the steamboat company. This was necessary to overcome the small canal running between the two places. At Carillon, passengers boarded the steamer PRINCE OF WALES for Montreal.

In 1885, in mid-season, as the PEERLESS approached Montebello from Grenville, she was discovered to be on fire. Quick work by Captain Alexander Bowie and crew put the steamer alongside the wharf, and all on board scrambled to safety. Reportedly a disgruntled crew member who had been dismissed set fire to the vessel.

The superstructure was entirely destroyed, but her iron hull was cut in two so it could be towed through the Ottawa canals to Montreal. In 1886, she was shortened and rebuilt by W. C. White in Montreal, and renamed EMPRESS (185'3" × 28' × 8'1"; 678 gross tons, 372 net tons). The same beam engine was used.

As EMPRESS, she remained on the Ottawa-Grenville route until 1907. In that year she received new boilers (two water tube, 7'6" × 13', built by McDougall of Montreal in 1907). She also was transferred to the lower route, between Montreal and Carillon, to replace the SOVEREIGN, which burned in March, 1906. The slower DUCHESS OF YORK replaced the EMPRESS on the upper route.

The EMPRESS remained on this route on a daily excursion basis, which included shooting the Lachine Rapids, until she was laid up at the end of the 1931 season. In 1920, the Ottawa River company went into receivership. Williamson F. Stuart, of the Central Railway of Canada, Montreal, served as receiver. In 1921, W. H. Dwyer, Ltd., of Ottawa, owned the ship. Apparently he headed up a syndicate, called the Empress Navigation Company, Ltd., of Ottawa, which operated the vessel for the ten years following 1921.

In 1932 the EMPRESS was laid up at Lachine. She was scrapped in 1935.

EN-AR-CO

This iron hulled barge entered service as a propellor built for the east coast coal trade and was launched on April 29, 1874. Her first owners were the Philadelphia and Reading Railroad. Her original name was BERKS (US 2905). Her original engine was a compound 2 cylinder 20-1/2" + 34" Diameter × 30" Stroke built by her owners.

By the early 1900's, she had been superseded by newer and more efficient coastal colliers. She was sold in 1906 to the Canadian Transit Co., Ltd., Toronto, and was brought to the Lakes as the barge b) W. S. CALVERT under Canadian Registry.

In 1909 she was acquired by the National Refining Company (later to become Canadian Oil Companies, Ltd., Toronto) and in 1910 was transferred to their subsidiary, the Sarnia and Toledo Transit Company, and used in the bulk oil trade. In 1921 she was given the name c) EN-AR-CO, representing the initials of her owner's corporate name.

The barge was laid up in the late 1920's and remained idle until 1934 when she was sold to John E. Russell, a prominent Toronto shipping figure. She was being refitted at Toronto for carrying crude oil to the Lloyd Refineries at Port Credit, Ontario, when on July 23, 1934, the ship was damaged by a tremendous explosion which was followed by a stubborn fire fed by oil in the bilges. The explosion took the life of John E. Russell who was on deck at the time.

In 1935 EN-AR-CO was sold to Pyke Salvage and Navigation Co., Kingston, Ontario. She was converted to a coal barge and lighter with a steam driven whirly crane mounted on deck. She put in good service on many occasions for her owners who later became McAllister-Pyke Salvage, Ltd., but her assignments became fewer as the years passed and she spent much of her time idle at Kingston.

One of her last jobs was removing the molten rubber and other damaged cargo from the hull of the Greek salty ORIENT TRADER which burned and sank in Toronto Harbor July 21, 1965.

After several years of inactivity at Kingston, EN-AR-CO was sold in 1969 to United Metals and Refining Co. at Hamilton, Ontario, and was dismantled at their yard in the autumn of 1969.

W. S. CALVERT awaiting a cargo

W. S. CALVERT in 1916

Berks,
b) W. S. Calvert,
c) EN-AR-CO

BUILT: Delaware River Iron
Shipbuilding and Engine Co.,
J. Roach & Sons,
Chester, Pennsylvania

LENGTH: 189
BREADTH: 29
DEPTH: 14.4
GROSS REGISTERED
TONNAGE: 565
REGISTRY NUMBER: C. 112113

EN-AR-CO at Kingston, Ontario, tug CAPT. M. B. DONNELLY at left

FAVOURITE

FAVOURITE at Collingwood

The wooden passenger and freight vessel, FAVOURITE, was built in 1889 for the Meaford Transportation Company (Charles A. Farrar) and was intended for Georgian Bay service. In 1892, the Meaford firm worked out an arrangement with the North Shore Navigation Co., Ltd., of Collingwood. The following year the North Shore company absorbed the Meaford firm and renamed the vessel CITY OF PARRY SOUND. In 1899 the corporate name of the firm was changed to the Northern Navigation Company, Ltd., but the CITY OF PARRY SOUND did not last long. She burned on October 9, 1900 at Collingwood.

The hull of the passenger steamer was saved and, in 1906, was built as a completely new vessel, a tug called the A. F. BOWMAN (C. 116385), which was built by Robert

J. Morill at Collingwood. The dimensions of the new vessel were: 76' × 22' × 12'; 112 gross registered tons. Her engine was a fore and aft compound, 18" and 36" diameter by a 26" stroke, built by the Doty Engine Works, Toronto, Ontario in 1889. The vessel was owned by the Canadian Towing and Wrecking Co., Ltd., James Whalen, president.

In 1907, the vessel's ownership was transferred to the Great Lakes Dredging Company Ltd., of Port Arthur, Ontario but, in May of 1912, reverted back to Canadian Towing and Wrecking. From January, 1929 to April of the same year she belonged to the Dominion Towing and Salvage Co., Ltd., of Montreal and after that date belonged to the United Towing and Salvage Co., Ltd., also of Montreal. The vessel was finally dismantled at Port Arthur in 1941.

FAVOURITE,	
b) City of Parry Sound,	
c) A. F. Bowman	
BUILT:	Chisholm, Meaford, Ontario
LENGTH:	130'
BREADTH:	25'

DEPTH:	10'
GROSS REGISTERED TONNAGE:	491
REGISTRY NUMBER:	C. 94762
ENGINES:	Compound 15" & 27" Diameter × 24" Stroke
ENGINE BUILDER:	T. Doty Engine Co., Toronto, Ontario

GEORGE R. FINK (I)

J. Q. RIDDLE in 1907

The J. Q. Riddle was a bulk steel freighter built in 1906 for the Hawgood-managed Milwaukee Steamship Company and was launched on June 30, 1906.

Her days under the Hawgood management ended in 1911, when she passed to the management of the M. A. Hanna Company of Cleveland, Ohio. Thereafter this ore carrier was transferred to various fleets managed by Hanna; into the Commonwealth Steamship Company in 1911 which renamed her J. J. TURNER in 1915; the Scott Steamship Company in 1916; the Calumet Transportation Company in 1919; the Producers Steamship Company in 1931, which renamed her GEORGE R. FINK (I); and the National Steamship Company in 1936. The last two firms were divisions of the National Steel Corporation. The vessel usually carried iron ore and coal cargoes, and occasionally handled grain.

On September 11, 1952, the FINK made headlines in Detroit, Michigan when she ran aground in the Amherstberg Channel, knocking the Livingstone Channel lighthouse into the water. The FINK was refloated and returned to service later that fall as THOMAS E. MILLSOP (I). Because of the new tonnage acquired by National Steel, the ship was sold to the Midwest Steamship Company and operated by

Troy H. Browning of Detroit in 1953, and in 1955 was renamed W. WAYNE HANCOCK. In 1957 the corporate name of this line was changed to Browning Lines, Incorporated.

The last year the HANCOCK operated was quite unusual. The idea of carrying containers on her deck for the "Chung King" Chinese food enterprise of Duluth, Minnesota was envisioned. The HANCOCK would load the containers at Duluth-Superior Harbor and carry them to Detroit, Cleveland and Buffalo, New York for distribution there. The idea was tried but did not succeed because of the difficulty of loading and unloading the containers. So the HANCOCK was in reality, the first container ship on the Lakes, however brief her attempt.

This vessel came to the end of her useful life and was excess tonnage by 1962 when sold for scrap to Marine Salvage of Port Colborne, Ontario, who in turn sold her to an overseas scrap yard. The HANCOCK left the Lakes in the summer of 1962 and headed across the Atlantic in tow of powerful transatlantic tugs. Enroute to Genoa, Italy, the HANCOCK sank 30 miles Southeast of the Azores on December 8, 1962, cheating the breakers of a grand old lady of the Lakes.

J. J. TURNER at Mission Point

GEORGE R. FINK in the Detroit River

a) J. Q. Riddle, b) J. J. Turner, c) GEORGE R. FINK (I), d) Thomas E. Millsop (I), e) W. Wayne Hancock

BUILT:	American Shipbuilding Company, Lorain, Ohio	*GROSS REGISTERED TONNAGE:*	6,832
HULL NUMBER:	344	*REGISTRY NUMBER:*	US 203377
LENGTH:	532	*ENGINES:*	Triple expansion 23½″, 38″, 63″ diameter × 42″ stroke
BREADTH:	56	*ENGINE BUILDER:*	American Shipbuilding Company, Cleveland, Ohio
DEPTH:	31		

THOMAS E. MILLSOP in the St. Mary's River

THOMAS E. MILLSOP in the Detroit River

W. WAYNE HANCOCK at Mission Point

W. WAYNE HANCOCK downbound in the St. Mary's River

EDMUND FITZGERALD

On February 1, 1957, the Northwestern Mutual Life Insurance Company, Milwaukee, entered into a contract with the Great Lakes Engineering Works for the construction of the first "maximum sized" Laker ever built. The builder laid the keel of Hull 301 at its yard at Ecorse, Michigan, on August 7, 1957, and the vessel was launched on June 7, 1958. On September 22, 1958, EDMUND FITZGERALD was delivered to her owner. She was to operate for her entire career under charter to the Columbia Transportation Division, Oglebay Norton Company, Cleveland.

EDMUND FITZGERALD made a name for herself by setting a number of cargo records over the years. She was an extremely handsome boat and was well known to both casual and serious shipwatchers, notably as a result of the antics of her longtime master, Capt. Peter Pulcer, who did his best to entertain anyone who might be watching his vessel.

The only major work, apart from some stiffening of hull members, ever done on the FITZGERALD was the installation of a bowthruster in 1969 and a conversion to oil fuel and the fitting of automated boiler controls over the winter of 1971–72.

The EDMUND FITZGERALD is, unfortunately, best known today for the tragic and violent manner in which she met her untimely demise. She cleared Superior, Wisconsin, on her last trip on November 9, 1975, with a cargo of 26,116 tons of taconite pellets consigned to Detroit. Travelling down Lake Superior in company with ARTHUR M. ANDERSON of the United States Steel Corporation's Great Lakes Fleet, she encountered heavy weather and, in the early evening of November 10th, suddenly foundered approximately 17 miles from the entrance to Whitefish Bay. Had she been able to manage those last few miles, she would have achieved the safety of calmer waters. All 29 of her crew, including Capt. Ernest McSorley who had commanded her since 1972, were lost and not one body has ever come ashore from the wreck. The broken hull of the steamer was located in 530 feet of water, the bow and stern sections lying close together.

The cause of the sinking is still a matter of controversy but, shocking as it is, the fact remains that the "FITZ" is gone. Her mangled lifeboats, mute testimony to her violent end, can be seen aboard the museum ship VALLEY CAMP at Sault Ste. Marie, Michigan.

On the ways—Str. ALPENA at right

EDMUND FITZGERALD with a load of iron ore

BUILT:	Great Lakes Engineering Works, Ecorse, Michigan	*GROSS REGISTERED TONNAGE:*	13,632
HULL NUMBER:	301	*REGISTRY NUMBER:*	US 277437
LENGTH:	711.2	*ENGINES:*	Steam Turbine 2 Cylinder—7,500 SHP
BREADTH:	75.1	*ENGINE BUILDER:*	Westinghouse Electric Corporation
DEPTH:	33.4		

Upbound light on Lake Huron

CLARY FORAN

The lower lakes bulk carrier COTEAUDOC (1) was built in 1929 for Paterson Steamships Ltd., Fort William, Ontario. Requisitioned for east coast service by the Canadian Government in 1940, she was later transferred to the U.S. Maritime Commission. She was brought back to the Lakes in 1947 by Colonial Steamships Ltd., Port Colborne, and refitted for lake and canal service at Port Weller Drydocks Ltd. as b) MILVERTON.

She collided with the tanker TRANSLAKE in the St. Lawrence River near Morrisburg, Ontario, on September 24, 1947. A devastating fire followed the collision and seven members of MILVERTON's crew perished. She finally came to rest, her back broken, about a mile downstream from the collision scene. The wreck was declared a hazard to navigation.

Salvage was undertaken by E. B. Magee Ltd., Port Colborne, and work started on August 9, 1948. On November 29, 1948, she floated free. In April 1949, she sailed under her own power to Port Weller Drydock to be rebuilt. She came out in September 1949 as c) CLARY FORAN and remained in the Colonial Fleet until the opening of the St. Lawrence Seaway.

In the summer of 1959, she was purchased by Reoch Transports Ltd., Montreal, and renamed d) FERNDALE (1). Laid up in Toronto at the end of the 1962 season, she was fitted out for the last time in March 1963 and sailed to Hamilton, Ontario, for scrapping at the Steel Company of Canada Ltd., ending the interesting career of another small canaller.

COTEAUDOC Loading grain at Port Colborne

MILVERTON wrecked

Coteaudoc (1), b) Milverton, c) CLARY FORAN, d) Ferndale (1)

BUILT:	Barclay Curle & Co., Ltd.,	*GROSS REGISTERED*	
	Whiteinch, Glasgow, Scotland	*TONNAGE:*	1,975
HULL NUMBER:	630	*REGISTRY NUMBER:*	C. 149500
LENGTH:	252.7	*ENGINES:*	Triple Expansion
BREADTH:	43.3		15″, 25″ & 40″ Diameter × 33″
DEPTH:	17.9		Stroke
		ENGINE BUILDER:	Barclay Curle & Co., Ltd.,
			Glasgow, Scotland

CLARY FORAN in the Welland Canal

CLARY FORAN upbound in the Detroit River

FERNDALE in Lake Huron

FORT WILLDOC

JOHN J. ALBRIGHT passing Marine City

John J. Albright,
b) Regulus,
c) FORT WILLDOC

BUILT:	American Shipbuilding Co., Cleveland, Ohio
HULL NUMBER:	403
LENGTH:	422.1
BREADTH:	50.2

DEPTH:	23.7
GROSS REGISTERED TONNAGE:	4,542
REGISTRY NUMBER:	US 77456
ENGINES:	Triple Expansion 23″, 37½″ & 63″ diameter × 42″ Stroke
ENGINE BUILDER:	Shipyard

JOHN J. ALBRIGHT downbound in the St. Mary's River

Built in 1900 as JOHN J. ALBRIGHT for Captain John Mitchell's Cleveland Steamship Company, this steel bulk freighter was sold in 1916 to Interlake Steamship Co., Cleveland (Pickands Mather & Co.) and renamed b) REGULUS. She received an extensive rebuild in 1925. In 1926 she was sold to Paterson Steamships Ltd., Fort William, and renamed c) FORT WILLDOC under Canadian Registry (C. 153114).

FORT WILLDOC spent the next 38 years in the grain and coal trade. From 1961 to 1964 she operated almost exclusively in the coal trade from Lake Erie ports to Toronto and Hamilton. She was well suited for this trade with her 12 hatches spaced on 24' centers, which enabled dockside whirley cranes to lower their clams into the hold without damaging her hatch coamings. On December 2nd, 1964, she passed down the Welland Canal with her last load of coal, bound for Toronto. Two days later she sailed light from Toronto to Hamilton for scrapping by the Steel Company of Canada Ltd. and was cut up in the summer of 1965.

Once a familiar sight on the Lakes, this class of boat, designed by Capt. John Mitchell, is no more, but to ship watchers, all of them had a distinctive silhouette. The sleek lines of these vessels were a sight to behold but then again, these ships were built for economical operation and their small capacity doomed them in modern times because of their inability to carry sufficient cargoes to pay their way.

REGULUS, A. T. KINNEY, AUGUSTUS B. WOLVIN astern

FORT WILLDOC in the St. Clair River

FORT WILLDOC

W. C. FRANZ

URANUS in the St. Clair River

<table>
<tr><td colspan="2" align="center">Uranus,
b) W. C. FRANZ</td><td>GROSS REGISTERED</td><td></td></tr>
</table>

		GROSS REGISTERED	
		TONNAGE:	3,748
		REGISTRY NUMBER:	US 25339
BUILT:	Detroit Shipbuilding Co.,	*ENGINES:*	Triple expansion
	Wyandotte, Michigan		22″, 35″ & 58″ Diameter × 42″
HULL NUMBER:	140		Stroke
LENGTH:	346	*ENGINE BUILDER:*	Detroit S. B. Co. (Engine
BREADTH:	48		Div.),
DEPTH:	28		Detroit, Mich.

This steel bulk carrier was launched as URANUS by the Detroit Shipbuilding Co. on Saturday, April 20, 1901, for the Gilchrist Transportation Co., Cleveland.

When the Gilchrist Transportation Company was being liquidated in 1913 she was sold on January 15 to Roy M. Wolvin and resold immediately to Algoma Central Railway (C. 130775). She was renamed W. C. FRANZ and served in the Algoma Fleet until November 21, 1934 when she

was in collision with the Great Lakes Transit Corporation's EDWARD E. LOOMIS in Lake Huron, off Thunder Bay. The FRANZ was upbound light and foundered quickly. Four crewmen were lost. The LOOMIS, also badly damaged, proceeded to Buffalo where she was laid up without being repaired. She did not move again until she was towed to the Hamilton scrapyard in 1940.

W. C. FRANZ in the ice 1914

W. C. FRANZ in the Soo

HENRY C. FRICK

HENRY C. FRICK in the Detroit River

This bulk carrier was built in 1905 for the Pittsburgh Steamship Co., Cleveland, Ohio, later Pittsburgh Steamship Division, United States Steel Corp.

She operated in the "Steel Trust" fleet until 1960, and was sold in 1964 to the Providence Shipping Company, a Nassau, Bahamas, subsidiary of the Algoma Central Railway, Sault Ste. Marie, Ontario. Although registered in Nassau, she continued in service on the Lakes in the Algoma Central Fleet (C. 317342).

She was retired from service late in 1972. Sold for scrapping, she left Sorel, Quebec in tow of the ocean tug KORAL bound for a Spanish scrapyard on November 15, 1972. She broke adrift from the tug in very heavy weather in the Gulf of St. Lawrence on November 17, 1972 and broke in two off Anticosti Island. The bow section sank the same day but the stern section remained afloat until November 18th.

MICHIPICOTEN at Mission Point

HENRY C. FRICK,			GROSS REGISTERED	
b) Michipicoten			*TONNAGE:*	6,490
			REGISTRY NUMBER:	US 202443
BUILT:	West Bay City Shipbuilding		*ENGINES:*	Triple Expansion
	Co.,			24″, 39⅛″ & 65⅛″ diameter ×
	West Bay City, Michigan			42″ stroke
HULL NUMBER:	615		*ENGINE BUILDER:*	American Shipbuilding
LENGTH:	549			Company,
BREADTH:	56			Cleveland, Ohio
DEPTH:	26.4			

GARDEN CITY

The passenger vessel GARDEN CITY was built for the Toronto-Port Dalhousie service of the St. Catharines, Grimsby and Toronto Navigation Co., entering service on June 20, 1892, under joint management of Captain N. J. Wigle and A. W. Hepburn. Her running mate was Hepburn's EMPRESS OF INDIA. Captain Wigle operated LAKESIDE on the route owned by Lakeside Navigation Co. This joint management agreement did not last long.

By 1896 a rate war had driven EMPRESS OF INDIA off the route and in 1901 GARDEN CITY went to the Buffalo-Crystal Beach run. In 1901 the Lakeside Navigation Co. was merged with the St. Catharines, Grimsby and Toronto Navigation Co. GARDEN CITY returned to her original run in 1902 and in that year the line became a subsidiary of the Niagara, St. Catharines and Toronto Railway Co. The principals behind this merger were J. S. Flavelle, Z. A. Lash and J. H. Plummer of Toronto who had close connections with the McKenzie and Mann Railroad interests. GARDEN CITY remained in service until 1917,

latterly operating at times out of Toronto to Whitby, Newcastle and Port Hope and also to Olcott Beach, New York.

About 1920 she was sold for service to King Edward Park near Montreal. Ownership was transferred by the Niagara, St. Catharines and Toronto Navigation Co. on May 2, 1922 to Joseph Rinfret, Montreal. On April 30, 1927 she was transferred to Joseph and J. Herve Rinfret, Montreal, operators at that time of a ferry service to St. Helen's Island from Montreal. On May 31, 1930 the ship was sold to Joseph Henri Beaudoin, Montreal, but on September 19, 1930, Beaudoin was declared bankrupt. The trustee in bankruptcy sold her on November 24, 1932 to Martineau Lacomee. She was sold June 8, 1935 to J. L. Lachance, Montreal. On December 1, 1936, she was sold to Les Chantiers Manseau, Ltee., and towed to Sorel, Quebec, for scrapping. GARDEN CITY originally carried the melodious three-part chime whistle which saw service on NORTHUMBERLAND after GARDEN CITY left Lake Ontario.

GARDEN CITY on her way

BUILT:	Redway, Toronto, Canada
LENGTH:	177.9
BREADTH:	26.1 (over guards 44')
DEPTH:	10
GROSS REGISTERED TONNAGE:	637
REGISTRY NUMBER:	C 100035
ENGINES:	28" & 54" diameter × 48" stroke Inclined compound
ENGINE BUILDER:	John Doty Engine Co., Toronto

Leaving Toronto

GARDEN CITY

The wooden passenger and freight propeller GARDEN CITY was built in 1873. Her master carpenter's certificate was signed by Hugh Miller, superintendent, on October 14. About two weeks later, she was enrolled, on October 31, at Cleveland, Ohio, to the Northern Transportation Company, a subsidiary of the Central Vermont Railway. She joined several other vessels of this large fleet in providing a link between Ogdensburg and the upper lakes, stopping at Chicago, Detroit, Toledo, Cleveland, and Oswego.

When the company suffered financial reverses and went into receivership in 1876, the reorganization saw the development of the Northern Transit Company, under the leadership of Philo Chamberlain, A. W. French, and W. W. Butler. In the spring of 1879, the small vessel was sold to Frank W. Gilchrist, a prominent lumberman in Alpena, Michigan. She was cut down to a lumber carrier (351 gross tons, 276 net tons) to operate from the Lake Huron lumber ports to the lower lakes.

On May 26, 1897, while docked at Alpena, a watchman smelled smoke and roused the crew. The fire which started near the smokestack, gutted her cabins, engine, and boiler rooms, but the machinery was saved. The vessel was rebuilt and, in 1898, sold to John J. Boland, of Buffalo, New York.

She continued in the bulk lake trade until October 10, 1902 when, about four miles south of Bay City, Michigan, she again caught fire. Her crew was saved, but this second fire spelled the end for the GARDEN CITY.

GARDEN CITY at the Soo

BUILT:	St. Lawrence Marine Railway, Ogdensburg, New York	*GROSS REGISTERED TONNAGE:*	436
LENGTH:	133'4"	*REGISTRY NUMBER:*	US 85292
BREADTH:	26'	*ENGINES:*	Steeple Compound 21" & 38" Diameter × 36" Stroke
DEPTH:	11'8"	*ENGINE BUILDER:*	Cuyahoga Steam Furnace Co., Cleveland, Ohio

A. GEBHART

A. GEBHART at the Soo

The A. GEBHART was a wooden schooner barge built in 1869 for David Lester, one of the Lester brothers who built many fine wooden ships at Marine City, Michigan.

The GEBHART labored for many years in the lumber, stone, coal and miscellaneous trades for David Lester, the Toledo and Saginaw Transportation Company, J. O. Wolson of Bay City, Michigan, James D. Brown, Charles F. and Sarah F. Brown, John Stevenson, and Hugh R. Havey. Forty years of service for these various owners came to an end on the 4th of June 1909, when this vessel burned at Drummond Island in the St. Mary's River. At the time of the loss, the vessel was valued at $4,000 and the cargo of cedar posts she carried was valued at $5,000. Both, unfortunately, were uninsured.

Like many of the wooden vessels that plied the Lakes, the older they got, the more inflammable they became. The GEBHART was ripe with age, and the word "Fire" was the most feared among her sailors. Luckily, however, no one was injured when she burned.

BUILT:	David Lester, Marine City, Michigan
LENGTH:	145.6
BREADTH:	29.1
DEPTH:	12.3
GROSS REGISTERED TONNAGE:	354
REGISTRY NUMBER:	US 29504

GERMANIC

GERMANIC on the St. Mary's River

The wooden passenger and package freighter GERMANIC was built in 1899 and received the engines which were formerly in the steamers PACIFIC and EMERALD ex OSWEGO BELLE. She was laid down for the Great Northern Transit Co. of Collingwood and intended for service between Collingwood, Ontario and the head of the lakes. The Great Northern Transit Co. merged with the North Shore Navigation Company in 1899 to form the Northern Navigation Co. of Ontario, Ltd. Later in 1899, the new company absorbed the North West Transportation Co., Ltd. The result was the formation of the Northern Navigation Co., Ltd.

GERMANIC served on various upper lakes routes operated by the company and she continued in service for Canada Steamships Lines, Ltd., when Northern Navigation became a division of that company in 1913.

Her end came when she was destroyed by fire at a Collingwood dock on March 30, 1917. The burned out hull settled on the bottom but was later raised and towed to Collingwood's west harbour where it lay for several years. It was eventually towed out into Georgian Bay and beached near Wasaga Beach. The remains were broken up for firewood by the local residents in the hungry 1930's.

In 1914

BUILT:	Collingwood Dry Dock Co., Collingwood, Ontario
LENGTH:	184
BREADTH:	32
DEPTH:	12.1
GROSS REGISTERED TONNAGE:	1,014
REGISTRY NUMBER:	C. 107164
ENGINES:	Two Steeple Compound—Single Screw 17″ & 28″ Diameter × 21″ Stroke
ENGINE BUILDER:	Kelley & Beckett, Hamilton, Ontario (1875) Rebuilt 1883 by G. N. Oille

GLADIATOR

Tugs are the workhorses of the seas, and this fine wooden tug was one of the Lakes' best and longest lived. She was launched on May 6, 1871 from Leighton's yard at the mouth of the Black River to the witnessing of cheering crowds. At her launching party, guests were entertained with wine and dining and then were treated to speeches by enthusiastic rivermen and tugboat owners.

George E. Brockway, her first owner, operated her in the lucrative business of towing wooden schooners through the rapids of the St. Clair River at the foot of Lake Huron. The GLADIATOR was among the strongest in his fleet of tugs, and she would often speed out into the lake to be the first to tow the arriving schooners down past Port Huron. Often she towed more than three at a time, presenting to the onlooker a glorious scene, a majestic line of stately schooners behind a gleaming white tug whose funnel belched out great quantities of thick black smoke.

The ownership changes of GLADIATOR, especially in the late 1800's, seems endless. Among the owners of this tug were: Murphy (1879); Detroit Tug & Trans. Co. (1884); George Elsey, Jr., of Detroit, Michigan (1893); B. B. Moiles, Saginaw, Michigan (1896); Thomas D. Merrill, Duluth, Minnesota (1903); R. B. Knox, Duluth (1909); and the Duluth-Superior Dredging Company (1913).

On October 17, 1895, the tug burned to the waterline while at her dock at Sault Ste. Marie. She was raised during May of 1896, and towed to Port Huron, where she was rebuilt and re-engined, at a cost of $8,000. Her new dimensions were: 121.5 × 22.6 × 11.3; 177 gross tons. Her new engine was an 1892-built steeple compound constructed by S. F. Hodge & Co., engine builders at Detroit, and was a duplicate of her first engine. The tug was ready for business and was re-launched on the first of August, 1896.

GLADIATOR was given a thorough rebuild at Duluth in 1934, when her engines were refurbished and she received new boilers built by the Johnston Brothers in 1934 at Ferrysburg, Michigan. Her cabins were redone at that time.

GLADIATOR was stationed at Duluth for most of the rest of her life. The tug was moved around the Lakes by her owners as business demanded. She towed the huge dredges to and from their assignments in various locations where dredging contracts were being performed. She was often seen at Marysville, Michigan, where the Duluth-Superior Dredging Company kept parts of their fleet. Her last days were spent on the lower end of the Detroit River. She towed mud scows and equipment up and down the River, and was based at Stoney Island, across from Bob-Lo Island amusement park in the lower Detroit River. Here she spent her last days, until being dismantled due to old age in December, 1959.

Only her cabin remains at Stoney Island, and is now used as an office. Her remarkable career lasted for 88 years, a productive one when it is considered that she was originally built of oak planks.

GLADIATOR at Duluth

GLADIATOR in the St. Clair River

BUILT:	Leighton,	*REGISTRY NUMBER:*	US 85263
	Port Huron, Michigan	*ENGINES:*	22″, 40″ diameter × 30″ stroke
LENGTH:	115.8		Steeple compound
BREADTH:	22.3	*ENGINE BUILDER:*	Cuyahoga Steam Furnace
DEPTH:	12		Company,
GROSS REGISTERED			Cleveland, Ohio
TONNAGE:	220		

In the Detroit River

GLADSTONE

Probably one of the outstanding examples of a ship that refused to die was the steamer GLADSTONE. Until the early 1960's more of the vessel was visible, but now all that remains is some scrap steel from the engine and stern of the wooden freighter. This lies about a quarter of a mile above the Point Edward range light on the Canadian shore of Lake Huron just above Sarnia, Ontario.

In 1888 a wooden bulk freight vessel was built in Cleveland and sailed for many years in the fleet of M. A. Bradley. In 1909 she was rebuilt and refitted because of wear and tear from wind, wave and ice. After rebuilding, the ship had dimensions of 282′ × 40.3′ × 25.5′ and measured 2,453 gross tons. By World War I the GLADSTONE was near the end of her useful career, but was once again rebuilt to assist in the urgent raw materials movement on the Lakes necessitated by the war. This reconstruction resulted in a depth reduction to 23.7′ and a new gross tonnage assignment

of 2,348. The vessel was painted grey at this time.

In late 1918, GLADSTONE was sold to the Joan Steamship Company but never ran because winter closed navigation. As the vessel lay at her moorings in the Pine River at St. Clair, Michigan, she sank due to ice jams in the spring of 1919. It is quite probable that her wooden hull was not capable of sustaining such pressure. When she was raised and pumped out surveyors found the keel badly twisted and broken. Further repair for service was deemed impractical and the wreck was left idle and was stripped of remaining valuable parts.

In 1923 the hull was sold into Canada and towed to Point Edward to be sunk with its bow on the beach and to be used as a breakwater protection for the yacht harbor behind Point Edward light. Still partially visible in 1959, the wreck was removed during the winter of 1963 except for the engine and stern frames which still remain today.

GLADSTONE in the St. Mary's River

BUILT:	William Radcliffe, Cleveland, Ohio	*REGISTRY NUMBER:*	US 85996
LENGTH:	283	*ENGINES:*	20½″, 32″, 54″ diameter × 42″ stroke
BREADTH:	40		Triple expansion
DEPTH:	22	*ENGINE BUILDER:*	S. F. Hodge & Company, Detroit, Michigan
GROSS REGISTERED TONNAGE:	2,112		

WILLIAM T. GRAVES

WILLIAM T. GRAVES and schooner GENOA at Marquette

The WILLIAM T. GRAVES was built in 1867 as a three-masted sailing vessel. Though originally listed as a "bark," she was actually a three masted, topsail schooner. "Bark" to Lake men meant anything having three masts and some square sails on the foremast. The GRAVES was one of the largest sailing vessels built up to that time.

Thomas Quayle emigrated from the Isle of Man for America with his parents in 1827 when he was 16 years of age. In 1847 he went into the shipbuilding business in Cleveland and in a very short time became one of the most prominent shipbuilders on the Great Lakes. His firm built many large ships of the day and the WILLIAM T. GRAVES was one of the largest and finest of them.

In 1871 the WILLIAM T. GRAVES was rebuilt and powered with a steeple compound engine. She was built-up one deck and thereafter had a rather odd appearance.

In 1876 the ship was owned by O. L. Nims, prominent Buffalo shipowner, who sold her about 1880 to the Ohio Central Barge and Coal Company of Toledo, Ohio of which M. D. Carrington was the managing operator. The vessel sailed for the Carrington interests until October 31, 1885 when she stranded on North Manitou Island in Lake Michigan, and proved a total loss. Her engines were salvaged, taken to Milwaukee and rebuilt there by the Sheriffs Manufacturing Co. In 1888 they were placed in the new steam barge GEORGE H. DYER (later HENNEPIN), then under construction at Wolf and Davidson's yard in Milwaukee, Wisconsin.

The WILLIAM T. GRAVES is pictured as a steamer on an Isle of Man postage stamp, issued in 1975 to commemorate the emigration of prominent Manx citizens, including builder Thomas Quayle, to America.

BUILT:	Quayle and Martin, Cleveland, Ohio
LENGTH:	207
BREADTH:	35
DEPTH:	14
GROSS REGISTERED TONNAGE:	804
REGISTRY NUMBER:	US 26172
ENGINES:	Steeple Compound 20″ × 36″ Diameter × 30″ Stroke
ENGINE BUILDER:	Rebuilt by Sheriffs & Co., Milwaukee

GREATER DETROIT

GREATER DETROIT under the Ambassador Bridge

On April 28, 1922, the directors of the Detroit & Cleveland Navigation Company authorized the asking of bids on two passenger sidewheel steamers to be called the GREATER DETROIT and GREATER BUFFALO. The cost of both vessels was to be $6,800,000. Designed by Frank E. Kirby, they were destined to be called "the Wonderful Arks of the Great Lakes" and were the largest passenger sidewheel vessels in the world. The GREATER DETROIT was launched on September 15, 1923 amid many ship's whistles and the clamor of thousands who attended her christening. Her horsepower was 12,000 producing a speed of 21 miles per hour. She had 26 parlors and 829 staterooms and beds for some 1,200 passengers.

This mammoth steel-hulled passenger and freight vessel took her place on the Detroit to Buffalo run and was the envy of all the passenger operators then left on the Lakes. She continued this operation through the World War II era and was in service alone after her sister, GREATER BUFFALO, became a training aircraft carrier for the Navy during the hostilities of that war. At the end of the conflict, it was expected that a new vessel would be built to replace the GREATER BUFFALO, but this was not to be, because passenger traffic on the Lakes had passed its peak and these beautiful ships were no longer economically viable. Problems with labor contracts and a change of corporate ownership spelled the end of these magnificent vessels. Up to the late 1940's GREATER DETROIT had been painted the traditional colors of the fleet with black hull and white cabins. Her last year of operation saw her sporting an all white hull with blue lettering and trim. Along with the other members of the D&C fleet, the GREATER DETROIT lay idle from 1950 to 1956 at the dock on the Detroit River.

In June, 1956 she was sold to the Rosen & Abraham firm for scrapping. At an auction sale held while she was tied up to her dock, many people familiar with her opulence purchased the last remaining souvenirs of her faithful years of service. Silverware, dishes, blankets, and all moveable equipment was sold.

The vessel was then taken in tow, along with a smaller sister, the EASTERN STATES, up the Detroit River into Lake St. Clair, where their upper works were set afire and burned. Her funeral pyre was visible for miles, and the staunchest of Lake mariners who witnessed it wept as the flames devoured the stately ship. The remains of the once proud vessel were towed down the river to Hamilton, Ontario for scrapping. This event spelled the end of a fleet close to one hundred years old. The remains of GREATER DETROIT were scrapped by the Steel Company of Canada in early 1957. Thus came to an inglorious end the once proud "largest sidewheeler in the world."

BUILT:	American Shipbuilding Company, Lorain, Ohio	*GROSS REGISTERED TONNAGE:*	7,739
HULL NUMBER:	785	*REGISTRY NUMBER:*	US 223664
LENGTH:	518.7	*ENGINES:*	Inclined compound 66″, 96″, 96″ diameter × 108″ stroke
BREADTH:	58		
DEPTH:	21.3	*ENGINE BUILDER:*	Detroit Ship Building Company, Detroit, Michigan

GREATER DETROIT leaving Mackinac Island

After the cabins were burned off

GREAT WESTERN

The iron-hulled sidewheel railway car ferry GREAT WESTERN was built to provide the vital connecting rail link between Great Western Railway and Detroit and Milwaukee Railway, crossing the Detroit River. Her hull was fabricated by Barclay, Curle and Company in Glasgow, Scotland. All 10,878 pieces were shipped to Walkerville, now a part of Windsor, and assembled under the careful eye of Henry Jenkins. She was launched on September 6, 1866, and was considered a marvelous monster for her day. Her entire deck was covered, giving the appearance of a tunnel, with a pilothouse on either end and two towering smoke stacks from which belched black smoke. Her namesake company placed her in service between Windsor and the foot of Bruch Street, Detroit, on January 1, 1867.

During the summer of 1882, her deck housing was removed, reducing her tonnage (1080 gross tons, 662 registered tons). While this was being done, the Great Western Railway was acquired by the Grand Trunk Railway of Canada. In 1888, the Grand Trunk shops at Montreal built four new Scotch boilers for the GREAT WESTERN (9'6" × 14').

Over the years the hulking sidewheeler provided yeoman service. As traffic demands increased, new and larger car ferries were built. Finally, the GREAT WESTERN found herself spending time at the dock as the "spare" boat, with LANSDOWNE and HURON able to hold their own with the cross-river demands.

In December, 1923, she was sold to Essex Transit Company, of Ford, Ontario, who reduced her to a sand barge (220' × 40'2" × 10'; 973 gross tons, 973 registered tons). A few years later she was passed on to the Wallaceburg Sand and Gravel Company, Ltd., of Wallaceburg, Ontario. In 1938 the Pine Ridge Navigation Company, Ltd., also of Wallaceburg, became her owner. In 1941 she left the Detroit River region for the upper lakes as United Towing and Salvage Company, Ltd., of Port Arthur, Ontario, recognized the strength of the old iron hull. When the St. Lawrence Seaway was under construction, the hull reportedly was towed to that project. She dropped from the *Canadian List of Shipping* in 1965, after a century of faithful duty.

GREAT WESTERN ferrying railroad cars across the Detroit River

BUILT:	Henry Jenkins, Walkerville, Ontario	*REGISTRY NUMBER:*	C. 80576
LENGTH:	220'	*ENGINES:*	Two Horizontal Condensing
BREADTH:	40'2"		45" Diameter × 108" Stroke
DEPTH:	13'	*ENGINE BUILDER:*	Gartshore & Sons,
GROSS REGISTERED			Dundas, Canada West
TONNAGE:	1,252		(Ontario) (1866)

GRECIAN

GRECIAN in 1902

The steel freighter GRECIAN was built in 1891 for the Menominee Transit Company. GRECIAN was one of six sister vessels built by Globe in 1890 and 1891 for the same owners. The others were BRITON, GERMAN, NORMAN, ROMAN and SAXON. These ships had black hulls, black stacks with blue shield and monogram and natural stained wood cabins. Like so many of the Globe-built freighters of the early 1890's they were well proportioned and handsome in appearance. With the exception of NORMAN, lost by collision in 1895, these vessels became part of the Pittsburgh Steamship Company fleet at the time of its organization in 1901.

On June 7, 1906, GRECIAN ran aground on the rocky shore near Detour, Michigan and suffered considerable bottom damage. She was refloated and temporarily repaired at Detour and then taken in tow by the SIR HENRY BESSEMER, bound for Detroit and drydocking. In a storm on Lake Huron on June 16, 1906, the GRECIAN foundered.

The other four units of the original group were still on the Lakes when World War I broke, and all were sent to the coast after having been cut in two and bulkheaded through the old Welland and St. Lawrence canals. On the coast GERMAN was promptly renamed YANKEE, and on June 11, 1919 was sunk in collision off Fire Island, New York. ROMAN was sold French after the war and renamed LIBERTAS. She foundered 350 miles east of Sandy Hook, New Jersey, on November 11, 1919, while on delivery to France. SAXON was sold to Danish owners and drops out of Lloyd's Register around 1928, after having been renamed ANNE JENSEN. BRITON returned to the Great Lakes in the early 1920's and was wrecked near Buffalo on November 13, 1929.

BUILT:	Globe Iron Works, Cleveland, Ohio
HULL NUMBER:	40
LENGTH:	296.2
BREADTH:	40.4
DEPTH:	21.1
GROSS REGISTERED TONNAGE:	2,348
REGISTRY NUMBER:	US 86136
ENGINES:	Triple Expansion 24″, 38″ & 61″ Diameter × 42″ Stroke
ENGINE BUILDER:	Shipyard

HALCYON

HALCYON

Death on the bleak shore of Baffin Island in Canada's Arctic Archipelago was the unlikely fate that befell this vessel which began her life in 1926 as the Detroit and Walkerville Ferry Co.'s HALCYON. She made her last trip as a cross-river ferry in May, 1942. In August, 1942 she was towed to Todedo and rebuilt as the U.S. Coast Guard Cutter (b) CHAPARRAL. A decade later she was lying inactive when purchased by a group which transferred her to Canadian Registry (C. 313944) with the provocative name (c) TREASURE UNLIMITED. However, the vessel never went treasure hunting on the Lakes as proposed. She spent her time tied up, first at Windsor, Ontario and later at Amherstburg, Ontario.

Finally in 1961 the Levis Trading Company of Lauzon, Quebec bought the ship and rebuilt it as the diesel coaster (d) NEWFOUNDLAND CRUISER. In addition to service on the east coast, she operated on the St. Lawrence and made a number of trips into the Lakes. She stranded on September 15, 1963 at Cape Dorset on Baffin Island and was abandoned as a total loss.

Tug ATOMIC towing CHAPARRAL to Amherstburg

TREASURE UNLIMITED at Amherstburg

HALCYON, b) Chaparral, c) Treasure Unlimited, d) Newfoundland Cruiser

BUILT:	Great Lakes Engineering Works, Ecorse, Michigan	*GROSS REGISTERED TONNAGE:*	405
HULL NUMBER:	252	*REGISTRY NUMBER:*	US 225224
LENGTH:	128	*ENGINES:*	Fore and Aft Compound 20″ & 40″ Diameter × 28″ Stroke
BREADTH:	45	*ENGINE BUILDER:*	Shipyard
DEPTH:	15.3		

NEWFOUNDLAND CRUISER

HAMILDOC (2)

DEEPWATER on builder's trials

The steel steamer DEEPWATER, of canal size to carry cargoes through the then existing St. Lawrence River canals, was built in 1928. This vessel was operated by the Water Transports Company of Canada, Ltd., a subsidiary of Keystone Transports, Ltd., which in turn was a subsidiary of the Montreal Light, Heat and Power Co. It engaged mainly in the coal trade from Lake Erie to Montreal.

The year the DEEPWATER arrived on the Lakes was a troublesome one for owners and operators of vessels. On October 28, 1928, the DEEPWATER herself was in trouble. She went ashore near the west end of the Port Colborne, Ontario, breakwater on Sugar Loaf Point. The new ship was loaded with 90,000 bushels of wheat from Buffalo, New York, bound for Montreal. The weather had been foggy and the DEEPWATER missed the pier heads leading to the Lake Erie entrance of the Welland Canal. Four days she was stuck, really not in deep water. After 30,000 bushels of the grain had been lightered, the vessel

was released, proceeded to reload her cargo, and continued the journey. In 1939, DEEPWATER was renamed KEYMONT and transferred to the parent, Keystone Transports.

Requisitioned for war service in 1940 by the US War Shipping Administration, the vessel went to the Altantic. Her war service included the bauxite trade from South America and overseas trades. She served well, and in 1946 was returned to her former owners and brought back to the Lakes. KEYMONT was purchased by N. M. Paterson & Sons, Ltd. in 1947 and renamed HAMILDOC.

HAMILDOC remained active until the 1959 season, when she was idled by the demand for larger and more economical tonnage for the new St. Lawrence Seaway trade. The small canaller was sold to Newman Steel of St. Catharines for scrap and arrived in Port Dalhousie under tow on October 15, 1961. Scrapping of this vessel was completed at Port Dalhousie Drydock in June of 1962.

	Deepwater, b)Keymont, c) HAMILDOC (2)
BUILT:	Smith's Dock Co., Ltd., South-Bank-On-Tees, England
HULL NUMBER:	837
LENGTH:	253
BREADTH:	43.4

DEPTH:	18.4
GROSS REGISTERED TONNAGE:	1,796
REGISTRY NUMBER:	C 147797
ENGINES:	16", 26", 44" diameter × 33" stroke Triple Expansion
ENGINE BUILDER:	Shipyard

KEYMONT at Toronto

In the old St. Lawrence Canals

HAMONIC

HAMONIC in Lake St. Clair

The HAMONIC, a steel package and bulk freight as well as a passenger vessel, was completed in 1909 for the Northern Navigation Co., Ltd., which was absorbed by Canada Steamship Lines, Ltd., Montreal in 1913. She was launched November 26, 1908. It was originally proposed to name her PACIFIC.

In the eyes of many, this ship was the most beautiful passenger and freight vessel built for Lake Service. She spent her entire life on the Sarnia-Lakehead run. She came to a tragic end on Tuesday, July 17, 1945 when fire spread from the freight shed at Point Edward to the ship.

Although 400 persons were aboard HAMONIC, through personal bravery and thrilling rescue efforts all were saved except one freight handler who was drowned. Fifty survivors owed their lives to an ingenious operator who used his coal crane to lift them from the bow to the shore. The burned out hull was sold in September, 1945 to Romeo Roy, Windsor, Ontario. He sold her to Steel Company of Canada, Ltd., Hamilton, Ontario for scrapping in June, 1946.

BUILT:	Collingwood Shipbuilding Co., Ltd., Collingwood, Ontario
HULL NUMBER:	22
LENGTH:	349.7
BREADTH:	50
DEPTH:	24

GROSS REGISTERED TONNAGE:	5,265
REGISTRY NUMBER:	C 122553
ENGINES:	24″, 35″, 52″ & 80″ diameter × 42″ stroke Counterbalanced quadruple expansion
ENGINE BUILDER:	Shipyard

D. R. HANNA

D. R. HANNA ice-bound in Whitefish Bay

In 1906 the Pioneer Steamship Company, Hutchinson & Company managers, committed for construction and took delivery of the steel bulk freighter D. R. HANNA. For the next 13 years this ship ran in the iron ore, coal and grain trades with few eventful incidents except for being stuck with several other freighters in an ice jam in Whitefish Bay early one spring.

Collision is one of the most dreaded accidents that can befall sailors and formerly was one of the most frequent occurrences because of the narrowness of the waters traversed by the lakes' huge ore carriers. Areas of the connecting channels are more dangeous than open lakes and rivers and rank among the most feared in foggy weather. Converging courses on Whitefish Bay, Thunder Bay and Lower Lake Huron, along with Pelee Passage on Lake Erie, rank second on the statistical lists where vessels are most likely to encounter the danger of collision.

It was at the Thunder Bay "collision corner" in upper Lake Huron that the D. R. HANNA met her unfortunate fate. On May 16, 1919 the D. R. HANNA and QUINCY A. SHAW came into collision on a foggy day with the result that the HANNA was lost. Six miles Northeast of Thunder Bay Light on Lake Huron, the HANNA, loaded with wheat downbound, was hit headon by the SHAW at 1:50 P.M. and sank in a few minutes. The SHAW, coal laden, hit the HANNA, opening a gaping hole in her bow. The waters rushed in, but not quickly enough to trap any of the crew. Shortly after the accident the HANNA capsized and sank in deep water. Fortunately, the weather was calm and the crew of 32 men was taken off the sinking vessel by a fish tug and landed at Alpena, Michigan. Once again, "heads-up seamanship" prevented any loss of life.

About the middle of October of that year, a diver located the wreck of the HANNA, bottom side up, six miles Northeast by East of Thunder Bay Island Light. The steamer even today still lies in 90 feet of water. The bow of the QUINCY A. SHAW was severely damaged, but she returned to service after reapirs had been made.

In the St. Clair River

BUILT:	American Ship Building Company, Lorain, Ohio
HULL NUMBER:	346
LENGTH:	532
BREADTH:	56
DEPTH:	31
GROSS REGISTERED TONNAGE:	7,023
REGISTRY NUMBER:	US 203676
ENGINES:	Triple expansion 23½", 38", 63" diameter × 42" stroke
ENGINE BUILDER:	American Ship Building Company, Cleveland, Ohio

FANNIE C. HART

FANNIE C. HART at the dock

The wooden propellor FANNIE C. HART was built in 1888 for the Green Bay Transportation Company, (Hart Brothers), of Green Bay, Wisconsin. Launched originally as a steam barge, she was sent back to the shipyard at Manitowoc and redesigned for passenger and freight service. Another unusual aspect of this vessel was the fact that her original engine had been recovered from the wooden barge W. L. BROWN (US 80767 built in 1880 at Green Bay) which had foundered off Peshtigo, Wisconsin, in October, 1886. She was repowered with a more appropriate power plant in 1894.

FANNIE C. HART's area of service was upper Lake Michigan and Lake Huron between Green Bay ports, Mackinac Island and the Soo River. In the Eighties, Nineties, and early 1900's, there were a dozen similar small but sturdy craft plying between the cities along the north shore of these two lakes, and also calling at the numerous islands in those waters, carrying passengers, mail and general freight. The Hart Line was the largest fleet in this service and continued regular operation until about 1910, when it went out of business and its ships were sold to other owners.

The FANNIE C. HART was sent to the Atlantic Coast in 1911 and was owned briefly by the Cook Steamship Company of Miami. In 1912 she came back up the coast to New London, Connecticut, was renamed ROWE, and served for many years as a sort of "mother ship" and supply tender for a fleet of oyster boats. She lay idle from the mid-thirties until 1942 when she was transferred to Panamanian registry with new owners listed as Cia de Navigacion Marina and renamed c) MARINA. Her career ended in 1963 when the vessel was scrapped.

ROWE in drydock at New Haven, Conn.

FANNIE C. HART,
b) Rowe
c) Marina

BUILT:	Burger & Burger, Manitowoc, Wisconsin
LENGTH:	142.8
BREADTH:	30
DEPTH:	10.6
GROSS REGISTERED TONNAGE:	476
REGISTRY NUMBER:	US 120718
ENGINES:	Fore & Aft Compound (2nd Engine) 18″ & 34″ Diameter × 26″ Stroke
ENGINE BUILDER:	Manistee Iron Works, Manistee, Michigan (1894)

HELENA

The wooden bulk freighter HELENA was built in 1883 for the Milwaukee Tug Boat Line of Milwaukee, Wisconsin. She was equipped with four masts and two stacks and her triple expansion engine produced 1175 indicated horsepower.

The Milwaukee Tug Boat Line was owned by two brothers-in-law, Conrad Starke and William Meyer. The HELENA sailed out of Milwaukee for Starke and Meyer until 1901, when her home port shifted to Sandusky after her purchase by the Gilchrist Transportation Company. In 1903, her port of registry changed once again, this time becoming Cleveland. The change reflected some corporate shifting on the part of the Gilchrist firm, since that company retained ownership of her. In 1911, her home port once again changed, this time to Chicago. In that year she was purchased by the Armour Grain Company. Her new owners made the only drastic design change she ever underwent: a grain elevator structure was built on her deck and her two stacks were replaced by a single one. Most of her service was in the Chicago area, but occasionally she took a longer trip. It was on one of the latter voyages that she stranded on a reef in Lake Erie on September 17, 1918, after which she was abandoned.

HELENA at the dock at Toledo

As a grain elevator

BUILT:	Reiboldt & Wolter, Sheboygan, Wisconsin	*REGISTRY NUMBER:*	US 95970
LENTH:	275.5′	*ENGINES:*	Triple Expansion 20″, 32″ & 54″ Diameter × 42″ Stroke
BREADTH:	40′		
DEPTH:	20.3′	*ENGINE BUILDER:*	S. F. Hodge & Co., Detroit, Michigan—1888
GROSS REGISTERED TONNAGE:	2,083		

HUDSON

HUDSON at Buffalo

BUILT:	Detroit Dry Dock Company, Wyandotte, Michigan	*GROSS REGISTERED TONNAGE:*	2,294
HULL NUMBER:	82	*REGISTRY NUMBER:*	US 95953
LENGTH:	288	*ENGINES:*	Triple expansion
BREADTH:	41		23″, 36″, 62″ diameter × 48″ stroke
DEPTH:	22.7	*ENGINE BUILDER:*	Dry Dock Engine Works, Detroit, Michigan

In 1888 the steel package freighter HUDSON was built for the Western Transit Company of Buffalo, New York. She served this company all her life, and was one of the fastest steamers on the lakes. The HUDSON's hull was painted a light brown while the cabins were white. The stack was buff with orange and black bands at the top. She was one of the first ships on the lakes to have two stacks in line and was valued at $250,000. She and her sister ship, HARLEM, ran between Buffalo, Chicago, Illinois and Duluth, Minnesota.

The HUDSON survived many storms on the Lakes in her brief lifetime, but the one that struck the eastern half of Lake Superior on September 15, 1901 was the worst. She was bound from Duluth to Buffalo with a cargo of wheat and flax when the storm hit. For three days the storm raged. On September 19th wreckage from a steamer was sighted, and in the following days bodies came ashore in the vicinity of Keweenaw Point. The HUDSON had apparently foundered with all hands (24) somewhere off Eagle Harbor Light at the height of the storm on September 16th.

Reports filtered into the newspapers about the foundering of this big steel freighter and confirmed the worst. She had last been seen during the gale by another ship, which was in dire straits herself and could offer no help. The pilot house of the HUDSON was found a few days later many miles away. To this day the hull has not been found by the avid divers of the area and the cause of the sinking remains a mystery. The HUDSON's tale is one that records the terrifying strength of the storms that hit the lakes with fury in the dying days of each shipping season.

HUDSON in 1900

HURON

At 2 o'clock on the afternoon of June 3, 1875, Miss Jessie S. Hughes, of Toronto, Ontario broke the traditional bottle of champagne over the bow of the iron carferry propeller HURON, initiating her sideways launch into a slip at Sarnia, Ontario. Miss Hughes was the daughter of M. G. Hughes who, along with John H. Smith, supervised construction of the vessel for the Grand Trunk Railway. The ship's hull plates were fabricated in Scotland and shipped to Point Edward, Ontario for assembly. The awkward looking river craft made her trial trip between Fort Gratiot, Michigan and Point Edward on July 1st of that year, beginning a career that would last to the present day. The work of assembling her had begun on August 12, 1874. She was designed for service between Sarnia and Port Huron, Michigan.

Essentially during her long span of years, she has spent an uneventful life, splitting her service between the Sarnia-Port Huron and the Windsor-Detroit terminals. Twice her decks were covered with water, but in each instance even these accidents lacked the dramatics of a sinking. On April 12, 1901, she apparently struck a boulder on the bottom

of the Detroit River. Two days later, she began to settle forward and barely was able to make her Windsor slip before resting on the bottom. On August 20, 1907, while receiving repairs to her propellers at Windsor, her bow was tipped with loaded gondolas to raise the stern. While in this position, she was struck by waves created by the wake of the passing TASHMOO. The wash swept through some open deadlights, allowing the hull to fill and settle in the slip.

During the ensuing years, the HURON continued to ply the river with her sidewheel companion, the LANSDOWNE. The HURON was used regularly as the summer vessel. During the winter, she supplied steam for the Windsor passenger station. Finally, in 1974, she was chartered to the Windsor Detroit Barge Line, Ltd., of Windsor, to serve as a transfer barge, along with the LANSDOWNE, OGDENSBURG, and tug PRESCOTONT, for a rail flatcar container service between Windsor and Detroit, and vessels anchored in the Detroit River. In 1975, the grand old lady of the river was sold to the new firm, and as of this writing, though her engines are inactive, she still fulfills a useful existance.

HURON in the Detroit River

At Sarnia

BUILT:	John Smith, Port Edward, Ontario
LENGTH:	238.5
BREADTH:	53.9
DEPTH:	12.8
GROSS REGISTERED TONNAGE:	1,052
REGISTRY NUMBER:	C. 71216
ENGINES:	30″ × 30″ Two High Pressure Non-condensing
ENGINE BUILDER:	T. Wilson & Mac Farlane, Dundas, Ontario

HURONIC

HURONIC under full steam

The HURONIC, a steel passenger and package freighter, was built in 1901–02 for the Northern Navigation Co., Ltd. which was absorbed by Canada Steamship Lines, Ltd., Montreal, in 1913. She made her first trip on May 24, 1902. While upbound on Lake Superior on the night of November 21, 1902, HURONIC passed the ill-fated BANNOCKBURN. This was the last time BANNOCKBURN was ever seen.

It was proposed to lengthen her by 50' in 1912, but the plan was dropped with the building of NORONIC. On August 6, 1928, she stranded in spectacular fashion on Lucille Island, southeast of Pigeon Point, Lake Superior. A good portion of her hull was completely out of the water. After ten days of hard work, she was refloated by the Reid Wrecking Co., Ltd., Sarnia. Salvage and repair costs (including 55 bottom plates) amounted to $110,000.

During the late 1930's HURONIC was relegated to freight-only service. The cabins were removed from the upper deck in 1944. She continued in the package freight service until the close of the 1949 season. She was sold to Steel Company of Canada Ltd. and proceeded to Hamilton, Ontario under her own power in December 1949. She was scrapped there in 1950.

In the St. Mary's River

BUILT;	Collingwood Shipbuilding Co., Ltd., Collingwood, Ontario	
HULL NUMBER:	1	
LENGTH:	321	
BREADTH:	43	
DEPTH:	23.4	

GROSS REGISTERED TONNAGE:	3,330	
REGISTRY NUMBER:	C 107168	
ENGINES:	26", 42", & 70" diameter × 42" stroke Triple expansion	
ENGINE BUILDER:	John Inglis & Sons, Toronto, Ontario	

ILLINOIS

ILLINOIS was a steel passenger and freight ship built in 1899 for the Northern Michigan Transportation Company of Chicago. The vessel was designed by the very capable Mr. Washington I. Babcock, chief designer and superintendant of the Chicago Shipbuilding Company. ILLINOIS had a very strong hull for winter service and an excellent reputation as an icebreaker. The route of the NMTC ships was from Chicago to Ludington, Manistee, Frankfort, Traverse City, Charlevoix and Mackinac Island. ILLINOIS and her near sister ship MISSOURI of 1904 were the main source of freight and mail from Chicago before the days of busses and trucks. When these ships came in, half the town came down to the docks to witness the arrival of the "Chicago Boat." Today, in forgotten ports on Michigan's west shore, one may see abandoned wharfs where these ships once docked.

The ILLINOIS was involved in a great rescue effort on August 27, 1907 when she grounded while entering Charlevoix piers. Most of the 500 excursionists were on deck ready to greet friends and relatives on the dock when the ship, going full speed, veered to avoid a collision with a small craft which had cut across its course, and drove fast aground on a shallow sand bar south of the piers. With a storm brewing and waves lashing onto the decks and sweeping through the broken cabin windows of the helpless ship, surfmen from the nearby Charlevoix Lifesaving Station went about the task of removing the passengers. They first shot a breeches buoy, a canvas bag which slides along a rope on a pulley, from the south pier to the deck of the ship and started the tedious task of removing the passengers one by one. The following day, when the lake was calmer, a surf boat was used to remove most of those remaining. On August 29, 1907, the ILLINOIS was pulled free with no serious damage and resumed its run soon afterward.

In 1920 ILLINOIS was sold to the Chicago, Racine, & Milwaukee Steamship Company, operating out of Milwaukee to Chicago with stops at Racine in both directions. On March 22, 1922, she was purchased along with PILGRIM by Goodrich with whom they had been in direct competition. In the early thirties, ILLINOIS operated on the West shore route, from Chicago to Manitowoc with stops at Milwaukee, Racine, and Sheboygan, Wisconsin after the merger with Goodrich.

When the assets of the Goodrich Transit Company were sold at auction on May 10, 1933, the ILLINOIS was sold to attorney, Francis Bloodgood, Jr., of Milwaukee for $1,500 and the bond issue amounting to $60,000. Although the Wisconsin and Michigan Steamship Company purchased the vessel in 1934 and transferred her to the Sand Products Steamship Company in 1936 and then back in 1941, the ILLINOIS was laid up from the mid-thirties and her engines were removed in 1942 and placed in the barge LAKE FOLCROFT which was being repowered for the war effort. ILLINOIS was removed from documentation in 1945, towed to Hamilton, Ontario in 1947, and scrapped there in 1948.

ILLINOIS in Chicago

ILLINOIS

At Petoskey

Entering MANISTEE HARBOR

BUILT:	Chicago Shipbuilding Company, Chicago, Illinois
HULL NUMBER:	35
LENGTH:	225
BREADTH:	40
DEPTH:	24.7
GROSS REGISTERED TONNAGE:	2,427
REGISTRY NUMBER:	US 100680
ENGINES:	Triple Expansion 20″, 32″ & 54″ Diameter × 36″ Stroke
ENGINE BUILDER:	Shipyard

INDIA

INDIA at Duluth

INDIA, b) City of Ottawa, c) INDIA, d) Sault Ste. Marie, e) INDIA

BUILT:	King Iron Works,	*GROSS REGISTERED*	
	Gibson and Craig	*TONNAGE:*	1,239
	subcontractors,	*REGISTRY NUMBER:*	US 100008
	Buffalo, New York	*ENGINES:*	Low Pressure
LENGTH:	210		36″ Diameter × 36″ Stroke
BREADTH:	32.6	*ENGINE BUILDER:*	H. G. Trout,
DEPTH:	14		Buffalo, New York

At Sault Ste. Marie

CITY OF OTTAWA

This famous iron-hulled passenger and package freight propellor was built at Buffalo in 1871. She had two sister ships, CHINA and JAPAN, and many consider these three sister ships to have been the most handsome passenger and freight vessels ever to operate on the Lakes.

INDIA was built for J. C. and E. T. Evans of Buffalo, whose operations later became the nucleus of the Anchor Line, the marine affiliate of the Pennsylvania Railroad. From 1872 to 1892 she operated as a unit of the Lake Superior Transit Company, a pool fleet operating out of Buffalo to Duluth. She reverted to operation by the Anchor Line in 1892.

In 1906 after the Line took delivery of the new JUNIATA, INDIA became surplus tonnage and was sold to the Montreal and Lake Erie Steamship Co., Toronto, and was placed under the management of Jaques & Co., Montreal. Registered in Canada as b) CITY OF OTTAWA (C. 122018) and given a new engine (Fore and Aft Compound 22″ & 44″ Diameter × 36″ Stroke built in 1907 by the Polson Iron Works, Toronto), she operated between Montreal, Toronto and Lake Erie ports. She was later absorbed into the Merchants Mutual Line, which in 1913 was merged into Canada Steamship Lines, Ltd., Montreal.

About 1914 she ceased carrying passengers and was placed on the Montreal-Toronto-Hamilton express package freight service. Soon after entering this new service her passenger accommodations were removed. CITY OF OTTAWA remained on this run until 1926. Replaced by newly built tonnage, she was laid up from 1926 through 1928. She was sold in 1928 to Charles F. Mann, Marine City, Michigan and reverted to U.S. registry under her original name of INDIA. In 1929 she was sold to the Algoma Steamship Co., Hamilton, Ontario, and brought back to Canadian Registry. This company placed her in operation on an unsuccessful package freight run between Toronto and Fort William as d) SAULT STE. MARIE.

In 1930 she was sold at a bailiff's sale in Detroit for $7,000 to the Pine Ridge Coal Company, Detroit. Reverting to U.S. Registry once again, under her original name of INDIA, her new owners cut her down to a barge. INDIA was sold to C. W. Bryson's Copper Steamship Company, Cleveland, in 1934.

In 1942 she was requisitioned by the U.S. Maritime Commission and taken down the Mississippi for proposed salt water service. Her conversion never took place and she was abandoned on the shore of Lake Pontchartrain near New Orleans. She is reported to have been scrapped in 1945.

INDIA as a barge

INDIANA

The wooden passenger and freight propellor INDIANA was launched on April 5, 1890 for the Goodrich Transportation Company. She was designed as a night boat with accommodations for 200 passengers and hold space for 1,000 tons of general freight. Assigned initially to the Chicago-Racine-Milwaukee night service, she ran opposite her near sister ship, CITY OF RACINE b) ARIZONA. In 1895 INDIANA was assigned to the cross-lake route from Chicago to Muskegon and Grand Haven, until being replaced by ALABAMA in 1910.

INDIANA returned to a Manitowoc shipyard for the winter of 1915–16, this time to the Manitowoc Shipbuilding Company, for a major overhaul including a 22 foot lengthening (223 × 35.4 × 14.3; 1979 gross tons). When INDIANA returned to service, she was placed on the west shore route to Washington Island, Wisconsin.

Always a lucky ship, INDIANA avoided serious trouble but did have several minor accidents. On January 14, 1917, she was making Chicago harbor in heavy ice, with steam and vapor reducing visibility, and struck an extension of the Chicago outer breakwater. She proceeded to Manitowoc under her own power for repairs. On January 30, 1918 she was trapped in ice off the Racine entrance and all perishable freight had to be rushed ashore. A wind shift several days later allowed INDIANA to free herself. Finally, INDIANA struck the Carter H. Harrison water intake crib off Chicago during a dense fog in the summer of 1922, and again went to Manitowoc for repairs.

Retired in 1928 and laid up at Manitowoc, INDIANA was sold in 1931 to the P. L. Connolly Contracting Company of Duluth for $16,200 and taken to the Soo River where she served as a powerhouse and barracks for the workers on the West Neebish Rock Cut Project. In 1934 she was purchased by George Mills & Company of Detroit for the Livingstone Channel work in the lower Detroit River. Finally abandoned as unfit for further use, INDIANA was taken first to Monroe, Michigan and then to Toledo, Ohio where she was allowed to rot away on the Maumee River close to her long-time running mate ARIZONA.

INDIANA at Muskegon

INDIANA at Toledo

BUILT:	Burger & Burger, Manitowoc, Wisconsin	*GROSS REGISTERED TONNAGE:*	1,177
LENGTH:	201	*REGISTRY NUMBER:*	US 100471
BREADTH:	35.4	*ENGINES:*	Fore & Aft Compound
DEPTH:	14.3		26″ & 50″ Diameter × 36″ Stroke
		ENGINE BUILDER:	C. F. Elmes, Chicago, Illinois

INDIANAPOLIS

Despite spending most of her life on the West Coast, the steel day passenger vessel INDIANAPOLIS, launched May 4, 1904 for the Indiana Transportation Company of Chicago, has left a memory for many people in the Chicago area. The vessel was intended for the excursion route between Chicago and Michigan City, Indiana, on which her owners had used the wooden propellor MARY of 1881 and several chartered vessels. This popular route jammed the INDIANAPOLIS with passengers and she soon proved to be too small for the trade. The owners replaced her in 1906 with the THEODORE ROOSEVELT which had more than double her capacity and nearly twice the speed (she reached 28 knots in trials). INDIANAPOLIS became surplus and was sold to the Alaska Steamship Company in 1906.

She made the long voyage via the St. Lawrence, Atlantic, Straits of Magellan and the Pacific to her new home port, Seattle.

She was immediately placed on the Seattle to Victoria, British Columbia, day run. Two well-proportioned masts with gaffs were added, replacing her thin steel masts, improving her appearance greatly. In 1912 *Indianapolis* was sold to the International Steamship Company and in 1922 to the Puget Sound Navigation Company. In 1932 she was converted into an automobile ferry with bow loading ramp and operated across Puget Sound between Port Townsend, Washington and Edmonds, Washington. Rendered obsolete by newer vessels, INDIANAPOLIS lay idle in the late 1930's and was abandoned and scrapped in 1940.

INDIANAPOLIS at Chicago

BUILT:	Craig Shipbuilding Company, Toledo, Ohio
HULL NUMBER:	99
LENGTH:	180
BREADTH:	32
DEPTH:	18.6
GROSS REGISTERED TONNAGE:	765
REGISTRY NUMBER:	US 200920
ENGINES:	Triple Expansion 18″, 30″ & 50″ Diameter × 30″ Stroke
ENGINE BUILDER:	Shipyard

INDIANAPOLIS as an auto ferry

IOWA

The wooden passenger and freight vessel IOWA of the Goodrich Transportation Company had quite a history. In 1896 the old wooden steamer MENOMINEE was retired by the company and sent to Manitowoc for scrapping. After stripping the vessel of her cabins it was found that the hull was in very good condition. Thereupon the owners decided to build a new vessel on the old hull, this work costing $146,000. The new steamer came out as the IOWA. The hull was covered with sheet iron fastened to the hull with extra long nails and a reinforced bow to enable the ship to smash her way through ice.

IOWA was placed in regular cross-lake service and on the Muskegon to Grand Haven route opposite the INDIANA. Perhaps some vessels are lucky and others are not. It soon became obvious that IOWA was Goodrich's "jinx steamer." In the severe winter of 1897, IOWA was stuck in a mid-lake ice floe and finally made it to Milwaukee with the help of the steamer CITY OF LUDINGTON. On November 2, 1905 the IOWA went ashore north of Milwaukee, a grounding which necessitated major repairs. In early 1906 the cranky vessel rammed into a dock in the Milwaukee River and destroyed it. In November of 1907, IOWA stranded on Hill's Point in Sturgeon Bay. By now two of her captains had lost their jobs and the IOWA was firmly entrenched as the jinx ship of the fleet.

After nearly three years of smooth sailing, the IOWA again made the newspapers by going aground north of Kenosha, Wisconsin on April 23, 1910, an accident which again required major repairs. Another captain was out of a job—number three! On the foggy morning of July 17, 1913, the SHEBOYGAN, a sister fleet ship, collided with the IOWA in the Chicago River. The IOWA made it to the dock but there she settled. The SHEBOYGAN was at fault but again the IOWA's captain, and also that of the SHEBOYGAN, were both fired. More repairs were finally completed and IOWA successfully survived the "Big Storm" on Lake Michigan in November of that year.

However, in September of 1914, the vessel was again in trouble, crushing a small tug against a dock in the Milwaukee River due to the swift current and a malfunctioning bridge.

After 28 years in and out of service, IOWA finally fell victim to Lake Michigan's severe ice laden winters. On February 4, 1915, while attempting to make Chicago Harbor, she was caught in the ice three miles ENE of the entrance. Despite efforts of tugs and the sister vessel RACINE to reach her to offer help, the IOWA was crushed. The crew and passengers hurriedly scrambled off the vessel onto the ice and watched horrified as the ship settled. There were no casualties among the 71 persons aboard, all of whom walked over the ice to approaching tugs. In spite of all the unlucky incidents in which this ship was involved, not a single life was lost in any of her escapades or accidents. The sunken hulk of the IOWA was determined to be a hazard to navigation and was destroyed by dynamiting the following year.

IOWA leaving Manitowoc

IOWA at Chicago

BUILT:	Burger & Burger,
	Manitowoc, Wisconsin
LENGTH:	202.5
BREADTH:	36.4
DEPTH:	13

GROSS REGISTERED	
TONNAGE:	1,157
REGISTRY NUMBER:	US 100613
ENGINES:	Steeple Compound
	21″ & 42″ Diameter × 36″ Stroke
ENGINE BUILDER:	C. F. Elmes,
	Chicago, Illinois

IROQUOIS

IROQUOIS at Duluth

The almost exact sister of CHIPPEWA was built in 1901 at Toledo for the Arnold Transit Company of Mackinac Island, Michigan. The IROQUOIS was intended for express and day passenger service between Mackinac Island and the Soo. After a few years it was found too expensive to operate two big ships on this route, and IROQUOIS was leased out for operations elsewhere on the Lakes.

In 1903 she was chartered to W. H. Singer of Duluth, Minnesota who operated the vessel between Duluth and Isle Royale in Lake Superior. In 1906 the Dunkley-Williams line chartered the vessel for use in Lake Michigan and also ran excursions out of Oswego, New York, on Lake Ontario for some time.

In 1908, however, Arnold sold both ships to the Pacific coast, necessitating a voyage for them around Cape Horn. IROQUOIS gave good service in the Puget Sound area for the Alaska Steamship Company which purchased her in

1908 and the Puget Sound Navigation Company to which she passed in 1912. In 1920 IROQUOIS returned to the Lakes for the Chicago and South Haven Steamship Company and operated on Lake Michigan until 1927. Once again she was purchased by the Puget Sound Navigation Company in 1928 and returned to the Pacific. During the winter of 1927–28 she was rebuilt as an auto ferry and continued in this service out of Seattle. (Her new dimensions were 213.8 × 46 × 15.2; 1,767 gross tons.)

In 1948 she was retired for five years, but in 1953 she was rebuilt once again as a diesel truck ferry for the Black Ball Transportation Company. (213.7 × 46 × 15.2; 949 gross tons.) Her diesel engines were 10 cylinder Fairbanks-Morse. This operation proved a success. In 1973 the IROQUOIS was renamed ALASKA SHELL under which name she now serves.

IROQUOIS,		*DEPTH:*	21.2
b) Alaska Shell		*GROSS REGISTERED*	
		TONNAGE:	1,169
BUILT:	Craig Shipbuilding Company, Toledo, Ohio	*REGISTRY NUMBER:*	US 100730
		ENGINES:	Triple Expansion
HULL NUMBER:	83		21″, 34″ & 58″ Diameter × 30″
LENGTH:	214		Stroke
BREADTH:	34.4	*ENGINE BUILDER:*	Shipyard

As a diesel auto ferry on Puget Sound

JESSE JAMES

JOHN E. MEYER at Manitowoc

In 1923, the steel tug JOHN E. MEYER was built for the Barnet and Record Company of Duluth, Minnesota and was used both as a harbor tug and as a long haul tug for dredging equipment. The Pringle Barge Line of Detroit bought the tug in 1940, and she became a familiar sight on the Detroit River, towing the self-unloading barge MAIDA, her usual consort, to and from Toledo, Ohio in the coal trade. Renamed the JESSE JAMES in 1940, she carried this name until leaving the Lakes. She did a splendid job for the Pringle Barge Line. Often the little tug could be seen twice daily, since the run from Toledo to the Detroit Edison plants on the Detroit River was so short, and the coal loading facilities at Toledo so efficient.

In 1964 the vessel was sold to the Seaway Cartage Company, and lay idle a few years in the Rouge River. The Nickerson Marine Company of Tampa, Florida bought her in 1966, and she left the Lakes that year via the Mississippi River in tow of another Lake tug, the CENTRAL. At Tampa she was used to tow oil barges and for miscellaneous harbor duties. Her old steam engine was worn out by 1967 and was replaced by a new diesel, giving the tug new life for another few years. In 1970, the tug was sold

to the Baleen Towing and Transport, Inc. of Bath, Maine, who renamed her BALEEN that same season. Her duties at Bath were about the same as at Tampa, towing the huge oil barge BFT 50. The largest load ever brought into Bangor, Maine, 48,000 barrels of oil, was towed to that port by the BALEEN on her first trip.

The most dreaded tragedy on board any ship is fire. Sailors of every nation brave storms and the furies of nature, hurricanes, gales, snow, sleet, fog, and even tidal waves, but the word "fire" is the most feared. It was just this catastrophe that struck the BALEEN in November of 1975. Her after end caught fire, and the crew was unable to put it out. The U.S. Coast Guard came to the rescue on November 27, 1975 and saved the crew. The fire became so fierce and uncontrollable that the owners decided to let the tug burn out. She sank on November 29–30, after several attempts to salvage her proved futile. The BALEEN had been a good tug in her lifetime (according to the many sailors who labored aboard her) and she will be remembered both on the Lakes and the East Coast for a long time to come.

JESSE JAMES in the Detroit River

JESSE JAMES, towing the barge MAIDA

John E. Meyer (2),
b) JESSE JAMES,
c) Baleen

BUILT:	Manitowoc Shipbuilding Company, Manitowoc, Wisconsin
HULL NUMBER:	206
LENGTH:	102.8
BREADTH:	24.1
DEPTH:	13.9
GROSS REGISTERED TONNAGE:	205
REGISTRY NUMBER:	US 222858
ENGINES:	15½", 26", 44" Diameter × 26" Stroke Triple Expansion
ENGINE BUILDER:	Hewes & Phillips, Newark, New Jersey—1918

BALEEN on the East coast

ROY A. JODREY

ROY A. JODREY downbound loaded.

This modern steel self unloader was built in 1965 for Algoma Central Railway, Sault Ste. Marie, Ontario, as part of its fleet modernization and expansion program.

On November 21, 1974, while upbound with ore from Sept Iles, Quebec to Detroit, she veered off course in the Alexandria Bay Narrows in the St. Lawrence River. She collided with buoy 194 and ran aground on Pullman Light Shoal. She immediately began to take on water and developed a list. Five hours after the stranding this fine ship slipped off the shoal and sank in 200 feet of water. All 29 crew members were taken off by the U.S. Coast Guard.

Subsequent surveys by the Underwriters determined that salvage was impossible, and the JODREY has been declared a constructive total loss.

BUILT:	Collingwood Shipyards Ltd., Collingwood, Ontario
HULL NUMBER:	186
LENGTH:	619.7
BREADTH:	72.1
DEPTH:	39.11
GROSS REGISTERED TONNAGE:	16,154
REGISTRY NUMBER:	C 318689
ENGINES:	2 Diesel 1) 10 Cylinder 8⅛″ Diameter × 20″ Stroke 2) 12 Cylinder 6¼″ Diameter × 8″ Stroke
ENGINE BUILDER:	1) Fairbanks Morse Ltd., Canadian Locomotive Ltd., Kingston, Ont. 2) Caterpillar Tractor Co., Peoria, Illinois Geared to Single Screw Shaft

JOLIET (1)

The steel bulk freighter JOLIET (1) was built in 1890 for the Lake Superior Iron Company of Ishpeming, Michigan. She was an exact duplicate of GRIFFIN, LA SALLE, and WAWATAM. These four ships were among the earliest freighters to have the more modern design of placing the pilot house atop the forecastle and as a result were very distinctive. They carried three large masts, single black stack with a white "S", black hull and dark gray cabins.

In 1899 the four Lake Superior iron ships and three others were purchased by Henry W. Oliver, who was trying to organize a Great Lakes fleet for Andrew Carnegie. Oliver's seven freighters made up the fleet of the first Pittsburgh Steamship Company. They were given dark red hulls, white cabins, and a black stack with a white "P."

In 1901 Elbert H. Gary and J. Pierpont Morgan bought out Carnegie's steel empire and formed the United States Steel Corporation. The JOLIET and her sisters then became part of the 112 vessel second Pittsburgh Steamship Company, or "Steel Trust" as it was commonly called in those days. After serving these last owners well for another ten years, JOLIET collided with the 600 foot "Steel Trust" ore carrier HENRY PHIPPS on September 22, 1911 and was sunk opposite Port Huron. Her hull was dynamited as a menace to navigation, but final removal did not take place until 1963.

JOLIET in 1911, her last year

BUILT:	Cleveland Shipbuilding Company, Cleveland, Ohio	GROSS REGISTERED TONNAGE:	1921
		REGISTRY NUMBER:	US 76873
HULL NUMBER:	7	ENGINES:	Triple Expansion
LENGTH:	266		17" , 29" & 47" Diameter × 36"
BREADTH:	38.2		stroke
DEPTH:	19.8	ENGINE BUILDER:	Shipyard

In the St. Clair River

JUNIATA

In the 1870's the Erie and Western Transportation Company, known as the "Anchor Line," the Great Lakes arm of the Pennsylvania Railroad, began naming its ships after the rivers of Pennsylvania. As a result, the ships of this fleet carried some of the most attractive names seen on the Great Lakes.

The steel passenger and freight propellor JUNIATA was built for the "Anchor Line" in 1905 and carried on the company's naming tradition. She was the second of a trio of nearly identical passenger ships. TIONESTA of 1903 was the first, while the OCTORARA was last in 1910. All three had green and white hulls, white cabins, and single crimson stacks. They were identical in hull and machinery but differed slightly in arrangement of spars and superstructure. Their main route was from Buffalo to Duluth with stops at way ports.

When the railroads were forced to divest themselves of their fleets in 1916, JUNIATA was one of the acquisitions that made up the Great Lakes Transit Corporation. New safety requirements as well as declining passenger trade forced the layup of the three passenger ships in 1936.

In 1941, however, JUNIATA was purchased by the Wisconsin & Michigan Steamship Company and taken to Manitowoc for a complete rebuild and modernization (4,272 gross tons). She was renamed MILWAUKEE CLIPPER and resumed service as a passenger and automobile carrier across Lake Michigan between Milwaukee and Muskegon. She operated in this trade for another thirty years until declining trade again forced her layup at Muskegon.

MILWAUKEE CLIPPER was towed from her Muskegon berth on June 12, 1977 by the tug AMERICAN VIKING. Her destination was Sturgeon Bay, where new owners, ironically named Great Lakes Transit Company, had arranged for Bay Shipbuilding to drydock the veteran and make the necessary repairs to pass Coast Guard inspection prior to placing her in the excursion trade out of Chicago as CLIPPER. More than $300,000 was spent on the boat but the Coast Guard still would not pass CLIPPER, and any future operation and ownership is now clouded.

JUNIATA upbound in the St. Mary's River

JUNIATA passing a slow freighter

	JUNIATA, **b) Milwaukee Clipper,** **c) Clipper**	*DEPTH:*	28
		GROSS REGISTERED *TONNAGE:*	4,333
		REGISTRY NUMBER:	US 201768
BUILT:	American Shipbuilding Company, Cleveland, Ohio	*ENGINES:*	Quadruple Expansion 22″, 31½″, 45″, & 65″ Diameter × 42″ Stroke
HULL NUMBER:	423	*ENGINE BUILDER:*	Detroit Shipbuilding Company,
LENGTH:	346		Detroit, Michigan
BREADTH:	45		

MILWAUKEE CLIPPER leaving Muskegon

KAMLOOPS

One of the steel "Northwestern type" package freighters, KAMLOOPS was built in 1924 for Canada Steamship Lines Limited, Montreal. Built to replace obsolete wooden tonnage, she operated between Montreal and the head of Lake Superior usually carrying package freight westbound and grain and flour on the return trip.

Bound for Fort William, she disappeared in heavy weather in the vicinity of Isle Royale on Lake Superior on December 6, 1927. All hands were lost. Although an extensive search was made for the vessel, her remains were only discovered in 1977 by skin divers. She was found off Isle Royale's 12 o'clock Point within the boundaries of Isle Royale National Park.

KAMLOOPS in 1925

BUILT:	Furness Shipbuilding Co., Ltd., Haverton-Hill-on-Tees, G.B.	*GROSS REGISTERED TONNAGE:*	2407
HULL NUMBER:	68	*REGISTRY NUMBER:*	C 147682
LENGTH:	250	*ENGINES:*	Triple expansion
BREADTH:	42.9		18″, 30″ & 50″ Diameter × 36″ Stroke
DEPTH:	26.6	*ENGINE BUILDER*	Richardsons, Westgarth & Co., Ltd., Hartlepool, England

KANSAS

After being completed in 1870, the wooden passenger and freight propellor CHAMPLAIN operated on the Ogdensburg to Chicago route for the Northern Transportation Company and its successor, the Northern Transit Company, until the firm went out of business in 1882. CHAMPLAIN, along with LAWRENCE of 1868, was then sold to the Northern Michigan Line of Chicago. The same colors, white hull and cabins with green trim, and a black stack with white top, were retained by the new company.

On June 16, 1887, CHAMPLAIN was swept by fire on Grand Traverse Bay between Norwood and Charlevoix, a disaster that claimed 22 lives and left only the hull intact. Her place was then taken by the ill-fated VERNON, chartered from the Booth Line of Chicago. Meanwhile, CHAMPLAIN was rebuilt and lengthened (165.4 × 28.4 × 12.4; 711 gross tons) and reentered service in 1888 as CITY OF CHARLEVOIX. She was repowered in 1892 with a fore and aft compound steam engine (19″ & 46″ Diameter × 36″ stroke) built by S. F. Hodge at Detroit. Her original simple steam engine went into the tug ALFRED J. WRIGHT in 1893.

CITY OF CHARLEVOIX suffered a second fire in 1894 and was again rebuilt and lengthened (185.5 × 33.3 × 12.6; 835 gross tons). She continued in the Northern Michigan Line after its merger with the Seymour Line in 1896, running with PETOSKEY. When the new steel liners ILLINOIS of 1899, MISSOURI of 1904 and MANITOU, purchased in 1906, joined the fleet, PETOSKEY was sold and CITY OF CHARLEVOIX was renamed KANSAS. At this time the Northern Michigan liners were painted with all black hulls and black stacks.

In 1918 the old line was reorganized as the Michigan Transit Company, having five ships, KANSAS, ILLINOIS, MISSOURI, MANITOU, and the recently acquired PURITAN. By this time KANSAS was old and slower, and was used for a few short cruises and mostly for freight. After several years of partial inactivity, this venerable old hull succumbed to the third fire in her history on October 27, 1924 while laid up at Manistee, Michigan.

CITY OF CHARLEVOIX

In the ice

KANSAS

Champlain,
b) City of Charlevoix,
c) KANSAS

BUILT:	A. C. Keating, Cleveland, Ohio
LENGTH:	135.2
BREADTH:	26

DEPTH:	11.6
GROSS REGISTERED TONNAGE:	438
REGISTRY NUMBER:	US 5848
ENGINES:	High Pressure Non-Condensing 24″ Diameter × 36″ Stroke
ENGINE BUILDER:	Cuyahoga Iron Works, Cleveland, Ohio

KEARSARGE

This steel 'tween-decked package freighter was built in 1894 for the Interlake Transportation Company managed by Pickands Mather. This fine example of naval architecture, designed by Washington Irving Babcock, was the first Lake ship that employed the use of the channel system of construction.

She had two masts and one stack with the pilot house behind number one hatch. She operated for her original owners and part time under charter to the Western Transit Company in the bulk and package freight trade until 1907 and was then sold to the Elphicke interests of Chicago, becoming a unit of the Canada-Atlantic Transit Company. Mr. Elphicke was the U.S. agent of the Line. For close to 30 years the KEARSARGE sailed in this fleet, mostly between Georgian Bay ports and Chicago and Milwaukee. The colors were black hull, white forecastle and cabins, and dark yellow stack with a black smoke band on top.

By the late 1930's she was pretty well worn out and lay idle at Chicago. In 1942 KEARSARGE became a part of the U.S. War Shipping Administration Fleet, but unlike her many sister package freighters, did not go to the coast during World War II. After more idle time, she was towed by one of Captain John Roen's tugs to Nicholson's dock at Ecorse, Michigan and partially scrapped. Her lower hull was acquired by Sabadash Brothers of Detroit and her bow portion was converted into the barge SABADASH I in 1951. The stern section was later converted into a barge which eventually became barge 225. The rest of the vessel including her upper works and engine were scrapped.

There are no U.S. flag package freighters in service on the lakes today. The American type, of which the KEARSARGE is a good example, disappeared after World War II.

KEARSARGE in 1922

		GROSS REGISTERED	
BUILT:	Chicago Shipbuilding Company, Chicago, Illinois	TONNAGE:	3,092
		REGISTRY NUMBER:	US 161061
HULL NUMBER:	10	ENGINES:	Triple expansion
LENGTH:	328		23″, 38″, 62″ diameter × 40″ stroke
BREADTH:	44.2		
DEPTH:	23	ENGINE BUILDER:	Cleveland Shipbuilding Company, Cleveland, Ohio

IDA KEITH

Schr. IDA KEITH, Schr. ZAPOTEC at left, Str. GEORGE W. MORLEY

The three-masted schooner IDA KEITH was built in 1873 for William O. Keith, of Chicago, Illinois, who supplied the necessary $35,000 to pay for her. She passed Detroit, Michigan on her maiden voyage August 21, 1873, having been officially enrolled at Chicago twelve days earlier. The vessel continued to serve the Keith interests until 1893 with few interruptions and only modest expense.

One large expense, however, resulted from a stranding in 1880. Early on April 10th of that year, bound from Chicago to Buffalo, New York, with a cargo of corn, the jaunty vessel found herself in a severe noreaster and blizzard. It was driven ashore about 4-1/2 miles south of the North Manitou Island Life Saving Station in northern Lake Michigan. About 8 a.m. the life saving crew arrived on the beach opposite the distressed ship. They succeeded in shooting a line across to the vessel on their second attempt, but as a small boat was being hauled out to her, the line snapped. All other efforts that day were thwarted and the KEITH's captain finally floated a shingle ashore with the message to cease efforts until the seas subsided. The following morning, the nine crew members were taken off by a boat manned by the Life Savers. The IDA KEITH was recovered, much the worse for wear, a short time later.

In June, 1893, the ship was sold to M. J. Galvin, Edward Gaskin, and George W. Lennon, all of Buffalo. Galvin and Gaskin were connected with the Union Dry Dock Company. In July, 1894, Gaskin and Lennon were the sole owners, and in June, 1895, Harry Richardson, also of Buffalo, acquired a one-third interest in the ship.

Early in 1901, F. G. Andrews of Detroit, purchased the KEITH. A short time later, Homer Warren, also of Detroit, acquired her. On March 26, 1902, the KEITH, along with the steamer HOMER WARREN, were sold at a United States Marshall's Sale, through the efforts of the Union Trust Company of Detroit. Bay City shipbuilder James Davidson acquired the KEITH and sold her to the Saginaw shipping firm of Shannon & Garey. In May, 1910, she was sold to C. A. Osborne, of Marine City.

In about 1914, Captain Theobald Emig, of St. Clair, Michigan, bought the tired old schooner. He sold her to William Somerville, of Sandusky, Ohio in 1916. In 1920, now owned by Judge Claude J. Minor, also of Sandusky, she was pulled onto a mud flat at the foot of McEwan Street in Sandusky. There on January 16, 1922, she was set on fire, presumably by skaters building a bon fire. Still later, on July 14, 1922, what still remained of her again caught fire, spelling her final end.

BUILT:	Arch S. Stewart, Saugatuck, Michigan	*DEPTH:*	13
LENGTH:	163.3	*GROSS REGISTERED TONNAGE:*	489
BREADTH:	30.6	*REGISTRY NUMBER:*	US 100110

KEYBELL

The early steel canaller KEYBELL was built in 1912 for Keystone Transports Ltd., Montreal. This was a joint venture established by Montreal Light, Heat and Power Co., Ltd., Montreal, and the Koppers Coal Co., Pittsburgh. The ship's main trade was between the Lake Erie coal ports and the Montreal Light, Heat and Power Co. plant on the Lachine Canal in Montreal West. On occasion she carried pulpwood from the Gulf of St. Lawrence to Thorold. It was not uncommon for her to deliver a cargo of coal a week to Montreal. This was a rather remarkable accomplishment, particularly during the years that the Third Welland Canal was in use. It involved navigating 44 locks upbound and 41 downbound.

Three facts made KEYBELL a unique unit in the Keystone Transports Fleet. Firstly, she was the only unit built on the Lakes—the other 12 came from U.K. yards. Secondly, she was the first of many canallers to become inoperative in the years immediately preceding and following the opening of the Seaway; 1957 having been her last year in active service. Lastly, when Keystone Transports Ltd. became the Laverendrye Line Ltd. late in 1957, she was the only one of the nine vessels transferred that never saw service for her new owners. Her last four years were spent in idleness tied up to a dock in the Cataraqui River at Kingston, Ontario. In 1961 she was towed to the nearby Kingston Dry Dock where she was soon reduced to scrap.

KEYBELL departing Dickinson's Landing westbound, Cornwall Canal

BUILT:	Collingwood Shipbuilding Co., Ltd., Collingwood, Ontario	*GROSS REGISTERED TONNAGE:*	1,730
HULL NUMBER:	37	*REGISTRY NUMBER:*	C 131111
LENGTH:	258	*ENGINES:*	Triple Expansion 16″, 26″ & 44″ × 36″
BREADTH:	42.6		Two Scotch Marine Boilers 10′6″ × 11′9″
DEPTH:	17.3	*ENGINE BUILDER:*	Collingwood Shipbuilding Co., Ltd.

KEYPORT

KEYPORT

The KEYPORT was built in 1909 for Keystone Transports Ltd., Montreal, for the Lake Erie–Montreal coal trade. During the winter of 1915–16 she was chartered to operate on salt water. She left Montreal in December 1915 for Halifax. However, she spent the winter locked in the ice near the Gaspe peninsula in the Gulf of St. Lawrence. When the ice broke up in the spring of 1916, the vessel headed back up the St. Lawrence to resume her regular passages in the coal trade. Her total service spanned 52 years.

In 1957 the Keystone Fleet became the LaVerendrye Line Ltd., and early in 1962 control passed to the Hall Corporation of Canada, Ltd. By that time KEYPORT had outlived her usefulness and she spent the 1962 season laid up in Kingston Harbor. On June 5th, 1963 she was towed to Port Dalhousie by the tug GRAEME STEWART. She ended her days in the Port Dalhousie Dry Dock where she was cut up during September 1963 by A. Newman Co. Ltd., St. Catharines.

KEYPORT

BUILT:	Swan Hunter and Wigham Richardson, Ltd., Wallsend on Tyne	GROSS REGISTERED TONNAGE:	1,721
HULL NUMBER:	818	REGISTRY NUMBER:	C 125459
LENGTH:	250	ENGINES:	Triple Expansion 15″, 25″, & 42″ diameter × 30″ stroke
BREADTH:	42	ENGINE BUILDER:	North Eastern Marine Engineering Co., Ltd., Newcastle on Tyne
DEPTH:	18		

KINGSTON

KINGSTON c. 1919

KINGSTON was a classic passenger vessel built in 1901 of steel up to and including the main deck. Both in the interior fittings and especially in exterior line and silhouette, KINGSTON resembled a smaller version of the well remembered sidewheelers of the famous Fall River Line of Long Island Sound.

She was originally owned by the Richelieu and Ontario Navigation Co., Ltd., Montreal, which was absorbed by the Canada Steamship Lines, Ltd. in 1913. Her entire life was spent on the Toronto–Thousand Islands–Prescott run, her running mate being the slightly smaller TORONTO. This ship was retired in 1938 and KINGSTON then carried on alone. KINGSTON made her last trip from Toronto on September 17, 1949, the day NORONIC burned at the C.S.L. Terminal in Toronto. During the winter of 1949–50 it was decided to retire KINGSTON and she was towed to Hamilton for scrapping in 1950.

KINGSTON from a timetable

BUILT:	Bertram Engine Works Co., Ltd., Toronto, Ontario	*GROSS REGISTERED TONNAGE:*	2,925
HULL NUMBER:	37	*REGISTRY NUMBER:*	C 111654
LENGTH:	288	*ENGINES:*	28″, 44″, & 74″ diameter × 72″ stroke
BREADTH:	36.2 (over all 65)		Direct connecting inclined triple expansion
DEPTH:	13.3	*ENGINE BUILDER:*	Shipyard

KINGSTON c. 1930

KINGSTON in the Thousand Islands

FRANK E. KIRBY

FRANK E. KIRBY in the Detroit River

The "Flyer of the Lakes," as the steel passenger sidewheel steamer FRANK E. KIRBY was known, was launched on February 14, 1890. It was equipped with an engine formerly used in the revenue cutter JOHN SHERMAN and later in the passenger steamer ALASKA. She was built to operate between Detroit and Sandusky for the Ashley & Dustin Steamer Line. Her first enrollment was issued at Detroit on June 19, 1890, to Walter O. Ashley; a second one was issued in 1900 to Edward A. Dustin. For twenty-nine years, the KIRBY left Detroit at nine a.m., stopped at Put-In-Bay, Middle Bass, Kelleys Island, and Sandusky, then left the latter place at three p.m. for the return trip to Detroit. She would make occasional moonlight trips as well as special excursion runs to Port Huron and Toledo. During the early fall, special trips were advertised to the Lake Erie Islands as she transported the fruit crop, especially grapes and peaches, back to Detroit. For twenty-one of those years, Arthur J. Fox served as her master. Her fastest run over the sixty miles from Detroit to Put-In-Bay was two hours and fifty-four minutes.

During the famous race between the steamers TASHMOO and CITY OF ERIE in 1901, the KIRBY kept pace with the speeding ships even though she carried passengers with a vested interest in the outcome! But such an occasion was a rarity on an otherwise hum-drum and pocketwatch career. In 1911, when the owners decided to construct the larger steamer PUT-IN-BAY, a new corporation was formed with a capitalization of $345,000. Principal stockholders included Edward A. Dustin as president and general manager, Oliver S. Dustin, Florence C. Ashley, Alice E. Atcheson, W. H. McFall, C. G. Edgar, and Captain A. J. Fox.

In 1920, the KIRBY laid up before her season had been completed. After lying idle for over a year, she was sold to the Nicholson Transit Company (William Nicholson) and refurbished by the Great Lakes Engineering Works. On July 4, 1922, the vessel was placed on the Detroit-Kingsville, Ontario run, with stops at Ecorse and Wyandotte, Michigan. In 1923, under the firm name of Detroit and Kingsville Navigation Company, she continued on this route. In 1924, with the burning of the Cleveland and Buffalo Transit Company steamer STATE OF OHIO, the KIRBY was chartered to C&B to operate between Toledo, Put-In-Bay, and Cedar Point. In 1925, she again resumed her Detroit-Kingsville route. The following August, her name was changed to SILVER SPRAY and she left the Detroit area to run between Erie, Pennsylvania, and Port Dover, Ontario. This proved successful and for the next two seasons, 1927–1928, now under the name of DOVER, she ran cross-lake service with the steamer ERIE (ex PENNSYLVANIA, OWANA).

While in lay-up at Ecorse, Michigan, the DOVER caught fire on February 2, 1929. Work was begun to prepare her for the 1929 season, but as general business conditions worsened, repairs were stopped. Finally, on June 23, 1932, the DOVER, along with KEYSTONE, ENTERPRISE, and LEWISTON, were destroyed by a fire of major proportions. The proud old Flyer of the Lakes lay sunken in her slip until 1939, when she was raised and scrapped. The fine Fletcher beam engine was removed to Henry Ford's Greenfield Village for possible display, but reportedly was scrapped in the late 1940's.

FRANK E. KIRBY

FRANK E. KIRBY,		*DEPTH:*	10.2
b) Silver Spray,		*GROSS REGISTERED*	
c) Dover		*TONNAGE:*	532
		REGISTRY NUMBER:	US 120796
BUILT:	Detroit Dry Dock Company,	*ENGINES:*	48″ diameter × 108″ stroke
	Wyandotte, Michigan		Beam condensing
HULL NUMBER:	101	*ENGINE BUILDER:*	W. & A. Fletcher Company,
LENGTH:	195.5		Hoboken, New Jersey
BREADTH:	30.1		

DOVER, Str. ERIE after the fire

LADY ELGIN

LADY ELGIN at Chicago

BUILT:	Bidwell & Banta, Buffalo, New York
LENGTH:	252
BREADTH:	32.8
DEPTH:	13
GROSS REGISTERED TONNAGE:	1,037
ENGINES:	Vertical Beam, with wheels 32′ in diameter
ENGINE BUILDER:	Unkown

LADY ELGIN at Northport, Michigan

The elegant wooden sidewheel passenger/freight steamer LADY ELGIN was built in 1851. She was enrolled at the Buffalo customhouse in November, 1851, to Aaron D. Patchin of Buffalo and Gilman Appleby of Conneaut, Ohio. In October, 1852, Aaron Patchin became sole owner and, in May, 1853, Thaddeus W. Patchin also of Buffalo, became sole owner. Obviously the vessel was being kept within the family! During the following few years (May, 1855–May, 1856), Aaron Patchin again resumed full ownership. During the "Patchin Years" the LADY ELGIN remained on the lucrative Buffalo-Chicago, Illinois service for which she had been designed.

In the spring of 1856, the sidewheeler was transferred to the Chicago-Lake Superior run and ownership was changed to Albert T. Spence & Company and Gordon S. Hubbard, both of Chicago. In July, 1860, Hubbard came into sole possession of the vessel and she engaged in the Chicago to Collingwood, Ontario, trade. Also in that year she was readmeasured (231′ × 31′8″ × 11′5″, 880-53/95th tons).

On the evening of September 7, 1860, the LADY ELGIN departed Chicago with 385 passengers and crew members. About 300 were returning to Milwaukee, Wisconsin after attending a Republican political rally in Chicago. The vessel

was under the command of Captain Jack Wilson, who had guided the first steamer, the ILLINOIS, through the Soo Locks in 1855. At midnight, the weather picked up and the visibility became poor. About 2:30 a.m., September 8th, when about ten miles off Winnetka, Illinois, the schooner AUGUSTA sliced through the darkness and rammed the passenger vessel, ripping off her port wheel. At the time of the collision, a dance was in progress and the ship was well lit; the schooner showed no running lights.

Captain Wilson immediately headed the stricken ship for the beach, but she began to settle rapidly. As she slid beneath the waves, her upper works floated free. Several persons rode the wreckage safely to shore, only to be lost in the heavy surf. Edward Spencer, a young divinity student at the Methodist Garret Biblical Institute (now Northwestern University), saved several lives by swimming through the surf to assist them to shore, this at the ultimate expense of his health. Only ninety-eight people survived the loss, but Captain Jack Wilson was not among them.

The AUGUSTA reached Chicago safely, though leaking badly. She lived a long but stormy career on both salt and fresh water under the name COLONEL COOK. But she was never able to live down the disaster that she had caused through the sinking of the LADY ELGIN.

SIMON LANGELL

SIMON LANGELL in the St. Mary's River

On April 14, 1886, the wooden steamer SIMON LAN-GELL was launched. It had been ordered by Capt. J. Pringle of St. Clair who also was her skipper. The ship was sold in 1889 to A. R. Sinclair of Bay City, Michigan and was in his fleet through 1915 when she was owned by the Sinclair Transportation Company. In 1919 Argo Steamship Co. became the owners with Fisher and Wilson of Cleveland the managers. Later in 1919 the ship was sold to Scott Misener of Sarnia, Ontario, as one of the first vessels of his fleet. In 1923 it was again sold, this time to A. E. Millard of Sarnia. He ran her under the name of Langell Transportation Co. The ship's Canadian official number was 138373. In 1896 the ship had received a Cleveland-built Globe Iron Works engine of 27″ and 50″ cylinders and a 36″ stroke, a fore and aft compound. To help restore hull life, the aging ship was also reboiled in 1921, and the first cylinder was relined to 24″ in 1910.

On November 23, 1936 she was tied up alongside the steamers SIMLA, PALMBAY and STORMOUNT in Portsmouth Harbor, Kingston, Ontario. It was thought, but never proven, that a spark from the steamer RAPIDS PRINCE started a fire on board the PALMBAY, which spread to the other vessels. The SIMON LANGELL was burned beyond repair. The remains were taken out of the harbor and sunk in deep water at 9 Mile Point, Simcoe Island, in Lake Ontario where her bones now rest. The SIMON LANGELL was one of the last wooden steamers seen on these waters. The LANGELL's appearance during the years changed little. The vessel came out as a three masted steambarge, but her heavy masts were later cut down and replaced by two pole masts, and the upper pilot house was enclosed in later years.

With a load of coal in the St. Clair River

BUILT:	Simon Langell, St. Clair, Michigan	GROSS REGISTERED TONNAGE:	845
LENGTH:	195.3	REGISTRY NUMBER:	US 116091
BREADTH:	34.6	ENGINES:	Simple Steam Engine 12″ diameter × 20″ stroke
DEPTH:	13.7	ENGINE BUILDER:	Samuel F. Hodge #121, Detroit, Michigan

LANGELL BOYS

The wooden steambarge LANGELL BOYS was launched on July 8, 1890. Built at a cost of $50,000, the new ship ran for the Simon Langell and Sons Steamship Co. In 1893 the vessel was sold to F. W. Bradley and others of Bay City, Michigan. In 1903 it was sold to Eddy Brothers, and in 1904 to J. W. Ritchie. The ensuing years were spent in the ownership of the following: 1906—C. A. Eddy et al.; 1907—Mershon, Schuette, Parker Company; 1910—Mershon, Eddy, Parker Co.; and 1911—Carrollton Steamship Company.

She served her owners well, but had a few mishaps that cost them much in upkeep, as well as worries about the safety of her crew. Six years after her launching, she met her first serious accident. On the 27th of April 1896 the steambarge left Buffalo, New York with her consort, UNITED STATES, bound for Deer Park, Lake Superior with a cargo of coal. When six miles northeast of Presque Isle, near Alpena in foggy weather, LANGELL BOYS struck an object, disabling her propellor. She was picked up by the steamer JOHN N. GLIDDEN and towed back to Port Huron. Another incident occurred on September 19, 1920 when a fire started from the explosion of an oil lamp while the ship was tied up at the Mershon, Eddy, Parker dock in Saginaw. It caused $8,000 damage to the hull and $1,000 damage to the half-unloaded cargo of white pine. The Saginaw Fire Department worked from 9:30 p.m. to 3:00 a.m. to put it out. As a result of this mishap, the vessel was taken to Marine City and completely rebuilt in 1920 by Sydney C. McLouth, shipbuilder and repairer, to 156.6 × 33.8 × 10.6 and 467 gross tons. A broken crank shaft on July 27, 1924 while she was bound for Blind River, Ontario, cost her owners another $2,000.

On Saturday, June 13, 1931, her days ended. She was bound without cargo from Saginaw to Spragge, Ontario when smoke was discovered aboard ship and the cargo hold was opened to ascertain the location of the fire. This evidently gave draft to the blaze for the flames spread rapidly. Water was turned into the bunker but the flames were soon out of control. Orders were given to abandon ship and the crew and two guests took to the lifeboats. The Coast Guard from Tawas met the lifeboats and brought them to shore safely. She drifted and sank two miles off Au Sable, Michigan in 18 feet of water.

LANGELL BOYS at Saginaw, Mich.

LANGELL BOYS at Marine City

BUILT:	Simon Langell, St. Clair, Michigan
LENGTH:	151
BREADTH:	30
DEPTH:	11.2
GROSS REGISTERED TONNAGE:	387
REGISTRY NUMBER:	US 141067
ENGINES:	Fore & Aft Compound 16" & 32" diameter × 30" stroke
ENGINE BUILDER:	S. F. Hodge & Company, Detroit, Michigan

LEECLIFFE HALL (2)

Some ships have short but spectacular careers, while others labor in obscurity for years. The LEECLIFFE HALL certainly was the former, because when she was launched on May 8, 1961, she was the largest dry cargo ship built in the United Kingdom up until that time. After sailing the Atlantic, another first, the new flagship of the Hall Corporation Fleet sailed from Montreal on September 25, 1961 on her maiden Great Lakes voyage. A cargo record soon fell when LEECLIFFE HALL hauled 1,030,979 bushels of mixed grain to the Bunge Elevator at Quebec City on her first downbound trip. In June, 1964, the vessel's last cargo record was established. LEECLIFFE HALL set a new two-way high in carrying 28,300 net tons of Labrador ore from Sept-Isles, Quebec to Ashtabula, Ohio and 924,577 bushels of wheat from the Canadian Lakehead to Montreal on the return trip back down the St. Lawrence Seaway.

Shortly after, on September 5, 1964, the LEECLIFFE HALL's short career came to an end when she set her final record as the first maximum-size 730 foot laker to be lost. Upbound in the St. Lawrence River with a cargo of iron ore, the big laker collided with the Greek freighter APOLLONIA. All of the crew (except one) and the passen-gers, including the President of Hall Corporation, Frank A. Augsbury, Jr., his wife Lee (after whom the ship was named) and their children, abandoned ship safely. Later, two crew members returned to the ship, and with the assistance of the tug FOUNDATION VIBERT, attempted to get the stricken laker into shallow water where she could be beached. These efforts were to no avail, however, and the LEECLIFFE HALL sank in 90 feet of water in the shadow of Ile Aux Coudres where the deep water runs right up to the shore. The three crewmembers lost their lives in the effort, and all that remained were the tops of the masts at low tide and a wreck buoy marking the location.

Salvage attempts started almost immediately, but these efforts also proved futile. During the winter of 1964–65 and after, more attempts were made but finally all hope was abandoned. In 1966, the hull was dynamited to clear the area, and on September 12, 1966, the LEECLIFFE HALL was declared a constructive total loss. Thus, the short but spectacular career of the first 730 footer to be lost had ended.

LEECLIFFE HALL upbound in the St. Mary's River

Downbound past the Blue Water Bridge, Port Huron

BUILT:	Fairfield Shipbuilding & Engineering Co. Ltd., Glasgow, Scotland	*GROSS REGISTERED TONNAGE:*	18,071
HULL NUMBER:	811	*REGISTRY NUMBER:*	C 314366
LENGTH:	714.4	*ENGINES:*	Steam Turbine 2 cylinder
BREADTH:	75.3	*ENGINE BUILDER:*	Shipyard
DEPTH:	35.3		

ALEXANDER McDOUGALL

The culmination of the dream that Alexander McDougall had of building steel vessels which would withstand any type of weather was the steel whaleback. The only one with a conventional bow was the ALEXANDER McDOUGALL, launched on the 25th of July, 1898. She was an odd creature as can be seen in the photographs, but Alexander's "patented" steam vessels were a huge success. In later years they proved difficult because of the rounded sections of their hulls. Unloading equipment had a difficult time negotiating the narrow hatches. In heavy seas, the water would run off the decks as intended, but no crewman could walk from bow to stern without fear of being washed overboard. In spite of these difficulties, the conventional bow on the McDOUGALL was a great improvement over the spoon-shaped bows of the other whalebacks built.

In 1900, McDougall sold this newest steamer to the Bessemer Steamship Company who in turn sold it to the Pittsburgh Steamship Company the following year when the entire Bessemer fleet became a part of the United States Steel fleet. In 1936, the McDOUGALL became a part of

the Buckeye Steamship Company, operated by Hutchinson. She proudly carried this flag until her final days afloat.

The War Years (1941–45) were difficult ones for every company on the Lakes, and the government decided on a plan to improve the capacity of Great Lakes shipping by trading in old vessels for new. Each operator was given the opportunity to retire its older vessels and obtain brand-new "Maritime Class" ships in return at a discount price. The Buckeye Steamship Company received the new steamer JOHN T HUTCHINSON to replace the old and small freighters MARIPOSA, MARITANA and ALEXANDER McDOUGALL. The Maritime Commission took over the ownership of these vessels in 1943, allowing the company to operate them for the duration of the war. At the end of the conflict, the trade-ins were retired from service and anchored in a vast armada, 47 ships altogether, in Erie Bay on Lake Erie. From here each was towed to Hamilton, Ontario for scrapping. The ALEXANDER McDOUGALL was cut up for scrap by the Steel Company of Canada in 1946.

ALEXANDER McDOUGALL—ice-covered at the Soo

ALEXANDER McDOUGALL leaving the locks at the Soo

In 1919

BUILT:	American Steel Barge Company, West Superior, Wisconsin	*GROSS REGISTERED TONNAGE:*	3,686
HULL NUMBER:	140	*REGISTRY NUMBER:*	US 107372
LENGTH:	413	*ENGINES:*	Quadruple expansion 19″, 28½″, 42″, 66″ diameter × 40″ stroke
BREADTH:	50		
DEPTH:	22	*ENGINE BUILDER:*	Cleveland Shipbuilding Company, Cleveland, Ohio

In the Detroit River

JOHN M. McKERCHEY

JOHN M. McKERCHEY, an early photo in Lake Erie

All steamers are necessarily functional, but the first vessel ever designed to carry coal and lumber as well as being equipped for sand dredging, certainly met this quality of adaptability. She was the JOHN M. McKERCHEY, a small steel sandsucker built in 1906.

The first owner was its namesake, Mr. John M. McKerchey of Detroit, Michigan who was in the construction, sand and gravel business. The ship's usual site of operations was in the Detroit River-Lake St. Clair-St. Clair River area. Here she dredged the bottom for the clean sand and gravel so necessary for the construction business and the making of concrete. Upon the death of Mr. McKerchey in 1912, the vessel was taken over by the C. H. Little Company of Detroit. In 1915 it was sold to the United Fuel & Supply Company of Detroit and carried coal and lumber as well as sand.

The last owners, Kelley Island Lime & Transport Company, bought the ship in 1923. She was slightly rebuilt in 1929: her dimensions were: 161.2 × 37.1 × 11 with 506 gross tons. The McKERCHEY sailed for KILT until sunk during a violent storm in 1950. On October 16, 1950, she capsized in a heavy sea nearly opposite the entrance to the harbor of Lorain, Ohio. All her crew were rescued except the captain, Horace Johnson, but the vessel was a total loss. She was abandoned in place, on the bottom but not in deep water. Her wreck was a hazard to navigation, and the remains were dynamited to remove the obstruction to the harbor entrance. To people around Detroit, the little steamer was a familiar sight, but to cottagers on the lake and rivers she was a menace. They always feared that she would suck away their golden beaches.

BUILT:	Great Lakes Engineering Works, Ecorse, Michigan	GROSS REGISTERED TONNAGE:	732
HULL NUMBER:	23	REGISTRY NUMBER:	US 203204
LENGTH:	161	ENGINES:	Steeple compound, Non-Condensing
BREADTH:	37.1		11″ & 23″ diameter × 14″ stroke
DEPTH:	11	ENGINE BUILDER:	Shipyard

In Lake St. Clair

PRICE McKINNEY

On June 16, 1961, the Steamer PRICE McKINNEY passed downbound in the Welland Canal on the first leg of its journey to a European scrap yard. Just five weeks ahead of her, the bulk freighter J. F. DURSTON made the same trip. It was fitting that these two veterans of the Lakes should pass out together as they both were launched the same day, Saturday May 23, 1908. While the DURSTON was being launched at Superior Wisconsin, the McKINNEY was sliding into the Black River beside the American Ship Building Company at Lorain, Ohio. The McKINNEY was named for Price McKinney, a partner of the famous James Corrigan, a highly successful vessel and ore broker.

McKinney, Corrigan, and M. A. Bradley were all on hand for the launching to watch Miss Grace Rardon christen the new ship. The vessel was to sail initially not for any of the above named men but for J. J. Rardon's Island Transit Company. In 1913 it was taken over by Corrigan, McKinney & Co. and it was sold to the Pioneer Steamship Company, managed by Hutchinson & Company, in 1915.

During PRICE McKINNEY's final years (1959–61), she was chartered to the Buckeye Steamship Company. She was sold for scrap and arrived at Hamburg, Germany on July 17, 1961.

BUILT:	American Ship Building Company, Lorain, Ohio
HULL NUMBER:	363
LENGTH:	432
BREADTH:	54
DEPTH:	28
GROSS REGISTERED TONNAGE:	5,250
REGISTRY NUMBER:	US 205324
ENGINES:	Triple expansion 22″, 35″ & 58″ diameter × 40″ stroke
ENGINE BUILDER:	American Ship Building Company, Cleveland, Ohio

PRICE McKINNEY

MACASSA

MACASSA,
b) Manasoo

BUILT:	William Hamilton Co., Glasgow, Scotland
LENGTH:	155
BREADTH:	24.1
DEPTH:	16.3
GROSS REGISTERED TONNAGE:	574
REGISTRY NUMBER:	C 93932
ENGINES:	15″, 24″ & 40″ diameter × 27″ stroke Triple expansion
ENGINE BUILDER:	Kemp. Glasglow

MACASSA

This steel day passenger propeller (twin screw) was built in 1888 for the Hamilton Steamboat Co., Hamilton, Ontario. She arrived at Hamilton from Glasgow Thursday, June 7, 1888, and immediately entered Hamilton-Toronto service. She was lengthened in 1905 at Collingwood to 178.4. Control of the Hamilton Steamboat Co. passed to Toronto's T. Eaton Co., Ltd. (department store operators) in January, 1909. Eatons also controlled the opposition line, Turbinia S. S. Co. which operated TURBINIA, but the two companies were operated independent of each other until both lines were taken over by the Niagara Navigation Co., Ltd. in 1911.

Niagara Navigation Co., Ltd. was absorbed by the Richelieu and Ontario Navigation Co., Ltd., Montreal in 1912. The R. & O. became part of Canada Steamship Lines, Ltd. in 1913. MACASSA remained on the Toronto-Hamilton run operating at times from Toronto or Hamilton to Grimsby Beach until the close of Navigation in 1927.

She was then sold to Owen Sound Transportation Co., Ltd., rebuilt as an overnight boat for the Owen Sound-Soo service operating via the North Channel, and renamed MANASOO. She left Owen Sound on the new run for the first time on April 22, 1928. She foundered in Georgian Bay on September 15, 1928 when she rolled over in a heavy gale with the loss of 16 lives.

MANASOO at Owen Sound

MACKINAC

MACKINAC entering Hessel, Mich.

In Arnold colors

The steel hulled passenger/freight steamer MACKINAC was launched on May 25, 1909. She was designed by George L. Craig, son of the venerable Toledo, Ohio shipbuilder, John Craig, for George Arnold of the Arnold Transit Company, Mackinac Island. In her first year she was chartered to the Crawford Transit Company, of Chicago, Illinois, but the following year, 1910, returned to the Mackinac Island run.

In 1917, the MACKINAC was taken to Manitowoc, Wisconsin, where she was lengthened (162' × 28'2" × 12'; 512 gross tons). That same year, she was sold to the Virginia–Carolina Navigation Company, and taken to the Atlantic Coast for service between Norfolk, Virginia and Baltimore, Maryland. In about 1923, the ship was purchased by the Mackinac Company (R.I.), Pawtucket, Rhode Island, and placed in the freight business between Pawtucket and Newport. In 1925, it was placed in the passenger trade between the same two ports and operated by the Blackstone Transportation Company.

On August 18, 1925, with an estimated 700 excursionists on board, a boiler exploded as the vessel departed Newport, killing forty-nine persons. Oddly enough, Captain George McVay was in command; he had commanded the steamer LARCHMONT when she was sunk during a blinding snowstorm through collision with a schooner in February, 1907. The latter accident claimed between 125–175 lives off the coast of Rhode Island. The MACKINAC was towed to the Todd ship repair yard in Brooklyn in November, 1925 for rebuilding.

She was sold to the Pawtucket & New York Transportation Company and was renamed WOONSOCKET in 1926. In 1929, the firm name was changed to Pawtucket & New York Steamship Company and in 1931, the vessel again was sold, this time to the Colonial Navigation Company of New York. Finally, in 1935, the Norfolk, Baltimore & Carolina Line, of Norfolk, Virginia, acquired the old passenger ship. The next year, she received a Fairbanks Morse diesel (6 cylinders, 14" × 17"; 630 base h.p.; 168'2" × 28'2" × 12'; 434 gross tons). She was dropped from documentation in 1968 and sold to the Harry Lundeberg Seamanship School operated by the Seamens' International Union at Piney Point, Maryland. After conversion to a training ship at the Old Dominion Repair Corporation yard at Norfolk, she was renamed CLAUDE "SONNY" SIMMONS and today serves in that capacity at Piney Point.

MACKINAC in Lake Michigan

MACKINAC,
b) Woonsocket

BUILT:	Johnston Brothers, Ferrysburg, Michigan
HULL NUMBER:	35
LENGTH:	138.1
BREADTH:	28.2

DEPTH:	12
GROSS REGISTERED TONNAGE:	350
REGISTRY NUMBER:	US 206658
ENGINES:	18″, 40″ Diameter × 30″ Stroke Steeple Compound
ENGINE BUILDER:	Montague Iron Works, Montague, Michigan

With Str. GEORGEANNA at Baltimore, Md.

LIZZIE MADDEN

The double-decked wooden freight propellor CHENAN-GO was launched on July 2, 1887. She was enrolled at Detroit on July 23, 1887, to C. D. Waterman (1/3), of Grosse Ile, Michigan, and W. W. Waterman (2/3), of Detroit. She was launched with little fanfare, the local newspapers even neglecting to carry her name!

On April 10, 1890, the vessel departed Detroit bound for Buffalo with a cargo of wheat on her first trip of the season. The following day fire was discovered alongside her boiler as she neared Long Point, Lake Erie. The passing steamers EBER WARD and TECUMSEH tried to help fight the fire and later were joined by the MAJESTIC. Finally the WARD and MAJESTIC took the CHENANGO in tow and dropped her near the entrance to Erie, Pa., where she settled. The WARD took her crew to Maumee Bay where the tug DEXTER took them off.

The sunken hulk posed a threat to navigation and by the end of the month local fishermen were threatening to dynamite her if something was not done. Perhaps inspired by this, the underwriters sent a representative and a diver to inspect her. They found that she was burned from forward of the main mast down about three feet and back aft to the load line. After more negotiations, the wheat was sold to Henry and Pfohl of Buffalo for $10,000, and Henry McMorran of the Port Huron Wrecking Company submitted the low bid of $15,000 to deliver her inside Erie harbor. Wrecking master Charley Diefenbach brought in his crew and raised her by June 23. Then the sand dredge ENTER-PRISE, owned by Erie's J. C. Tanner, pumped her out. On June 28 the tugs HEBARD and GEE towed the CHEN-ANGO and the remnants of her rotting, smelling wheat cargo into Buffalo. She had been insured for $55,000, and the underwriters estimated that wrecking bill and rebuild would come to $46,000.

She was sold to James Davidson, shipbuilder at Bay City, Michigan, and later in the year the tug JUSTICE FIELD towed her to Bay City. Davidson cut the hull down to one deck so she could enter the flourishing lumber trade (175′ × 34′ × 13′; 690 gross tons, 517 net tons). In July he renamed her the LIZZIE MADDEN and sold her to T. F. Madden, of Bay City. After Madden's death she was owned by his estate, but operated by M. J. Lynn, also of Bay City.

On November 22, 1907 the MADDEN left Bay City to pick up another lumber cargo at Little Current, Ontario. As she cleared the river, fire was discovered in the lamp room. It spread rapidly and the crew took to her two life boats. They were picked up by the steamer LANGELL BOYS and taken to East Tawas, where Captain Ralph Pringle reported the incident. The burning hulk ultimately came to rest on Little Charity Island in Saginaw Bay where, in December, the Bay City Wreckage and Salvage Company retrieved her engine and boiler. Today even the bones have been picked clean by the scuba divers. Thus ended the CHENANGO/LIZZIE MADDEN.

LIZZIE MADDEN at the Soo

Chenango,
b) LIZZIE MADDEN

BUILT:	John Oades, Detroit, Michigan
LENGTH:	175′6″
BREADTH:	33′8″
DEPTH:	20′4″
GROSS REGISTERED TONNAGE:	938
REGISTRY NUMBER:	US 126431
ENGINES:	Steeple Compound 24″ & 46″ Diameter × 36″ Stroke
ENGINE BUILDER:	Frontier Engine Works, Detroit, Michigan

MAGNET

This iron side wheeler was built on the Clyde in 1847. (There is little doubt that Dennys were the builders although records are hard to trace.) The hull was shipped in sections and assembled at Niagara by the Niagara Dock Company. She was originally owned by J. W. Gunn and Capt. James Sutherland of Niagara and operated on Lake Ontario as a unit of the Royal Mail Line. Her upper cabins were added in 1853. Back on November 10, 1849, she missed the piers at Port Darlington, was holed when she hit bottom and settled in shallow water. She was quickly salvaged and returned to service. In due course, the Royal Mail Line became the Canadian Navigation Co., Ltd., and was merged into the Richelieu and Ontario Navigation Co., Ltd., Montreal in 1875.

During the Fenian Raids in 1866 MAGNET operated as a gunboat on Lake Ontario being manned by a crew from H.M.S. AURORA. MAGNET received a rebuild at Sorel in 1875. In 1883 she went to the Upper Lakes under charter to the Owen Sound Steamship Co., for service between Owen Sound and Fort William carrying supplies for the Canadian Pacific Railway's transcontinental line then under construction. On June 5, 1883 she ran aground on Cedar Island in the St. Joseph Channel between Bruce Mines and Thessalon, Ontario. The only damage was a badly twisted stern. In 1884 her usual route was Owen Sound-Sault Ste.

Marie. MAGNET continued to operate out of Owen Sound until the end of the 1892 season, and returned to her old run on Lake Ontario in 1893.

She received a major rebuilt at Sorel in 1895 after which her dimensions were 175.2 × 25.2 × 10.8; gross tonnage 938. She continued to be operated by the Richelieu and Ontario Navigation Co., Ltd., but from 1895–1907 she was actually owned by the Montreal Safety Deposit Co., Montreal. She was renamed b) HAMILTON in 1905, as she was then operating on the Montreal-Toronto-Hamilton run. Late in 1907 the Montreal Trust and Deposit Co., turned ownership over to the R. & O.

The ship was sold on December 31, 1909 to the Empire Refining Company of Wallaceburg, Ontario and converted into a five compartment barge; she was re-registered on August 11, 1910. In 1918 the barge was sold to Grant Cooper of Toronto. In 1928 it was sold to Louis Goodchild of Amherstburg, Ontario and he towed her to his private dock. Expected business did not develop, so Goodchild towed her two miles up the Detroit River to an old slip once used by the Canada Southern Railway. After some time the hull settled on the bottom. When a new compensating dike in the river directed more current over to the Canadian shore, the old iron hull was undermined, causing it to break in two and disappear.

MAGNET in the St. Lawrence River

HAMILTON shooting the rapids

MAGNET b) Hamilton		DEPTH:	11
		GROSS REGISTERED TONNAGE:	433
BUILT:	Alexander Denny, Dumbarton, Scotland	REGISTRY NUMBER: ENGINES:	C 103337 (allotted in 1895) Vertical beam engine 43½″
LENGTH:	173		Diameter by 10′ stroke
BREADTH:	26	ENGINE BUILDER:	Doubtful

MAJESTIC

MAJESTIC with a huge crowd of passengers at Midland, Ont.

The wooden passenger and freight propellor MAJESTIC was built in 1895 for the Great Northern Transit Co. (The White Line) of Collingwood. She was launched April 23, 1895. With 800 passengers aboard she took part in the ceremonies at the opening of the Canadian Soo Canal on September 7, 1895. In 1899 the Great Northern Transit Co. was merged with the "Black Line" (The North Shore Transit Co.) and the Beatty Line of Sarnia to form the Northern Navigation Co., Ltd. Originally she was painted all white with a black stack sporting a broad white band. After the 1899 merger she operated with hull painted black up to the main deck rail, white upper works and a red stack with a black smoke band over a narrow white band.

Northern Navigation Co. first employed her on the Sarnia-Lakehead and Duluth Service. When newer ships entered service, she sailed on the Georgian Bay-Mackinaw service. This handsome wooden vessel was destroyed by fire while in winter quarters at Point Edward, Ontario on December 15, 1915. Her burning hull drifted against SARONIC and set her on fire too, but unlike MAJESTIC, the SARONIC was not totally destroyed.

MAJESTIC entering Mackinac Island Harbor

BUILT:	Collingwood Dry Dock Co., Collingwood, Ontario	*GROSS REGISTERED TONNAGE:*	1,578
LENGTH:	209	*REGISTRY NUMBER:*	C 100950
BREADTH:	35	*ENGINES:*	Fore and Aft 28″ & 54″ diameter x 36″ stroke
DEPTH:	12.6	*ENGINE BUILDER:*	John Inglis, Toronto, Ont.

In the St. Clair River

MAJOR

The wooden freighter JOHN MITCHELL was built in 1889 for Gratwick, et al., of Buffalo, New York who did much business with the vessel's namesake. The ship was sold to Capt. John Mitchell himself (Mitchell & Co., organized in 1891) and in 1902 was renamed MAJOR.

She rode through the great storm of 1913 on a crossing of Lake Superior and on November 13, 1913 was found 30 miles northwest of Whitefish Point in a sinking condition. The Tomlinson freighter GEORGE G. BARNUM (formerly SOCAPA, later HENNEPIN) removed the crew and towed the MAJOR to Sault Ste. Marie, Michigan. So damaged was the ship it was abandoned to the underwriters who sold it in 1914 to the Great Lakes Transportation Co. of Midland, Ontario (Playfair Fleet). They repaired her and put the ship back into service. She now carried the Canadian registry number 134263 and had a gross tonnage of 2,150. For the next seven years the vessel carried crushed quartz from the Killarney Quarries to the Electro-Metal plant at Welland, Ontario.

In 1920 the Georgian Bay Wrecking Co. of Midland bought her and converted the vessel into a floating drydock by removing her aft portion, engines and adding a watertight gate with sluice valves to admit water, which was removed by pumps after a vessel entered. After a few years in this service fire of an unknown origin caused the complete destruction of the vessel. The date of this fire is unknown since the vessel was stricken from the shipping registries upon her decommissioning and conversion to a drydock in 1920.

MAJOR leaving the Soo Locks

John Mitchell,		*GROSS REGISTERED*	
b) MAJOR		*TONNAGE:*	1,864
BUILT:	F. W. Wheeler,	*REGISTRY NUMBER:*	US 76792
	Bay City, Michigan	*ENGINES:*	Triple expansion
HULL NUMBER:	47		20″, 32″, 52″ diameter × 42″
LENGTH:	283		stroke
BREADTH:	41	*ENGINE BUILDER:*	Frontier Iron Works,
DEPTH:	22		Detroit, Michigan

MANITOBA

The wooden side wheel passenger and freighter MANITOBA was built in 1871 for William Beatty of Thorold, Ontario. She was registered at St. Catharines, Ontario on August 19, 1871 as owned by Henry, J. H. and William Beatty Sr. of Thorold. In 1871 she made four trips between Collingwood and Fort William, Ontario where ships had previously anchored outside the bar and transferred their cargo to lighters. The Beattys, now of Sarnia, transferred the ownership of MANITOBA to the Northwest Transportation Company of Sarnia. In October 1883 she was wrecked on Chantry Island off Southampton, Ontario in Lake Huron.

Salvaged in the Spring of 1884, she was towed to Detroit and rebuilt as CARMONA. Prior to this stranding the ship had operated under charter to the C.P.R. for several years.

In 1890 it was brought to Toronto and in 1891 operated from Toronto to Grimsby and Lorne Park. Beginning in 1892 it operated to Rochester (Charlotte) and even made occasional trips to the Thousand Islands.

In 1896 she was acquired by Brown & Co., St. Catharines. In 1900 she was rebuilt and lengthened at Collingwood. She was renamed PITTSBURGH and now measured 223 × 28 (45.5 over guards) × 12. The 40′ section was added to the hull aft of the paddle boxes. This lengthening process was not a success as it reduced her speed to 6 MPH. The ship burned at Queen's Dock, Sandwich, Ontario, on August 13, 1903. What was left of the hull was broken up at Port Dalhousie in 1904.

MANITOBA at right with Str. ALGOMA

	MANITOBA,	DEPTH:	11
	b) Carmona,	GROSS REGISTERED	
	c) Pittsburgh	TONNAGE:	338
		REGISTRY NUMBER:	C. 92653
BUILT:	M. Simpson,	ENGINES:	Beam engine 45″ diameter
	Port Robinson, Ontario		× 108″ stroke
LENGTH:	173	ENGINE BUILDER:	G. N. Oilles,
BREADTH:	25		St. Catharines, Ont.

MANITOBA

MANITOBA in dry dock at Port Huron

This passenger and package freighter was built in 1889 by the Canadian Pacific Railway Co. to take the place of the wrecked ALGOMA. For the first few years MANITOBA saw only part time service as passenger traffic was dropping off in the Upper Lakes due to improved rail service. MANITOBA served on the Georgian Bay-Lake Superior service of the C.P.R. all her life. Although the C.P.R. moved its base of operations from Owen Sound to Port McNicoll on May 1st, 1912, MANITOBA continued to call at Owen Sound until she was retired at the end of the 1949 season. She was towed to Hamilton, Ontario for scrapping by the Steel Company of Canada Ltd. in June, 1950.

BUILT:	Polson Iron Works Co., Ltd., Owen Sound, Ontario
HULL NUMBER:	23
LENGTH:	303
BREADTH:	38.1
DEPTH:	14.7
GROSS REGISTERED TONNAGE:	2,616
REGISTRY NUMBER:	C 94879
ENGINES:	Came from wrecked ALGOMA of 1883—35″ & 70″ diameter × 48″ stroke
ENGINE BUILDER:	David Rowan, Glasgow, Scotland

In 1926

MANITOU

MANITOU

The steel passenger propellor MANITOU was built in 1893 as an overnight steamer for the Lake Michigan and Lake Superior Transportation Company. She had two masts and one stack, considerably raked. Her stack was originally black with a red band, but later had a large white "M." MANITOU was fast, steady and easily maneuvered in restricted harbors. Although subsequently owned by the Manitou S.S. Co. in 1903, the Northern Michigan Transportation Company in 1908 and the Michigan Transit Corporation in 1920, MANITOU nevertheless ran in the same Chicago to Mackinac Island express service for 40 years,

making three round trips weekly. She was very popular with Chicago's socially elite. On regular schedule she entered the Strait of Manitou at about 10:30 P.M. and played her searchlight on the white lightship "Manitou" and blew the traditional salute with her whistle. MANITOU's best remembered commanders were Captains Finucan and Bright.

Renamed ISLE ROYALE in 1933, she ran to Lake Superior for the Isle Royale Transportation Company, then lay idle at Manistee, Michigan until partially destroyed by fire in 1936. She was cut down to a barge and then finally broken up for scrap metal during World War II.

Aground in the St. Mary's River   Str. ACE at left—lighter RELIEF at right

ISLE ROYALE at the Soo

MANITOU,
b) Isle Royale

BUILT:	Chicago Shipbuilding Company, Chicago, Illinois
HULL NUMBER:	8
LENGTH:	274.7
BREADTH:	42.2
DEPTH:	20.8

GROSS REGISTERED TONNAGE:	2,944
REGISTRY NUMBER:	US 92521
ENGINES:	Triple Expansion 23″, 38″ & 63″ Diameter × 36″ Stroke
ENGINE BUILDER:	Cleveland Shipbuilding Company, Cleveland, Ohio

Being reduced to scrap at Manitowoc

MANITOULIN

MODJESKA

The steel day passenger steamer MODJESKA was built in 1889 for the Hamilton Steamboat Co., Ltd., Hamilton, Ontario and operated Toronto-Hamilton along with MACASSA. She was rather slow and lumbering and prone to accidents. In addition, she always seemed to ride with a list which did not help her looks. She did not have MACASSA's fine lines. Control of Hamilton Steamboat Co. passed to the T. Eaton Co., Ltd., Toronto in 1909. The line was absorbed by the Niagara Navigation Co., Ltd. in 1911. The Richelieu and Ontario Navigation Co., Ltd. took over Niagara Navigation Co. in 1912 and itself became part of Canada Steamship Line, Ltd. in 1913.

On July 5, 1924 when leaving Toronto for Hamilton, MODJESKA was in a collision with TORONTO. Several days later MODJESKA had the misfortune to get off course in a dense fog and ran into the cement breakwater off Toronto's western gap. As her bow was badly damaged, she was laid up in Toronto and remained on the wall until sold in 1926 to the Owen Sound Transportation Co., Ltd., Owen Sound.

Refitted, she operated in Georgian Bay out of Owen Sound as a day boat for the balance of the 1926 season. During the winter of 1926–27, she was converted to the overnight passenger and freight steamer MANITOULIN at Owen Sound. She entered service in 1927 between Owen Sound and the Soo until she was retired at the end of the 1949 season. She was towed to Port Dalhousie on Lake Ontario and stripped to the main deck in 1951. The hull was finally cut up in Port Weller dry dock in November, 1953.

MODJESKA in CSL colors

Modjeska,
b) MANITOULIN

BUILT:	Napier Shanks and Bell, Yoker, Glasgow, Scotland
HULL NUMBER:	46
LENGTH:	178
BREADTH:	31.1
DEPTH:	12.3

GROSS REGISTERED TONNAGE:	678
REGISTRY NUMBER:	C 96058
ENGINES:	18″, 24″ & 40″ diameter × 27″ stroke Two triple expansions
ENGINE BUILDER:	Dunsmuir and Jackson, Glasgow, Scotland

MANITOULIN upbound in the St. Mary's River

MANITOULIN

IMARI in the Welland Canal

This bulk canal freighter was built in 1929 as a) IMARI in England and purchased upon arrival on the Lakes by the St. Lawrence Steamships, Ltd., of Welland, Ontario; E. S. Crosby & Co., Buffalo, New York, managers. The second of her six names was given the vessel in 1931 when she was renamed b) DELAWARE. For more than a decade this fine steamer served her owners in the St. Lawrence canal trade, seeing much service on the upper Lakes as well. Taken over by the British Ministry of War Shipping in 1943 because of the dire need of vessels to transport war material overseas, the ship was renamed again as c) EMPIRE ROTHER, and came under the management of William Cory & Son, Ltd., London, England.

At the cessation of hostilities, this vessel and many others lay idle for some time. In 1949 she was purchased by the Quebec and Ontario Transportation Company, Ltd., Mon-

treal (a subsidiary of the Ontario Paper Co., Ltd., of Thorold, Ontario) and renamed d) MANICOUAGAN. This name lasted only two years when the vessel was again renamed e) WASHINGTON TIMES-HERALD. The main trade of the ship was still in the canals but her cargoes consisted of pulpwood and paper along with the usual coal and grain.

The final name of this vessel was given in 1954 when she was renamed f) MANITOULIN. Shortly after the opening of the St. Lawrence Seaway in 1959, the need for small vessels diminished because of their uneconomical cargo capacity and the MANITOULIN was sold for scrapping to the A. Newman Co., of St. Catharines, Ontario in 1962. This much renamed and well traveled vessel was finally scrapped at Port Weller, Ontario in the winter of 1962–63.

DELAWARE

**Imari, b) Delaware, c) Empire Rother,
d) Manicouagan,
e) Washington Times-Herald,
f) MANITOULIN**

BUILT:	Swan Hunter and Wigham Richardson Ltd., Sunderland, G. B.
HULL NUMBER:	1383
LENGTH:	252.8
BREADTH:	43.4
DEPTH:	17.8
GROSS REGISTERED TONNAGE:	1,940
REGISTRY NUMBER:	C 149497
ENGINES:	Triple Expansion 15″, 25″ & 40″ diameter × 33″ stroke
ENGINE BUILDER:	MacColl and Pollock Ltd., Sunderland, G. B.

DELAWARE in the locks

WASHINGTON TIMES-HERALD at Thorold, Ontario

MANICOUAGAN

MANITOULIN upbound into Lake Huron

MARGUERITE W.

In need of a fire tug at Duluth, Superior, and Two Harbors, Minnesota, the Duluth and Iron Range Railroad had a twin screw tug built in 1908, which they named the WILLIAM A. McGONAGLE. From her building, until she way sold in 1922 to the Duluth, Missabe and Northern Railroad, she performed her tasks ably. Many times she was called to the aid of firefighters ashore and afloat, as well as performing other tugging tasks.

In 1937, she was again sold this time to the Pigeon Timber Company of Fort William, Ontario and renamed the MARGUERITE W. (C. 153120). Here she was employed in towing lumber rafts in the Canadian Lakehead area. In 1938, the Lakehead Transportation Co., was organized and most of the ships of the Pigeon Timber Company went into the new fleet. Her dimensions were slightly changed in 1939 to—110 × 28:1 × 15.4—416 gross tons—by a rebuild of her cabins.

MARGUERITE W. towed the barges FLORENCE J., MERLE H. and MAUREEN H. down the lakes to the paper mills on Lake Ontario and the Welland Canal. In 1948, the Great Lakes Lumber and Shipping Co. became the successor to the Lakehead Transportation fleet. The colors the MARGUERITE W. possessed in these days were quite vivid: light green hull, white cabins, with a black stack encircled with wide white and green bands.

In 1953, the tug was sold to the Hindman Transportation Co. of Owen Sound and renamed RUTH HINDMAN (1). Now her scene of operations was changed as well as her colors, gray hull, purple cabins, buff stack with a red "H," but this color scheme did not last too long. When in her last years, she towed the DELKOTE, MITSCHFIBRE, or SWEDEROPE, her colors were the same as the other Hindman boats, black hull, white cabins, black stack with the white diamond and red "H." She was renamed LYNDA HINDMAN in 1965, but her days ended in 1966 when she was retired, her cabins stripped and loaded aboard the MITSCHFIBRE, and towed to Ashtabula for cutting up. Her hull remained at Goderich for a time, her new owner hoping to make her into a fish tug, but that project was never completed.

WILLIAM A. McGONAGLE

William A. McGonagle (1), b) MARGUERITE W., c) Ruth Hindman (1), d) Lynda Hindman

BUILT:	American Shipbuilding Company, Lorain, Ohio	*GROSS REGISTERED TONNAGE:*	275
		REGISTRY NUMBER:	US 205880
HULL NUMBER:	364	*ENGINES:*	20″ & 20″ Diameter × 24″ Stroke
LENGTH:	110		High Pressure Non-Condensing
BREADTH:	28		(2) on one shaft
DEPTH:	15	*ENGINE BUILDER:*	Shipyard

MARGUERITE W.

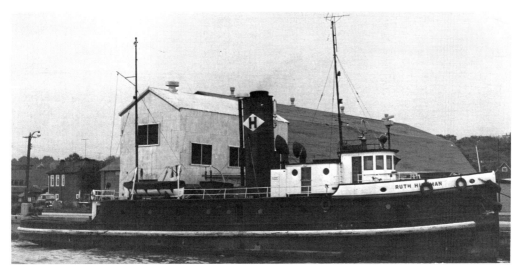

RUTH HINDMAN at Owen Sound

LYNDA HINDMAN at Detroit

MARICOPA

MARICOPA with barge MARSALA

This steel bulk carrier was built in 1896 for the Minnesota Steamship Co., subsidiary of the Minnesota Iron Mining Company. Pickands Mather & Co., Cleveland, were her managers. Minnesota Iron was absorbed by the Federal Steel Co. in 1900 and thus was swallowed up when the United States Steel Co. was put together in 1901. Ownership of the fleet passed to Pittsburgh Steamship Co., Cleveland in 1901.

MARICOPA was reboiled in 1914 and in 1923 was given an extensive rebuild by Pittsburgh Steamship Co. She remained in the U.S. Steel Fleet until 1936 when she was sold to the Geistman Transportation Co., Duluth and renamed b) JOHN P. GEISTMAN. She was transferred to Canadian registry in 1939 (C. 171063) when purchased by

the Lakehead Transportation Co., Fort William, Ontario. She was renamed c) E. E. JOHNSON (1) in 1941 and was transferred to the ownership of Great Lakes Lumber and Shipping Ltd., Fort William, in 1942.

From February 7, 1945 to March 6, 1945 ownership was in the name of Powell Transports Ltd., Winnipeg. On March 6, 1945, however, title passed to Paterson Steamships Ltd., Fort William as d) ALTADOC (2).

By 1962 ALTADOC was showing her age and Paterson sold her to the Goderich Elevator and Transit Co., Ltd., Goderich, Ontario for use as a grain storage barge. The new owners renamed her e) D. B. WELDON. She served as a storage barge at Goderich as needed until 1974 when she was sold for scrapping at Thunder Bay, Ontario.

With barge MAGNA at Mission Point

JOHN P. GEISTMAN with barge FLORENCE leaving the Soo

MARICOPA, b) John P. Geistman, c) E. E. Johnson (1), d) Altadoc (2), e) D. B. Weldon

BUILT:	Chicago Shipbuilding Co., South Chicago, Illinois	*GROSS REGISTERED TONNAGE:*	4,223
HULL NUMBER:	21	*REGISTRY NUMBER:*	US 92736
LENGTH:	406	*ENGINES:*	Triple Expansion 25″, 40″ & 68″ diameter × 42″ stroke
BREADTH:	48.2		
DEPTH:	23.4	*ENGINE BUILDER:*	Cleveland Shipbuilding Co., Cleveland

E. E. JOHNSON

ALTADOC in the ice entering the upper St. Mary's River

ALTADOC in the Detroit River

D. B. WELDON at Goderich, Ont.

MARIGOLD

The United States Lighthouse Service contracted to build an iron tender in 1890 and the new ship was launched on November 15, 1890. The MARIGOLD's duties on the Lakes were to bring the lighthouse keepers to their stations in the spring and retrieve them in the fall, fix all buoys, making sure the lighted ones were kept lit, and to completely provision the lighthouses in its district. She also went on rescue missions when the need arose. This vessel was a workhorse, but a different type than the commercial vessels.

Prior to World War II, in 1939, the Lighthouse Service was absorbed into the U.S. Coast Guard which then assumed the duties of caring for the lights on the Lakes. During World War II MARIGOLD was refurbished and her gross tonnage changed to 696. She was given the war numeral signification WAGL 235. A few of her interesting War duties were the convoying of the newly built warships down the St. Clair and Detroit Rivers into Lake Erie, where another group would take charge, and the patrolling of the coast in the Detroit area for "smugglers and spies," of which there were no dearth in the minds of the press.

After the War, the MARIGOLD was sold for commercial service in 1946 to the Lyons Construction Company of Whitehall, Michigan, where the ship received official #264968. In 1947 the vessel was renamed the MISS MUDHEN II and was rebuilt into a diesel dredge. The new dimensions were: 106.7 × 26.5 × 5.6, with gross tonnage becoming 124. She had been changed completely and her new duties took her to the rather lowly task of dredging channels in small harbors and at private construction sites. The ship was sold to the Michigan Dredging Company in 1965 and was based at Bay City for some time. The iron hull still holds out, and MISS MUDHEN II has been active in this new job with fervor even after some 75 years afloat.

MARIGOLD at Two Harbors

		DEPTH:	13
MARIGOLD,		GROSS REGISTERED	
b) Miss Mudhen II		TONNAGE:	454
BUILT:	Detroit Dry Dock Co., Wyandotte, Michigan	ENGINES:	Triple expansion 14¼″, 22″, 36″ diameter × 24″ stroke
HULL NUMBER:	105		
LENGTH:	149	ENGINE BUILDER:	Dry Dock Engine Wks., Detroit, Mich.
BREADTH:	27		

MARIGOLD in the Detroit River

MISS MUDHEN II in the Straits of Mackinac

MATOA

MATOA in the St. Mary's River

This steel bulk freight propellor was built in 1890 for the Minnesota Steamship Company. MATOA was painted in the Minnesota fleet colors, having a black hull with white stripe, white cabins, black stack with white triangle and red letter "M" on it.

In 1901 MATOA and all other vessels of the Minnesota fleet were absorbed into the newly formed Pittsburgh Steamship Company of United States Steel Corporation. MATOA sailed as a "tin-stacker" until 1913. In the Big Storm on Lake Huron in November of that year, the vessel was upbound loaded with coal when the full fury of that storm broke upon her. Many staunch ships disappeared without trace during that blow but the MATOA was rather lucky in this respect. She stranded about ten miles north of Harbor Beach, Michigan and became a constructive total loss. But, luckily, none of the crew was lost. She was abandoned to the underwriters who sold the hull to Reid Wrecking Company of Sarnia and Port Huron. They towed her to their Port Huron Shipyard after successfully salvaging the vessel from its stranded position.

After repairs MATOA was sold by Reid to the Warren Transportation Company of Boston, Massachusetts in 1915.

The hull was cut in two at Port Huron and both sections were towed down through the St. Lawrence River Canals to the coast. The sections were rejoined and the vessel was registered in Boston. During World War I her camouflage helped her elude German submarines.

In 1923 the vessel was sold Canadian (C. 151587) to the Playfair interests of Midland, Ontario. The Great Lakes Transportation Company again cut MATOA in two and brought it to Collingwood, Ontario where it was rebuilt and lengthened 36 feet. Her new dimensions were 326 × 40 × 24.2 with 2,723 gross tons. She was renamed GLENRIG in 1923. The new colors were gray hull, white cabins and rose stack with a black top. In 1926 the ship was sold to Canada Steamship Lines and renamed HUGUENOT. Under this flag she had a red hull, white cabins and forecastle and red stack with black top over a white band. HUGUENOT remained in the CSL fleet through the rest of its life, though laid up with many of the old timers in the depression. The aging vessel was sold for scrap in 1937 and broken up at Midland the same year. Thus ended a peculiar career for a lake steamer. Only nine or ten other lakers were cut in two twice to be taken to salt water and then returned.

Stern section—tug J. M. DIVER

Bow section—tug S. M. FISCHER

GLENRIG in 1924

MATOA,
b) Glenrig,
c) Huguenot

BUILT:	Globe Iron Works, Cleveland, Ohio	*DEPTH:*	21.1
HULL NUMBER:	34	*GROSS REGISTERED TONNAGE:*	2,311
LENGTH:	290.6	*REGISTRY NUMBER:*	US 92204
BREADTH:	40.3	*ENGINES:*	Triple expansion 24″, 38″, 61″ diameter × 42″ stroke
		ENGINE BUILDER:	Shipyard

HUGUENOT in 1928

MAUNALOA

MAUNALOA at the Soo

MAUNALOA,
b) Maunaloa II

BUILT:	Chicago Shipbuilding Company, South Chicago, Illinois
HULL NUMBER:	37
LENGTH:	430
BREADTH:	50.2
DEPTH:	24
GROSS REGISTERED TONNAGE:	4,951
REGISTRY NUMBER:	US 92974
ENGINES:	Quadruple expansion 18″, 27″, 40″, 62″ diameter × 42″ stroke
ENGINE BUILDER:	Shipyard

In the St. Clair River

MAUNALOA II passing Harsens Island

The Minnesota Steamship Company ordered a number of vessels near the close of the 19th century and all their vessels had names beginning with "M" and ending with "A." MAUNALOA, named after the volcano on the Island of Hawaii, was built in 1899 and was to have been called TENNESSEE by another firm that had originally ordered it from the Chicago Shipbuilding Company, but they changed plans and sold the uncompleted hull to the Minnesota Steamship Company.

In 1901 the Pittsburgh Steamship Company was organized and the entire Minnesota Steamship fleet was incorporated into the new corporation. Altogether, some 101 vessels came into that fleet in that one year. This was the lake transport arm of United States Steel Corporation, and since then has been the largest fleet on the Great Lakes. The MAUNALOA served in the fleet until 1945, then was sold to the Upper Lakes & St. Lawrence Transportation Company of Toronto, Ontario.

Her career started anew. Renamed MAUNALOA II, the ship was given the official Canadian registry number 174977. Very often, as the ship did for the Pittsburgh Steamship Company, she towed one of the fleet's barges behind her. Some of the more familiar steel barges owned by both firms at one time or another were the JOHN FRITZ and JOHN A. ROEBLING. The MAUNALOA's quadruple expansion engine served her well and gave her enough power to tow a heavy steel barge behind her as long as they were used. In the late 1950's these barges were retired to store cargoes of grain at Goderich, Sarnia and Toronto, Ontario.

Gradually, the usefulness of MAUNALOA II diminished as its cargo carrying capacity was small and the expense of running the ship rose. The aging vessel was finally retired from the active lists and was scrapped at Stratherne Terminals at Hamilton, Ontario in 1971. The "old lady" had completed some 70 years of sailing the Great Lakes.

Passing Mission Point in the St. Mary's River

MAYWOOD

The steel passenger and freight propellor MAYWOOD was built in 1905 for James B. Moran, managing owner of the Escanaba and Gladstone Transportation Co. MAYWOOD was intended primarily for service on Little Bay de Noc between Escanaba and Gladstone, Michigan, usually running opposite the older wooden propeller LOTUS, built in 1893. Both vessels also ran from these two ports to the Green Bay, the upper Wisconsin islands and nearby northern Lake Michigan cities.

In 1915 the vessel was sold to the Hill Steamboat Line of Kenosha, Wisconsin and sailed on Lower Lake Michigan briefly. In 1917 she was purchased by James W. Elwell & Company of New York, brokers, for the French Government. She left the Lakes via the St. Lawrence River in 1917 and was renamed INCA on her arrival across the Atlantic. The French Government operated INCA as a salvage tug during World War I.

The record of her demise is clouded. No record appears in the French "Bureau Veritas" listings after World War I, but she is still recorded in the "American Bureau of Shipping" until 1928. After this date, we have no information about the vessel.

MAYWOOD at Gladstone, Mich.

	MAYWOOD, b) Inca		
BUILT:	Manitowoc Dry Dock Company, Manitowoc, Wisconsin	DEPTH:	17
		GROSS REGISTERED TONNAGE:	398
HULL NUMBER:	6	REGISTRY NUMBER:	US 202202
LENGTH:	130	ENGINES:	Triple expansion 14″, 22″, 36″ diameter × 24″ stroke
BREADTH:	28	ENGINE BUILDER:	Marine Iron Works, Chicago, Illinois

M. F. MERICK

The large wooden tug M. F. MERICK was built in 1873, under the supervision of the veteran Buffalo shipbuilder George Hardison, who had moved to Detroit, Michigan. She was built on speculation and took her sea trials on May 28, 1873. She reportedly was designed by Captain Stephen R. Kirby, of Saginaw, Michigan, father of the well-known Detroit Shipbuilder Frank E. Kirby. Throughout her Detroit career, from 1873 to 1881, she was owned in part by John E. Edwards, William E. Edwards, J. P. Young, and later J. Emory Owen. Always, prominent stockholders of the Detroit Dry Dock firm maintained more than a half interest in her, however.

In July 1881, her enrollment was transferred to Buffalo, New York, and she was sold to the International Bridge Company (Elbridge G. Spaulding, President), of Buffalo. She was rebuilt in 1886 (92' × 24'5" × 10'2"; 133 gross tons, 77 net tons) and received a new high pressure, non-condensing engine (20" × 24"; 370 indicated horsepower) and boiler. It is interesting to note that in 1886, when the tug's enrollment was changed because of her readmeasure-

ment, she became "victimized" by the slip of a customs house clerk. The name of the tug should have been spelled MERRICK, but her name was inadvertently misspelled to M. F. MERICK, which is the way it appeared in official documents to her end.

In July 1891, the tug again was sold, this time to the Thompson Towing and Wrecking Company (C. D. Thompson) of Port Huron, Michigan. In August 1899, the Thompson firm was included in the formation of the Great Lakes Towing Company, and in December 1900, the tug was conveyed to a subsidiary firm, the Union Towing and Wrecking Company, of Duluth, Minnesota. She ended her towing career in 1907, when she was dismantled at the Dunham tug yard in Chicago, Illinois, but her engine was removed and served several more useful years in the new steel-hulled tug L. C. SABIN (later NORTH CAROLINA). Another account says that her stripped hull was used as a lighter in and around Chicago before being taken out and scuttled in Lake Michigan.

M. F. MERICK working in the river

BUILT:	Detroit Dry Dock Company, Detroit, Michigan	GROSS REGISTERED TONNAGE:	205.62
HULL NUMBER:	22	REGISTRY NUMBER:	US 90492
LENGTH:	92	ENGINES:	High Pressure Non-condensing
BREADTH:	24.5	ENGINE BUILDER:	Frontier Engine Works, Detroit, Michigan
DEPTH:	10.7		

MICHIGAN

CHARLES M. WARNER upbound in the St. Mary's River

The steel bulk freighter CHARLES M. WARNER was built in 1903 for the United States Transportation Company and was engaged in coarse freight trade until 1920. (The corporate name of the United States Transportation Company was changed in 1911 to the Great Lakes Steamship Company.)

In 1928 the WARNER was sold to the Great Lakes Dredge and Dock Company who had the steamer converted into a suction dredge at the yards of the Manitowoc Shipbuilding Company at Manitowoc, Wisconsin. The vessel was renamed MICHIGAN and its dimensions were: 377 × 48.2 × 24—3739 gross registered tons. At that time the ship was the largest sandsucker on the Lakes. Her unique paint job consisted of a bright red hull and cabins and black stack with red and white disc emblem.

In 1956 the vessel was sold to the Presque Isle Transportation Company of Erie, Pennsylvania. The vessel was again converted, this time to a self-unloading sandsucker by the American Shipbuilding Company at Chicago, towed to Erie by tugs and renamed LAKEWOOD. The gross registered tonnage was changed to 3751 when the vessel was dieselized in 1958 in Erie. She received a General Motors 16 cylinder 8-1/2 × 10″ diameter engine.

In 1970 Erie Sand Steamship Company took over the vessel which now appears painted a green hull, white cabins and orange stack with triangular emblem.

Entering Duluth harbor

288

MICHIGAN at Chicago

Charles M. Warner,
b) MICHIGAN,
c) Lakewood

BUILT: Chicago Shipbuilding Co.,
Chicago, Illinois
HULL NUMBER: 58
LENGTH: 370
BREADTH: 48

DEPTH: 24
GROSS REGISTERED
TONNAGE: 3,812
REGISTRY NUMBER: US 127752
ENGINES: 20″, 33½″, 55″ diameter × 40″
stroke
Triple expansion
ENGINE BUILDER: Shipyard

MICHIGAN being towed by tug JOHN ROEN V in St. Clair River

LAKEWOOD in Cleveland

In the Detroit River

MILWAUKEE

The Manistique, Marquette & Northern Railroad had a steel carferry built for their account in 1903, with the unimaginative name of MANISTIQUE, MARQUETTE & NORTHERN NO. 1. In 1909, this railroad was taken over by the Grand Trunk, and the carferry was renamed MILWAUKEE. She carried an average of 28 railroad cars across Lake Michigan from Grand Haven, Michigan to Milwaukee, Wisconsin. This water link was kept open throughout the winter months, and the MILWAUKEE had to combat Lake Michigan storms year-round.

On October 22, 1929, this carferry left Milwaukee at 2:30 p.m., bound for Grand Haven with 25 railroad cars, one of which carried new Nash automobiles. The seas were high and the fall storm that struck Lake Michigan that day wrought its fury on the ship with all its strength. The MILWAUKEE had crossed from Grand Haven that morning, and the captain routinely planned the return crossing. His staunch ship had weathered many such storms and proved she could take them in stride.

This trip however, proved to be different. The wind and waves were smashing on the stern when she left Milwaukee and there her story ends because the ship and crew of 47 suddenly disappeared. Wreckage came ashore near Milwaukee, but the mystery continued as to the hull's whereabouts.

A message was found by the lifeguards at the South Haven Coast Guard Station in a can typically carried on vessels to be used when in distress. Waterproof, about 18″ long and 3″ in diameter, this one was badly bent and some water had seeped in. Written in pencil the message read:

"S.S. MILWAUKEE
October 22, '29, 6″30 P.M.
Ship is taking water fast. We have turned and headed for Milwaukee. Pumps are all working, but sea gate is bent and won't keep water out. Flickers are flooded. Seas are tremendous. Things look bad. Crew roll about same as last payday.

Signed A. R. Sadon, Purser"

This last note was all that was ever heard from the ill-fated vessel.

In 1972 skindivers from Milwaukee located the MILWAUKEE, quite by accident, located about 10 miles from that port, somewhere near Wind Point or Fox Point (the divers did not reveal the exact spot). They investigated the wreck and found that it lay on an even keel, with the pilothouse wrenched off and lying a few yards away, and the tailgate smashed. Most of the railroad cars were off the tracks at the stern of the vessel, but the ones near the bow were intact and still on the tracks. Apparently, the captain had tried to turn her around in the heavy seas, and the cars had smashed their way into the tailgate, thus causing the MILWAUKEE to fill from the stern and sink. No one will ever know the exact answer, nor the plight of her crew those last few moments when she was sinking.

MANISTIQUE, MARQUETTE & NORTHERN NO. 1

MILWAUKEE leaving Grand Haven

**Manistique, Marquette, & Northern No. 1,
b) MILWAUKEE**

BUILT:	American Shipbuilding Company, Cleveland, Ohio
HULL NUMBER:	413
LENGTH:	383
BREADTH:	56
DEPTH:	19.5
GROSS REGISTERED TONNAGE:	2,933
REGISTRY NUMBER:	93363
ENGINES:	23½″, 37″, 62″ diameter × 36″ stroke Triple Expansion (2)
ENGINE BUILDER:	Shipyard

At Milwaukee

ANNA C. MINCH

ANNA C. MINCH in 1923

In 1903 many ships both large and small were built in Great Lakes shipyards. Among the steel freighters built was the ANNA C. MINCH. Named for the daughter of one of the executives of Kinsman Transit Company, the MINCH lived a varied life and met an untimely death.

The MINCH sailed for the Kinsman Transit Company until September of 1926, when it was sold to James Murphy, owner of the Western Navigation Company, Limited, of Fort William, Ontario. Her Canadian registry was obtained, being assigned number 153113. The bulk carrier was used mainly in the grain trade and carried these cargoes without mishap except for occasional minor damage. This happy career changed drastically in the fall of 1940. The Armistice Day storm of 1940 was to be the scourge of shippers that fall. The wind velocity reached hurricane force within a few hours after the front passed over Lakes Michigan and Superior. The resultant havoc the wind and seas caused are to be remembered by many sailors on these inland "mill-ponds" to this day. Salt water sailors visiting the Lakes in summer rarely meet the forces of our November storms, and think of our lakes in the endearing terms of mill-ponds. Only when they experience one of these storms in their own ships do they have any respect for them.

Along with the ANNA C. MINCH, the steamers WILLIAM B. DAVOCK and NOVADOC were lost in this fury on Lake Michigan, all near Ludington, Michigan, and the SPARTA was beached and wrecked on Lake Superior. November 11th is not a date favorable to Great Lakes sailors. In 1913, some 235 seamen lost their lives over a period of three days in the "Big Storm" on Lake Huron. Though not sinking quite as many vessels, the Armistice Day Storm of 1940 wrecked two ships and caused two more to disappear completely with all hands. The ANNA C. MINCH lies beneath the calm waters of Lake Michigan today near Pentwater, Michigan where she went down.

ANNA C. MINCH in 1938 at the Soo

BUILT:	American Shipbuilding Company, Cleveland, Ohio	GROSS REGISTERED TONNAGE:	4,285
HULL NUMBER:	415	REGISTRY NUMBER:	US 107846
LENGTH:	380	ENGINES:	22″, 35″, 58″ diameter × 40″ stroke
BREADTH:	50		Triple expansion
DEPTH:	28	ENGINE BUILDER:	Shipyard

MISSOURI

MISSOURI at Onekama, Mich.

Built in 1904, this passenger and freight vessel of the Northern Michigan Transportation Company was a near sister ship of the Steamer ILLINOIS. MISSOURI served on the route between Chicago, Illinois and northern ports of the lower peninsula of Michigan. The ship was designed by W. I. Babcock, Marine Architect and Consultant of Chicago, and had comfortable accommodations for over 200 passengers and a freight capacity of nearly 1,000 tons. In addition, the MISSOURI had a reinforced hull for winter service in ice and was known as a sturdy and reliable vessel.

In 1920 the Northern Michigan Transportation Company was reorganized as the Michigan Transportation Company. Warren A. Cartier became the owner of this ship in 1927, and the Wisconsin and Michigan Steamship Company took over the vessel in 1935, but ran her little. In 1942 her engines were removed and placed in the Ford Barge LAKE INAHA which was being repowered for war service. The latter vessel was lost by foundering in 1954 and presumably MISSOURI's engines went down with her. MISSOURI herself was towed to Hamilton, Ontario late in 1947 and was scrapped there in the following year.

BUILT:	Chicago Shipbuilding Company, Chicago, Illinois
HULL NUMBER:	65
LENGTH:	225
BREADTH:	40.1
DEPTH:	24.5
GROSS REGISTERED TONNAGE:	2,434
REGISTRY NUMBER:	US 200861
ENGINES:	Triple expansion 20″, 33″, 54″ diameter × 36″ stroke
ENGINE BUILDER:	Shipyard

MISSOURI at Ludington, Str. NEVADA in background

MOHEGAN

The wooden steam barge MOHEGAN was built in 1894 and was one of the larger ships of her type. She was used mostly in the lumber trade as a unit of the Curtis and Brainard fleet which was called the Miami Transportation Company. In 1904 the vessel was sold to the Buffalo, New York firm of Holland & Graves and in 1910 to Graves and Bigwood of the same city.

In 1916 the ship was sold to the Republic Mining and Manufacturing Company of New York, which in later years was known as the Aluminum Corporation of America. In this manner the MOHEGAN, a Great Lakes lumber hooker, became the pioneer ship of the Alcoa Fleet. Eventually the MOHEGAN was rebuilt for the Bauxite trade between New York and Demerara, British Guiana. The MOHEGAN entered this service in April, 1917 carrying machinery to the mines and bringing back bulk bauxite ore. She was attacked by a German submarine off Hampton Roads, Virginia in August, 1918, but escaped.

By the end of 1918, newer Alcoa ships replaced the aging vessel, and it was sold to a Mr. Shapiro of New York. On her maiden voyage under his flag, she exploded and burned while at anchor in the harbor of Rio de Janeiro, Brazil, on August 20, 1919, and was a total loss. No one of the 27 aboard was killed, but the boat was completely destroyed.

MOHEGAN in the St. Clair River

BUILT:	M. P. Lester, Marine City, Michigan	*GROSS REGISTERED TONNAGE:*	1,216
LENGTH:	225	*REGISTRY NUMBER:*	US 92561
BREADTH:	39.2	*ENGINES:*	Fore and Aft compound 25″ & 50″ diameter × 42″ stroke
DEPTH:	14.1	*ENGINE BUILDER:*	S. F. Hodge (#233), Detroit, Michigan

MONARCH

The combination wooden passenger and freight vessel MONARCH was built in 1890 at Sarnia, Ontario, for the Northwest Transportation Company (J. H. and J. D. Beatty), of Sarnia. In 1899, the Beatty Line merged with the Northern Navigation Company. She ran from Sarnia to Port Arthur, Ontario, during most of her lifetime.

On December 6, 1906, the vessel cleared Port Arthur at 6 o'clock in the evening with sixty-one persons on board and a cargo of flour and canned salmon on what was scheduled to be her last trip of the season. Three hours later, during a snowstorm that had reduced visibility to near zero, she struck Blake Point, bow-on, along an uninhabited stretch of Isle Royale. A line was made fast to a tree, but within an hour the stern was under water, with about thirty feet of the bow sticking out. The passengers and crew went hand-over-hand down the line to shore where they protected themselves with brush shelters and built a bonfire. One crewman was lost while sliding down the line. Captain Edward Robertson stayed on board the wreck until

the following day. Sometime during the night, the lighthouse keeper at Passage Island Light saw the bonfire, but the waves prevented him from landing in a small boat, but he successfully notified the outside world of the accident. After thirty-six hours of suffering from hunger and extreme cold, sixteen men and three women were rescued by the Steamer EDMONTON. Finally, on December 10, the tugs JAMES WHALEN and LAURA GRACE arrived with supplies and a doctor to complete the rescue. They returned to Port Arthur with the remaining forty-one souls, many of them suffering from frostbite. Chief Engineer Sam Beatty, of Collingwood, had received a preview of the MONARCH loss the year before when, as chief of the Algoma Central steamer MONKSHAVEN, he suffered under identical circumstances when she was lost on Pie Island. A few days later, the survivors reached Sarnia aboard the HURONIC. In the same storm, Northern Navigation Company's IONIC was driven shore near Whitefish Point, Michigan, but she was released on December 11 with little injury.

MONARCH in 1906

BUILT:	John Dyble, Sarnia, Ontario	*REGISTRY NUMBER:*	C 96843
LENGTH:	245	*ENGINES:*	21″, 33″, 54″ diameter × 42″ stroke Triple expansion
BREADTH:	35	*ENGINE BUILDER:*	Kerr Brothers, Walkerville, Ontario
DEPTH:	23		
GROSS REGISTERED TONNAGE:	2,017		

MONTAUK

The sidewheel passenger steamer MONTAUK was launched on March 31, 1891 for the Montauk Steamboat Company (Jackson and Sharp Company), of Sag Harbor, New York. She was built to run from New York to Sag Harbor, on the east end of Long Island. In June, 1895, her ownership was transferred to the Long Island Railway Company, New York, and in April, 1899, to the River and Harbor Transportation Company, New York. From 1895 she ran between Block Island and Fort Pond Bay.

On March 28, 1902, Edward V. Douglas, vice president of the Algoma Central and Hudson Bay Railway, of Sault Ste. Marie, Ontario, purchased the vessel and renamed her KING EDWARD (Br. 113897). Her registry was enrolled at St. Johns, Newfoundland, where it would remain until 1922. On May 8, 1903, ownership was transferred to the Algoma firm. She ran from Cleveland, Ohio, to the Canadian Soo.

In May, 1910, as a forerunner of things to come, the paddle steamer was renamed FOREST CITY, and the following May she was sold to the Ontario and Ohio Navigation Company, Ltd., for service between Cleveland and Port Stanley, Ontario, across Lake Erie. The next year saw a succession of official ownership changes—Richard Clayton Eckert, Everard Handel North, and the Silver Islet Navigation Company, Ltd. Her route again was changed, this time between Port Arthur, Isle Royale, Silver Islet, and the Canadian Soo. In 1918, Michael M. McCulloch, became her official owner.

In June, 1922, the thirty-year old sidewheeler returned to American documentation this time to Katherine Murphy, of Sturgeon Bay, Wisconsin, for excursions out of Chicago

as the MONTAUK (175' × 31' × 10'2"; 418 gross tons, 241 net tons). In 1923 ownership passed to Clow and Nicholson Transportation Company, of Duluth, Minnesota. She returned to Lake Superior to run excursions between Duluth and Fond du Lac under the name of the North Shore Steamship Company. During the winter of 1923-24 Marine Iron and Ship Building Company made extensive rennovations to her at Duluth. For the next twenty years MONTAUK became a familiar sight along the Duluth waterfront and, until she was dismantled in 1942, gained the distinction of being the last beam-engined sidewheeler on the Great Lakes. On January 20, 1942, the West End Iron and Metal Corporation of Duluth, took possession of her, and in October, 1943, Walter W. Bowe and A. B. Powers, both of Duluth, were her owners. During this period her upper works were stripped off and machinery removed.

In 1944 the hull was sold to Lyons Construction Company, of Whitehall, Michigan, for conversion to a barge. She was officially dropped from documentation in 1947, still as a sidewheeler.

Ultimately the hull was towed to West Bay City, Michigan and moored along the McNally and Nimergood property, the site of the old Wheeler ship yard, on the west side of the Saginaw River. One could still ser her trim, stylish lines, even if there was a small cabin perched on her deck aft. In about 1976 the hull partially submerged and in May, 1977, someone set fire to the remaining cabin.

As of this writing she still is there, mute evidence of a long and useful career and still representing a long-vanished era in lake "steamboating" history.

FOREST CITY

MONTAUK, b) Forest City, c) King Edward, d) Montauk

BUILT:	Harlan & Hollingsworth, Wilmington, Delaware	GROSS REGISTERED TONNAGE:	570
HULL NUMBER:	263	REGISTRY NUMBER:	US 92294
LENGTH:	175'	ENGINES:	Beam Condensing
BREADTH:	31'		38" diameter × 108" stroke
DEPTH:	9'6"	ENGINE BUILDER:	Shipyard

KING EDWARD at the Soo

MONTAUK at Duluth

MONTAUK as a barge at Bay City

DANIEL J. MORRELL

DANIEL J. MORRELL nearing the Soo

The West Bay City Shipbuilding Company turned out many big freighters in its short span of operation and the DANIEL J. MORRELL was one of them. Built in 1906, it was one of the standard 600 footers of the early 20th century and was built for the Cambria Steamship Company, managed by Bethlehem Steel Corporation.

Through almost 60 years of rather uneventful, but fruitful, steaming, the MORRELL was a familiar sight on the Detroit, St. Clair and St. Mary's Rivers. With the modernization of many of the older vessels in the 1950's, the MORRELL also took its turn. In May 1956, it came out with a new three-cylinder Skinner Uniflow engine, 30″ × 36″. This repowering gave the ore carrier added speed and increased her economical operation. Along with the added power also came new safety devices. The MORRELL already had radar which was installed just after World War II.

This steamer met the fate of many of her sisterships on the Lakes. On the night of November 28, 1966, she was upbound on Lake Huron in ballast and foundered about 28 miles Northeast of Harbor Beach, Michigan at 2:30 a.m. in a severe gale that had driven many other vessels to shelter. The ship broke in two, and the ship-to-shore radio could not be used to send distress signals to any other ships in the vicinity. The MORRELL, in fact, was nearly alone in that part of the Lake as many even larger vessels sought shelter. Some of the crew attempted to escape on a life raft after this disaster and succeeded in pulling away from the sinking vessel. Because no one sent any distress calls, the plight of these men went unheard. Only one crewman survived the ordeal. His life was saved while his fellow crewmen on top of him froze to death. The raft was picked up after a day and a half of wallowing over the rough seas of Lake Huron. Twenty-eight men lost their lives on this fateful day. The MORRELL was the first commercial vessel to sink in a Lake Huron storm since the steamer CLIFTON sank in 1924 about 29 miles East by North from AuSable Pierhead or approximately the same position as the MORRELL.

In the Detroit River

DANIEL J. MORRELL

BUILT:	Bay City Shipbuilding Company, West Bay City, Michigan	*GROSS REGISTERED TONNAGE:*	7,239
		REGISTRY NUMBER:	US 203507
HULL NUMBER:	619	*ENGINES:*	Triple Expansion
LENGTH:	580		24″, 39″, 65″ diameter × 42″ stroke
BREADTH:	58		
DEPTH:	27.4	*ENGINE BUILDER:*	Detroit Shipbuilding Company, Detroit, Michigan

DANIEL J. MORRELL, Windsor, Ont. in the background

MARTIN MULLEN

This steel bulk freighter was built in 1904 for the Lakewood Steamship Company, which was managed by Hutchinson & Company of Cleveland, Ohio. This company later (1908) became the Pioneer Steamship Company under the same management. Until late 1947 the MULLEN continued in her everyday task of carrying iron ore, grain, stone and coal cargoes to nearly all the ports of the lakes for the Hutchinson fleet.

On the 28th of November in 1947 the MULLEN was sold to the Paterson Steamships Limited of Fort William, Ontario and renamed SCOTIADOC. When she came out in 1948 under that name the official Canadian Registry number was 173186. Paterson's unique practice of naming ships after provinces and cities of Canada, with a suffix DOC refering to Dominion of Canada, distinguishes this fleet. The prefix of the name refers to Nova Scotia, hence SCOTIADOC in this case. This name was chosen to honor the province because the previous three vessels which were named for the same province had met with unfortunate accidents and used the term Nova instead of Scotia in the ship name. The first NOVADOC was lost, the second foundered, and the third was wrecked on the East Coast. Perhaps naming the MULLEN the SCOTIADOC would break the jinx.

Unfortunately, this was not to be. On June 20, 1953 just 15 miles out from Thunder Bay, Ontario, the SCOTIADOC, loaded with 239,000 bushels of wheat, collided with the Canada Steamship Lines Steamer BURLINGTON in foggy weather and winds reaching a velocity of 55 mph. The two steamers were on converging courses and did not see each other until it was too late. The SCOTIADOC went to the bottom at 6:40 p.m. off Trowbridge Island in Thunder Bay. All but one of her crew were saved by the BURLINGTON and brought into Thunder Bay, Ontario, a bit wet but happy to be rescued. The SCOTIADOC had loaded wheat for Georgian Bay ports and had left Fort William just a few hours prior to the sinking. Foggy weather had claimed yet another victim.

MARTIN MULLEN in the Detroit River

SCOTIADOC topside view

MARTIN MULLEN,
b) Scotiadoc

BUILT:	American Shipbuilding Company, Cleveland, Ohio
HULL NUMBER:	422
LENGTH:	416
BREADTH:	50

DEPTH:	28
GROSS REGISTERED TONNAGE:	4,635
REGISTRY NUMBER:	US 201025
ENGINES:	Triple expansion 22″, 35″, 58″ diameter × 40″ stroke
ENGINE BUILDER:	Shipyard

Awaiting lockage at the Soo

JAMES B. NEILSON

WASHBURN

The whaleback package freighter WASHBURN was built in 1891 for the Minneapolis, St. Paul & Sault Ste. Marie Railway, popularly known as the Soo Line, for the grain and package trade. After the vessel's acquisition by the Bessemer Steamship Company (Rockefeller Fleet) in 1896, the name was changed to JAMES B. NEILSON and she was converted to a bulk carrier. In 1901 the entire Bessemer fleet was absorbed into the newly formed Pittsburgh Steamship Company. The NEILSON and her barge consort, JOHN SCOTT RUSSELL, were taken over and painted the familiar colors of the "Silver Stackers."

In 1927 the NEILSON was sold to the Spokane Steamship Company of Detroit and renamed J. T. REID during the season of 1928. The vessel was decked over with a timber superstructure for the automobile trade on Lake Erie, and carried new autos from Detroit, Michigan to Cleveland, Ohio until retired and scrapped in 1936 at Cleveland.

Washburn,
b) JAMES B. NEILSON,
c) J. T. Reid

BUILT:	American Steel Barge Co., W. Superior, Wisconsin
HULL NUMBER:	124
LENGTH:	320
BREADTH:	42
DEPTH:	25
GROSS REGISTERED TONNAGE:	2,234
REGISTRY NUMBER:	US 81373
ENGINES:	23″, 37″, 62″ diameter × 40″ stroke Triple expansion
ENGINE BUILDER:	S. F. Hodge & Co., Detroit, Michigan 1892

JAMES B. NEILSON in 1925

J. T. REID as an auto carrier

NEVADA

This steel, single-screw package and passenger steamer was built in 1915 for the Goodrich Transit Company and intended for winter service on Goodrich's Lake Michigan routes. It was so successful the first winter, it was chartered by the Lake Carriers' Association for ice breaking in Whitefish Bay in Lake Superior in the Spring of 1916.

On March 29, 1917, Goodrich sold NEVADA to the Russian Government, who intended to use the new ship as an icebreaker at Vladivostok. NEVADA left the Lakes and proceeded to San Francisco, California, where she was rebuilt to 2,097 G.R.T. as a unit of the Russian Volunteer Fleet and renamed ROGDAY. Meanwhile, the Imperial Government of Russia had been overthrown by the Bolsheviks, and the ship was seized by the American government. She saw war duty in World War I under the American flag.

ROGDAY was returned to the Lakes in 1921 and purchased by the Pere Marquette Line Steamers who gave the vessel its original name again, and operated it between Ludington, Michigan and Milwaukee, Wisconsin. In 1936, NEVADA was owned by the Muskegon Dock and Fuel Company, and ran the Milwaukee to Muskegon service as an auto carrier and trailer transport after having been rebuilt to 1,685 G.R.T. at Manitowoc. In this class, NEVADA became America's first "Roll-on-roll-off" ship. In 1939 the parent firm, Wisconsin and Michigan Steamship Company, became direct owners. From 1936 onward Corporate ownership was basically that of Sand Products Corporation through wholly or jointly owned subsidiaries.

Because of the need for vessels during the World War II conflict, NEVADA was requisitioned by the U.S. Government and taken back to the coast in 1942. Her salt water duty, however, was short-lived, for NEVADA foundered in the North Atlantic on December 16, 1943.

NEVADA outward bound at Chicago

ROGDAY at San Francisco in 1918

NEVADA,
b) ROGDAY,
c) Nevada

BUILT:	Manitowoc Shipbuilding Company, Manitowoc, Wisconsin
HULL NUMBER:	70
LENGTH:	221.2
BREADTH:	42.2
DEPTH:	24.7
GROSS REGISTERED TONNAGE:	2,122
REGISTRY NUMBER:	US 213782
ENGINES:	Triple Expansion 21½″, 34½″, 56″ diameter × 36″ stroke
ENGINE BUILDER:	Great Lakes Engineering Works, Detroit, Michigan

NEVADA at Muskegon

NORONIC

The steel passenger and freight propeller NORONIC was built for the Northern Navigation Co., Ltd. service. Launched June 2, 1913, it had been planned to have the christening performed by Mrs. James Playfair, but due to the fatal illness of Mr. Playfair's father, the ceremony was performed by Mrs. Edward Bristol, wife of one of the company directors.

NORONIC made a few trips as a package freighter in 1913. During the winter of 1913-14 the cabin fittings and furnishings were installed at Sarnia. During the 1914 season NORONIC proved to be slightly unstable and was sent to the American Shipbuilding Co.'s dry dock at Lorain where her beam was increased by 6'. This change gave her both increased stability and an increase of speed of 1-1/2 M.P.H.

NORONIC operated from Windsor, Detroit and Sarnia to the Lakehead continually until the end of the 1949 passenger season. While on a post-season cruise, she was docked at Toronto and during the early hours of September 17, 1949, fire broke out in a linen closet. As a result, the ship was gutted and 139 passengers lost their lives. The burned out hull sank in the slip and was abandoned to the Underwriters. The hull was salvaged by Sin-Mac Lines, Ltd. and was towed to Hamilton, Ontario on Saturday, October 29, 1949 for scrapping by the Steel Company of Canada, Ltd.

NORONIC in 1914

BUILT:	Western Dry Dock and Shipbuilding Co., Ltd., Port Arthur, Ontario	GROSS REGISTERED TONNAGE:	6,905
HULL NUMBER:	6	REGISTRY NUMBER:	C 134014
LENGTH:	362	ENGINES:	29½", 47½", 58" & 58" diameter × 42" stroke
BREADTH:	52		4 cyl. triple expansion
DEPTH:	24.8	ENGINE BUILDER:	American Shipbuilding Co., Cleveland, Ohio

NORONIC in the 1940's

NORTHERN BELLE

This wooden passenger and freight propeller was launched May 20, 1875 by David Lester as GLADYS, a private venture for his Toledo and Saginaw Transportation Company. According to the Port Huron Daily Times of November 4, 1874, "The engines that were taken out of the J. S. ESTABROOK two years ago and previous to that were in use in the tug, DAN RHODES are to be placed in the new vessel." But this statement is in doubt because records state the engine was built in 1875. He sold her on November 1, 1876 to Thomas and John J. Long of Collingwood, Ontario who renamed her b) NORTHERN BELLE (C. 71111). She then was operated to the lumbering villages and camps on the east and north shores of Georgian Bay from Collingwood by the Georgian Bay Navigation Co. This company changed its name to the Great Northern Transit Co. after the tragic loss of the WAUBUNO in 1879. The NORTHERN BELLE continued to operate on the Georgian Bay route for 21 years. On November 6, 1898, however, she was totally destroyed by fire on the Magnetawan River at Byng Inlet, her value at the time being set at $15,000. Passengers and crew were rescued by a tug and taken to Parry Sound.

NORTHERN BELLE

Gladys,
b) NORTHERN BELLE

BUILT:	David Lester, Marine City
LENGTH:	135.4
BREADTH:	22.6
DEPTH:	9.5

GROSS REGISTERED TONNAGE:	337
REGISTRY NUMBER:	US 85422
ENGINES:	Fore and Aft Compound 17" & 28" Diameter × 21" Stroke
BUILDER:	Frontier Iron Works, Detroit, Michigan (1875)

NORTH LAND

NORTH LAND with three stacks

The second of two identical sisterships, NORTH LAND was completed in 1895 for James J. Hill's Northern Steamship Company. It and NORTH WEST were considered the finest and most luxurious passenger ships built on the Great Lakes up to that time. Originally the vessels carried three stacks painted light yellow with a white star on the side and two masts.

In 1902 the posh ships were rebuilt with fewer but more efficient boilers, two stacks, and an extra deck forward.

NORTH LAND operated between Buffalo, New York and Chicago, Illinois in cruise service from the time of her building until 1916.

During World War I, after a short lay-up, the vessel was cut in two and bulkheaded to be taken through the Welland and St. Lawrence Canals in 1918. Plans to operate the vessel as an ocean liner or troop ship never materialized and she lay at Montreal, Quebec until 1921 when NORTH LAND was broken up for scrap.

BUILT:	Globe Iron Works, Cleveland, Ohio
HULL NUMBER:	51
LENGTH:	358.5
BREADTH:	44
DEPTH:	23.2
GROSS REGISTERED TONNAGE:	4,244
REGISTRY NUMBER:	US 130690
ENGINES:	Quadruple expansion (2) $25\frac{1}{2}''$, 36″, $51\frac{1}{2}''$, 74″ diameter × 42″ stroke
ENGINE BUILDER:	Shipyard

NORTH LAND later, with two stacks

NORTH WEST

Like her sister, NORTH LAND, but built a year earlier in 1894, the NORTH WEST sailed on the Buffalo, New York–Duluth, Minnesota route during her active life as a passenger ship. Due to their elegance and high operating costs, these vessels always ran at a loss to their owner though usually sailing with full passenger lists. However, James J. Hill, the railroad-baron and owner considered them good advertising for his western railroads and always kept the ships in operation.

From the point of serving together in the passenger trade, these ships had quite differing careers. NORTH WEST was badly damaged by fire while in winter lay-up at Buffalo in 1911, and never ran as a passenger steamer again. From 1911 the vessel lay at the Buffalo wharf. Because of the shortage of steel hulls during World War I, the NORTH WEST was cut in two and prepared for transiting the old St. Lawrence River canals. While under tow, the bow section broke away on Lake Ontario on November 26, 1918 and sank in 100 feet of water. Of the crew of eleven, two drowned as the section of the hull sank and two others died of exposure after escaping in a raft.

The after end of the once proud vessel lay at Montreal and was sold to Canadian interests. A new bow section was added by the Davie Shipbuilding and Repairing Company at Lauzon, P.Q. in 1920. The virtually new vessel was renamed MAPLECOURT by Canada Steamship Lines, the new owners. The former quadruple expansion engine was removed and a triple expansion engine built by the Robb Engine Works of Amherst, Nova Scotia, was installed. The dimensions of the new engine were: 20″, 33″, 54″ diameter × 40″ stroke. The dimensions of the new vessel were now 365.4 × 44.8 × 23.4, 3,388 gross registered tonnage. Canadian official number: C 141766.

The quite distinguishable vessel returned to the Lakes in 1922 and ran principally in the grain trade. But again tragedy struck. On October 20, 1929 the steamer was wrecked on Cockburn Island's Magnetic Reef in Georgian Bay, Lake Huron during a severe storm. MAPLECOURT spent the winter on the rocks. The Sin-Mac Lines of Montreal succeeded in salvaging the vessel in early 1930. The new role of the MAPLECOURT was as a salvage vessel. In 1937 she was purchased by the United Towing and Salvage Company and served well in the salvage business.

The World War II need for ships became acute in 1940 when many ships were lost to the submarine warfare. The MAPLECOURT was requisitioned, cut in two at Kingston, Ontario and rejoined at Montreal for war service. The tragic end of the once posh steamer came at the hands of a U-boat in the North Atlantic on February 6, 1941 when the MAPLECOURT was torpedoed and sunk with all on board by Captain Hessler's U-107, approximately 300 miles from the Hebrides in the German Naval Quadrant AL 3871; 55.39 No. and 15.56 W. at 1732 hours.

NORTH WEST in the Soo Locks—three stacks

NORTH WEST in the Soo Locks—two stacks

NORTH WEST,
b) Maplecourt

BUILT:	Globe Iron Works, Cleveland, Ohio
HULL NUMBER:	50
LENGTH:	385.5
BREADTH:	44

DEPTH:	23.2
GROSS REGISTERED TONNAGE:	4,244
REGISTRY NUMBER:	US 130601
ENGINES:	Twin Quadruple expansion 25½″, 36¼″, 51½″, 74″ diameter × 42″ stroke
ENGINE BUILDER:	Shipyard

MAPLECOURT in 1924

NORTHUMBERLAND

The twin screw steel passenger vessel NORTHUMBER-LAND was built in 1891 to operate between Pictou, Nova Scotia and Charlottetown, Prince Edward Island across the Northumberland Strait for the Charlottetown Steam Navigation Co., Ltd. This company was taken over by the Canadian Government in 1916. She came to Lake Ontario in 1920 and it is generally agreed that she was one of the most interesting vessels to operate on the Lower Lakes.

At first she operated opposite DALHOUSIE CITY for Canadian National Steamers, a subsidiary of the Canadian National Railway Co., between Toronto and Port Dalhousie. Actually the registered name of the line was the Niagara, St. Catharines and Toronto Navigation Co. During 1920 NORTHUMBERLAND operated without change to her superstructure. During the winter of 1920–21, however, she

was altered by the Toronto Dry Dock Co., Ltd. Many of the individual cabins were removed and the upper deck was made suitable for the excursion trade. In 1927 a shade deck was built abaft the funnel and a dance floor installed. No change in engines or boilers was made during her life.

She continued on the Toronto-Port Dalhousie run until gutted by fire at Port Dalhousie on June 2, 1949, the day before commencing operations for the season. Damaged beyond repair, she was cut up for scrap at Port Weller Drydock. NORTHUMBERLAND inherited GARDEN CITY'S fine three-part chime whistle. After her demise the whistle saw service on the Toronto Dry Dock Co.'s tug J. C. STEWART and now reposes in the Marine Museum of Upper Canada in Toronto.

NORTHUMBERLAND leaving Toronto

		GROSS REGISTERED	
BUILT:	Wigham Richardson Co., Newcastle	*TONNAGE:*	1,255
LENGTH:	220	*REGISTRY NUMBER:*	C 96937
BREADTH:	33	*ENGINES:*	17½″, 27½″ & 46″ diameter × 33″ stroke Two Triple expansion
DEPTH:	20.4	*ENGINE BUILDER:*	Wigham Richardson Co.

Burning June 2, 1949 at Port Dalhousie

NOVADOC (2)

NOVADOC in the St. Mary's River

In the late 20's, various Canadian steamship companies ordered standard canal-type steel carriers from yards in Great Britain to traverse the St. Lawrence River canals. Among the companies ordering these vessels in 1928 was the Paterson firm from Fort William, Ontario. Cargoes of coal, grain, paper products, pulpwood, iron ore, gravel and various other products were the usual commodities carried by these unique ships. The Paterson firm's ships traveled all over the Lakes and the Rivers from the Lakehead to lower lake ports, the Welland Canal and the St. Lawrence River ports as far East as the Provinces of Prince Edward Island and New Brunswick on the Atlantic Coast. The NOVADOC was the second ship named for the Province of Nova Scotia, to which she frequently made trips.

During the Armistice Day Storm of November 11, 1940, the NOVADOC was embattled by the high hurricane force winds and heavy seas. She fought valiantly, but her northbound course made progress extremely difficult. Late that day, the ship was driven onto the beach near Pentwater,

Michigan, on Lake Michigan, and lay there, parallel to the beach, while huge combers swept over the hull time and again. The crew huddled in their cabins, but soon they provided little protection as the waves beat against them constantly, smashing through portholes. Two men were lost overboard during the struggle and the other 17 of her crew were desperate. Ice formed on every exposed part of the little steamer and hope of rescue was dim. Fortunately, the plight of the crew was known ashore. The steam fish tug, THREE BROTHERS, made two unsuccessful attempts to leave port and finally, on the third try, battled its way to the stranded ship. With expert seamanship, the tug was maneauvered carefully around the stricken ship and finally was able to rescue the remaining seamen from the NOVADOC. Such heroism is not uncommon on the Lakes, and the rescued sailors were grateful. They were alive because of the fortitude of a few men who risked their own lives to help others in dire need.

Broken in two off Pentwater

BUILT:	Swan, Hunter & Wigham Richardson, Wallsend-on-Tyne, England
HULL NUMBER:	1,345
LENGTH:	252.8
BREADTH:	43.3
DEPTH:	17.8
GROSS REGISTERED TONNAGE:	1,934
REGISTRY NUMBER:	C 149465
ENGINES:	15″, 25″, 40″ diameter × 33″ stroke Triple expansion
ENGINE BUILDER:	Shipyard

NYACK

In 1878 this wooden freight and passenger propellor was built for the Union Steamboat Company of Buffalo, New York, a division of the Erie Railroad. It was one of the largest and finest of the railroad ships. Operated on the Buffalo to Duluth express service until 1893, the vessel did much in her day to popularize travel on the Great Lakes. In the 1890's the NYACK was chartered to the Lake Superior Transit Company which was a consortiom of many vessels serving the same routes.

This operation was dissolved after 15 years of operation. All vessels used were returned to their former owners; NYACK, however, was immediately sold to E. G. Crosby and Associates.

The new service for E. G. Crosby (until 1903) and the Crosby Transportation Company of Milwaukee (1903–1916) took the vessel to Lake Michigan where she ran opposite the iron steamer NAOMI (ex WISCONSIN of 1881) across the Lake to Western Michigan ports.

While undergoing winter repairs at Muskegon, Michigan on December 30, 1915, the NYACK burned to the water's edge. The hull survived and was purchased by the Lake and Ocean Navigation Company of Milwaukee which used the old vessel as a stone and sand barge. In 1920 the NYACK was sold to Finn-Olsen Freighting Service. Finally the hulk was made a part of a breakwater and dock at Big Summer Island on Green Bay. She rested there along with the former Goodrich liner GEORGIA. The register was closed on February 1, 1933 with the notation "vessel abandoned."

NYACK at the Soo

BUILT:	Union Dry Dock Co., Buffalo, New York	*REGISTRY NUMBER:*	US 130125
LENGTH:	231	*ENGINES:*	20″, 40″ diameter × 36″ stroke Twin steeple compound
BREADTH:	33	*ENGINE BUILDER:*	H. G. Trout, Buffalo—1878
DEPTH:	14.7		
GROSS REGISTERED TONNAGE:	1,254.35 (readmeasured 1903-1,188 GT)		

OCTORARA

OCTORARA as she originally appeared

Designed by Frank E. Kirby, this steel passenger and package freight steamer built in 1910 was the last of the Anchor Line (Lake Erie & Western Transportation Co.) triplets to come out. She was slightly different from the other two, JUNIATA and TIONESTA, with one mast placed aft of the stack. OCTORARA carried round portholes in her middle deck similar to those of JUNIATA but in contrast to TIONESTA's square windows in that same area. The regular service of these triplets was between Buffalo, New York, and Duluth, Minnesota.

Because of the drastic conditions of business caused by the Depression of the 1930's, the OCTORARA was laid up in Buffalo in 1936 and saw no further service on the Great Lakes. In 1942 the vessel was requisitioned by the U.S. Army and taken to salt water via the Mississippi River and the Gulf of Mexico to the Pacific. It was converted to a troop transport and was used as an inter-island transport in the Hawaiian Islands. She served with distinction in the Pacific theatre of the war until its close. For some years the U.S.A.T. OCTORARA lay at the Army Base at San Francisco and was finally scrapped in 1952. The huge bronze bell now is a part of the Dossin Great Lakes Museum at Belle Isle, Detroit, Michigan and is rung each year at the blessing of the fleet in memory of the ships and sailors who have passed away.

U.S.A.T. OCTORARA in war colors

OCTORARA,		*GROSS REGISTERED*	
b) U.S.A.T. Octorara		*TONNAGE:*	4,329
		REGISTRY NUMBER:	US 207175
BUILT:	Detroit Shipbuilding Co., Wyandotte, Michigan	*ENGINES:*	22″, 31″, 45″, 65″ diameter × 42″ stroke
HULL NUMBER:	181		Quadruple expansion
LENGTH:	340	*ENGINE BUILDER:*	Detroit Shipbuilding Co., Detroit, Michigan
BREADTH:	45.2		
DEPTH:	28		

OGDENSBURG

OGDENSBURG in the St. Clair River

This steel canal-sized package freighter was built in 1906 for the Rutland Transit Company's Ogdensburg Line. Designed for fast freight service between Ogdensburg, New York, on the St. Lawrence River and Chicago, OGDENSBURG was a "full canaller," about 260 feet in overall length, the length permitted by the third Welland Canal. In the 1880's, the Ogdensburg & Lake Champlain Railroad (later the Rutland Ry.) began a line of express steamers over this route and eight wooden vessels composed the original fleet. These were supplemented in later years by six steel vessels, of which OGDENSBURG was the first.

In 1915 the railroads were required by legislation to dispose of their vessels and the Rutland boats were bought by salt water operators. The OGDENSBURG passed into the fleet of the Pacific Steamship Company, popularly known as the Admiral Line. The OGDENSBURG was renamed the ADMIRAL SEBREE in 1916, and was rebuilt topsides for ocean traffic. As a result, the gross tonnage was increased to 2,446 gross tons.

The ADMIRAL SEBREE sailed for nearly 30 years on the north Pacific coast. After a few years of inactivity following World War II, the ADMIRAL SEBREE was removed from Documentation in September of 1951, and scrapped.

ADMIRAL SEBREE at Seattle

OGDENSBURG,	DEPTH:	26.5
b) Admiral Sebree	GROSS REGISTERED	
	TONNAGE:	2,329
BUILT: American Shipbuilding Co.,	REGISTRY NUMBER:	US 203123
Cleveland, Ohio	ENGINES:	17½", 25½", 37", 54" diameter
HULL NUMBER: 432		× 36" stroke
LENGTH: 242		Quadruple Expansion
BREADTH: 43	ENGINE BUILDER:	Shipyard

MARGARET OLWILL

MARGARET OLWILL at Kelley's Island

This small wooden steam barge was built for L. P. and J. A. Smith of Cleveland, Ohio in 1887. Smith Brothers had a small yard in the Old River Bed at Cleveland, where they built some small tugs and scows. Henry Root had a shipyard in Lorain, Ohio at the foot of Sixth Street across the Black River from the present American Shipbuilding Company. He brought a gang of men to Cleveland and built the OLWILL in Smith's yard. She was named for Pat Smith's wife, who was Margaret Olwill.

On June 29, 1899, the steam barge loaded limestone at Kelley's Island for Calkins & Co. of Cleveland, leaving at midnight. This was usually an uneventful run, but at 4:30 a.m. of the 30th, having Lorain, Ohio abeam and about 8 miles off, the wheel chains parted. The wind being fresh, Northeast, the OLWILL fell off in the trough of the sea, rolling the cabin houses off. Part of the crew got away in a lifeboat which capsized. The OLWILL foundered about 6 o'clock.

The steamers STATE OF OHIO and SACRAMENTO picked up four of the crew, and later in the morning the tug CASCADE under the command of Capt. James F.

Bowen, picked up three more from the wreckage. Captain Brown, his wife and two children, with four members of the crew, were drowned. Later, most of the bodies washed up on the beach east of Vermilion, Ohio—one being that of Frank Hipp, fireman from Kelley's Island, Ohio. Considerable wreckage from the OLWILL came ashore on Cedar Point, Ohio. The brother of Captain Brown, George, was in command of the steamer ARROW when he sighted the wreckage; among it was the name board of the OLWILL off the pilot house. Tragedy had struck again, as it did so many times, when relatives sailed the lakes, and multiple deaths brought anxiety and sorrow to many households.

In later years members of the same immediate family were not permitted to be hired on the same vessel just because of the frequency of multiple deaths such as occurred on the MARGARET OLWILL. It is a great tragedy to lose even one member of a household, not to mention the deaths of a whole family. Even though the frequency of sinkings has diminished these days, this rule is still observed.

BUILT:	Henry D. Root, Cleveland, Ohio	GROSS REGISTERED TONNAGE:	554
LENGTH:	175.6	REGISTRY NUMBER:	US 91953
BREADTH:	34	ENGINES:	20″ & 36″ Diameter × 24″ Stroke Steeple Compound
DEPTH:	10.2	ENGINE BUILDER:	Cuyahoga Iron Works, Cleveland, Ohio

OTTAWA

Steamer "Ottawa," Thousand Islands, N. Y.

OTTAWA in the St. Lawrence River

The small wooden passenger and freight propeller A. B. TAYLOR was built in 1884. She was enrolled at Grand Haven, Michigan, for Bird and Rogers, of Saugatuck. In 1890 she was sold to John Houghton of Detroit and the following year enrolled at Marquette. In 1893 her tonnage was changed to 103 gross tons—72 net tons, but with the same dimensions. That same year her enrollment was transferred back to Grand Haven, where she was owned by Edward C. Dunbar. There the vessel engaged in the passenger and freight trade, especially between Chicago and Michigan City. As this small trade dwindled, she was laid up at Grand Haven in 1900.

After a year of inactivity, on the night of November 7, 1901, the TAYLOR caught fire. For a short while the entire waterfront was endangered as the wind picked up, but fortunately the local firefighters brought the fire under control with an estimated 600 dollars damage to the vessel. Early the next morning the fire flared up again and burned the vessel to her water line. The loss was set at 10,000 dollars.

In 1902 the burned hulk was rebuilt again as a passenger and freight steamer and was renamed OTTAWA (106′ ×

20′ × 7′8″; 94 gross tons, 64 net tons). Still owned by Mr. Dunbar, she operated under title of the Indiana Harbor Navigation Company.

In about 1904 the OTTAWA was chartered by the Goodrich Transportation Company for service between Manitowoc and Two Rivers, Wisconsin. On July 30, 1905, she departed Manitowoc bound for Rochester, New York for local Lake Ontario service. However, she returned to the upper lakes the following year, being sold by Dunbar to Clarence Parker, and was enrolled at Detroit. She was operated by the Bay Transportation Company of Sandusky, Ohio. However, she proved too small for her intended use. On January 7, 1907, she was sold to the Thousand Island Steamboat Company, of Cape Vincent, New York. As part of the arrangement, the steamer NEW YORK (ex SHREWSBURY) came to replace her at Sandusky.

For the next few years the OTTAWA engaged in the tourist trade on the eastern end of Lake Ontario. In September, 1909, she replaced the sidewheel steamer ISLANDER, which burned. Her career ended on December 14, 1910, as she burned at her dock at Clayton, New York. The loss was set at 20,000 dollars.

A. B. Taylor,	
b) OTTAWA	
BUILT:	R. T. Rogers, Saugatuck, Michigan
LENGTH:	106′
BREADTH:	20′
DEPTH:	7′8″

GROSS REGISTERED	
TONNAGE:	77
REGISTRY NUMBER:	US 106257
ENGINES:	High Pressure 16″ Diameter × 20″ Stroke
ENGINE BUILDER:	W. Hendrie, Montague, Michigan

OWANA

PENNSYLVANIA

Passenger boats generally were the most popular boats on the Great Lakes and the OWANA was no exception. She was a steel side-wheel passenger boat, built in 1899 as PENNSYLVANIA. At first she was operated by the Erie and Buffalo Steamship Company, but their tenure was brief. The side-wheeler was sold to the White Star Line of Detroit in November, 1902, renamed OWANA, and put on the run between Detroit and Toledo. She also made runs to Port Huron, when necessary, because she was classed as the spare boat and filled in on all of the company's runs as occasion dictated. Her best known duty was as the evening boat from Detroit. OWANA left at 6PM for the Flats with the cottagers returning from shopping in Detroit, or the tired businessmen commuting to their homes. They were always able to catch the early morning freight boat, the WAUKETA, coming down from Port Huron, or the OWANA later in the morning, and spend the day in Detroit.

In 1926, OWANA was sold to the Erie and Dover Ferry Line and commenced running between Erie, Pennsylvania and Port Dover, Ontario. Her name was changed to ERIE in 1927 and she ran along with the DOVER a) FRANK E. KIRBY. This run did not last long as she burned during layup at Nicholson's dock at Ecorse, Michigan on February 29, 1929.

Plans for her hull's conversion to a ferry still existed, but came to naught when the vessel was purchased as a barge by Thomas A. Ivey and Sons of Port Dover (C. 158138). She was renamed the T. A. IVEY in 1934, and ran as a coal barge for Mr. Ivey for many years. Harry Gamble bought her in 1968 and renamed her ERIE again. In 1975, she was removed from the Canadian Registry and used as a breakwater.

OWANA leaving Detroit

OWANA in the St. Clair River

Pennsylvania, b) OWANA, c) Erie, d) T. A. Ivey d) Erie

BUILT:	Detroit Dry Dock Company, Wyandotte, Michigan	*GROSS REGISTERED TONNAGE:*	747
HULL NUMBER:	129	*REGISTRY NUMBER:*	US 150813
LENGTH:	200.6	*ENGINES:*	Beam Compound
BREADTH:	32		48″ Diameter × 108″ Stroke
DEPTH:	12	*ENGINE BUILDER:*	Murphy Iron Works, New York, N.Y.—1865 for U.S.R.C. JOHN A. DIX

ERIE and M/V LIBERTY behind

T. A. IVEY

PACIFIC

The wooden passenger and freight propeller PACIFIC was built in 1883 for the Great Northern Transit Co., Collingwood. Her engines had previously seen service in EMERALD, a) OSWEGO BELLE built in 1875 and dismantled in 1882-1883. In part, PACIFIC was a replacement for the ASIA which was lost in 1882. She was commanded for a number of years by Captain Peter Campbell (widely known as "Black Pete" because of his dark whiskers). Campbell lost no opportunity to race with any rival ship in Georgian Bay, especially vessels of the opposition line, the North Shore Navigation Co.

Latterly PACIFIC operated between Collingwood and the Soo, stopping at way ports. She met her end when she burned at the Grand Truck Railway dock in Collingwood on Friday, November 4, 1898. The railway freight sheds and their contents were also destroyed. PACIFIC was valued at the time of loss at $65,000 and was insured for $25,000. After the fire her engines were salvaged and refitted in 1899 in the new GERMANIC which was built to replace PACIFIC.

PACIFIC

BUILT:	Capt. John Simpson, Owen Sound	*REGISTRY NUMBER:*	C 85323
LENGTH:	179	*ENGINES:*	Double Steeple Compound 17″ & 28″ Diameter × 21″ Stroke
BREADTH:	30.6	*ENGINE BUILDER:*	1875 Kelley & Beckett,
DEPTH:	11		Hamilton, Ont.
GROSS REGISTERED TONNAGE:	918		Rebuilt 1883 by G. N. Oille, St. Catharines

PEERLESS

PEERLESS,
b) Muskegon

BUILT: Ira Lafranier,
Cleveland, Ohio
LENGTH: 211
BREADTH: 39.9
DEPTH: 12.5

GROSS REGISTERED
TONNAGE: 1,199
REGISTRY NUMBER: US 20470
ENGINES: 56″ diameter × 54″ stroke
High pressure condensing
ENGINE BUILDER: Globe Iron Works,
Cleveland, Ohio

PEERLESS at Mackinac, Str. ISLANDER at left, CHIPPEWA behind

Built in 1872 for Leopold and Austrian's Lake Superior Line, this wooden propellor was an attractive boat with two arch frames, a full deck-line of cabins, octagonal pilot house and twin stacks. The main salon was 166 feet long, without obstruction its entire length and decorated in fine taste. The colors of this line were an all white hull and cabins with black stacks. This vessel's normal run was between Chicago, Illinois and Duluth, Minnesota in the passenger trade.

In 1879 Leopold's Line merged with Spencer's to form the Lake Michigan and Lake Superior Transportation Company. PEERLESS's colors were changed to an all black hull, with white cabins and a dark red band around her stacks. In 1906 the vessel was sold to Chicago Transportation Company and ran between Chicago and Milwaukee, Wisconsin. In 1907 PEERLESS was again sold, this time to the Muskegon and Chicago Navigation Company, and was renamed MUSKEGON. Late in 1908, now owned by the Buck-Mullen Steamship Company, the wooden ship was cut down to a freighter with one stack. In this venture the old ship failed to earn and was converted to a sand-sucker (941 tons) in 1910 under the ownership of the Independent Sand and Gravel Company.

Extensively damaged by fire at Michigan City, Indiana on October 6, 1910, the aging vessel was abandoned, sadly ending the colorful career of a once fine ship.

MUSKEGON on the bottom

PELEE

A single screw steel passenger, auto and freight ferry was built in 1914 for the Windsor and Pelee Island Steamship Co. In 1933 she was sold for $50,000 to the Pelee Shipping Co., Ltd. of St. Thomas, Ontario and placed on the cross-lake run through the Western Lake Erie Islands to Sandusky, Ohio.

Wide gangways with steel doors were located on each side opposite the pilot house and were used for embarking and disembarking cars and small trucks. Aft of these wide gangways were narrow ones for passenger use. There were two similar gangways on port and starboard sides for handling package freight and the use of the crew and receiving galley supplies.

In the spring of 1960 PELEE was withdrawn from service and replaced by the new PELEE ISLANDER.

BUILT:	Collingwood Ship Building Co., Ltd., Collingwood
HULL NUMBER:	41
LENGTH:	137
BREADTH:	24
DEPTH:	11.3
GROSS REGISTERED TONNAGE:	538
REGISTRY NUMBER:	C 130388
ENGINES:	Triple Expansion 12½", 21" & 34" × 21" Scotch Boiler 12'3" × 11'
ENGINE BUILDER:	Collingwood S. B. Co., Ltd.

PELEE in earlier years

Leaving Leamington

PERE MARQUETTE

PERE MARQUETTE

The twin screw, steel, railway carferry PERE MAR-QUETTE was launched on December 30, 1896, for the Flint & Pere Marquette Railway Company, of Ludington, Michigan. She was launched in a nearly completed state and arrived at Ludington, Michigan, on February 13, 1897 to begin her prosaic career. She was the first steel-hulled carferry on Lake Michigan and served as a prototype for most subsequent cross-lake carferries on both fresh and salt water for the next fifty years. During her career, the railroad company went through several corporate names, such as Pere Marquette Railway Company (1902), Pere Marquette Steamship Company (1904), and again the Pere Marquette Railway Company (1922). In 1929, the company came under the total control of the Chesapeake & Ohio system.

The PERE MARQUETTE led a most uneventful life—at least for a Lake Michigan carferry. She was readmeasured in 1897 (337'1" × 57'7" × 17'; 2443 gross tons), and received new boilers at Manitowoc, Wisconsin, in 1921. Although company officials referred to her as "No. 15" as early as 1905, her name was not officially changed to PERE

MARQUETTE 15 until November 24, 1924. Normally, she ran between Ludington and Milwaukee, Manitowoc, or Kewaunee, Wisconsin, carrying thirty rail cars on her four tracks. During the 1910 and 1915 seasons, she was chartered to Marquette & Bessemer on Lake Erie, from Conneaut, Ohio, to Port Dover, Ontario, to replace the lost MARQUETTE & BESSEMER NO. 2. Other than that, she was noted as one of the most dependable of the Lake Michigan carferries.

Only two incidents checkered her career for safety. On February 21, 1897, she struck and sunk the small steam fish tug T. M. FERRY, at the Pere Marquette Lumber Company dock at Ludington. On May 28, 1900, while navigating in the fog about twelve miles off Manitowoc, she collided with and sank the sailing scow SILVER LAKE. One life was lost on the scow and the car ferry brought the remainder of the crew into Manitowoc. As newer and more powerful ferries were built, and as the Depression crept in, the "15" was laid up in 1930 at Ludington. In 1935, she crossed to Manitowoc, where she was scrapped.

P.M. 19, P.M. 20 alongside P.M. 15 at right

PERE MARQUETTE,			*DEPTH:*	34.9
b) Pere Marquette 15			*GROSS REGISTERED*	
			TONNAGE:	5,580
BUILT:	F. W. Wheeler Shipbuilding		*REGISTRY NUMBER:*	US 150740
	Company,		*ENGINES:*	22", 56" diameter × 36" stroke
	West Bay City, Michigan			Two Fore & Aft compound
HULL NUMBER:	119		*ENGINE BUILDER:*	Frank W. Wheeler & Company,
LENGTH:	338			West Bay City,
BREADTH:	57.7			Michigan—1897

PERSEUS

FRANK J. HECKER upbound at the Soo in 1909

This steel bulk freighter was built for the Gilchrist Transportation Co. It was one of two laid down by the Columbia Iron Works at St. Clair, Michigan in 1904. The firm went into receivership before much work could be done on the vessels and Great Lakes Engineering Works of Detroit took over the contracts.

Originally designed to be 50 feet shorter, the keel had been laid in 1904, and the vessel was launched on September 2, 1905. The new builders lengthened this hull on the ways.

In 1913 the Hecker and her sister ship, GEORGE H. RUSSEL, were sold to the Interlake Steamship Co. The HECKER was renamed the PERSEUS, and the RUSSEL became the CANOPUS. Together these twins served in the Interlake Fleet without incident until both were sold to the Nicholson Transit Co. in 1945. A few years later the twins parted ways. After a few years in the grain traffic CANOPUS became an auto carrier with a flight deck, while PERSEUS remained a bulk carrier but with an auto elevator amidships to handle cars on the upbound trip to Duluth. For fifteen years the PERSEUS served the Nicholson Fleet well, running primarily between the Capital Elevator in Duluth and the Lake & Rail Elevator in Buffalo for the International Milling Company, with occasional "dips" at Detroit.

In 1961, both ships were sold to shipbreakers for scrap. The CANOPUS was scrapped at Ashtabula and the PERSEUS was destined for Italian wreckers. Filled with a cargo of scrap iron, PERSEUS left Quebec City in tow of the English deep-sea tug ENGLISHMAN. She was all "buttoned-up" (port holes and any openings were welded shut and the propeller removed) and was ready to make the final crossing.

On September 11, in a North Atlantic gale, PERSEUS broke loose from her tug at 44° North, 33° West. The tug abandoned the vessel because it could not approach it in the gale and the PERSEUS was lost from view. It was later found about 90 miles from Fayal by the Dutch tug WITMARSUM. Again she was taken in tow, but she broke loose once more, this time sinking on September 21, 1961 at 42°41′N 31°00′W.

Tugs L. C. SABIN and S. C. SCHENCK pull a heavy laden HECKER

PERSEUS in Interlake colors

	Frank J. Hecker,	GROSS REGISTERED	
	b) PERSEUS	TONNAGE:	4,978
		REGISTRY NUMBER:	US 202475
BUILT:	Great Lakes Engineering	ENGINES:	Triple Expansion
	Works,		22′, 36″, 60″ diameter × 40″
	St. Clair, Michigan		stroke
HULL NUMBER:	12	ENGINE BUILDER:	Great Lakes Engineering
LENGTH:	462		Works,
BREADTH:	50		Detroit, Michigan
DEPTH:	24		

Passing under the Ambassador Bridge

PETOSKEY

PETOSKEY at the launch

This wooden passenger and freight propellor was built in 1888 for the Seymour Brothers' Seymour Transportation Company for service between Chicago, Illinois and Mackinac Island, Michigan via way ports. The original colors were black hull to the main deck, white upper hull and cabins and black stack. Extra heavy ribs and planking enabled PETOSKEY to operate in the winter. In 1895 the Seymour Transportation Company and the Northern Michigan Line combined to form the Northern Michigan Transportation Company. This vessel continued in this service until 1932.

The vessel's operators from 1898 were: Chartered by the Crosby Transportation Company 1898–1899; chartered by Graham & Morton—1895; sold to H. W. Hart and C. B. Hart (Hart Transportation Company of Green Bay, Wisconsin) 1899–1901; chartered by the Pere Marquette Steamship Company 1900–1901; sold to G. P. Gory and S. J. Dunkley (Dunkley-Williams Company) Chicago and South Haven Steamship Company 1901–1927; chartered by George F. Arnold 1908; chartered by Crosby Transportation Company 1919; sold to LeRoy Woodland, Jr., (Wisconsin-Michigan Transportation Company) 1927–1928; sold to Francis Bloodgood, Jr. (West Ports Navigation Company) 1928–1934; Capt. John Roen 1935.

PETOSKEY was laid up in 1932. Captain Roen bought the vessel in 1935 with the intent of converting it to a barge, but the work was never done. Laid up in the boneyard of the Roen-Walter Company shipyard at Sturgeon Bay, Wisconsin, the old vessel was destroyed on the night of December 5, 1935 by a fire which also seriously damaged the E. G. CROSBY (ii), WAUKEGAN and SWIFT.

PETOSKEY

BUILT:	H. B. Burger, Manitowoc, Wisconsin
LENGTH:	171.3
BREADTH:	30
DEPTH:	12.2
GROSS REGISTERED TONNAGE:	770.96
REGISTRY NUMBER:	US 150425
ENGINES:	20″, 40″ diameter × 36″ stroke Fore and aft compound
ENGINE BUILDER:	H. G. Trout, Buffalo, New York

PLEASURE

PLEASURE

In 1894, the Detroit, Belle Isle & Windsor Ferry Company ordered the new wooden ferry boat PLEASURE, for service on the Detroit River, from the F. W. Wheeler shipyard at West Bay City. In 1909 the owning firm was reorganized as the Detroit & Windsor Ferry Company. The PLEASURE served for the next 46 years and became a fixture on the river.

There is not much glory in a plain, working boat such as the cross-river ferry, which daily, for years on end, shuttles passengers and freight back and forth. Occasionally, PLEASURE was chartered for a daylight excursion or a moonlight ride, but her primary task was menial but necessary.

The advent of the Windsor Tunnel and the Ambassador Bridge in 1929 meant that the ferry line became redundant. The Great Depression in the 1930's further dampened the business. The automobile was taking over, and use of the boats became more and more infrequent. One by one the ships of the line were retired or sold to other uses. By 1938, when the last ferries served Detroit and Windsor, there were only two boats left.

The PLEASURE was one of the first to be retired, and she lay idle for a few years before being purchased by the Nicholson Transit Company in 1940. Again, the times and her age proved her undoing.

When it came time for the inspection survey, the ancient mariner had settled to the bottom of her slip. The antiquated timbers could no longer support her. The deterioration that had set in was too much. She was dismantled on the spot but a few parts of her hull were saved. Someone bought the pilot house and had it taken to his Grosse Isle, Michigan home, where it was installed on the top of his boat-house. There it stood for years, sadly overlooking the staid river it once crossed so frequently. All who passed this reminder of the "good old days" and looked at the forlorn cabin of this once proud steamer knew it was a sad fate to befall this river workhorse. Remember her? Many did for a while, but soon forgot her again as they sailed on, past her dying timbers, to their own pleasures.

BUILT:	F. W. Wheeler Shipbuilding Company, West Bay City, Michigan
HULL NUMBER:	104
LENGTH:	128
BREADTH:	51
DEPTH:	12

GROSS REGISTERED TONNAGE:	489
REGISTRY NUMBER:	US 150670
ENGINES:	24″, 34″ diameter × 24″ stroke Fore & Aft Compound
ENGINE BUILDER:	Shipyard

CHARLES S. PRICE

CHARLES S. PRICE in 1910

The "Mystery Ship," CHARLES S. PRICE, was a steel steamer belonging to the Mahoning Steamship Co. of Cleveland, Ohio. It was built in 1910 and operated by M. A. Hanna Company. During her short existence she carried iron ore downbound, and coal upbound on the Great Lakes.

The first few years were uneventful, but on Saturday, November 8, 1913, loaded with coal from Toledo, her travail began. Upbound past Port Huron, Michigan, on Sunday, November 9, 1913, she sailed into history as the "Mystery Ship" of the Big Storm of 1913. On Monday, a ship completely turned-over was sighted above Port Huron. This was the first sign of any disaster. For six days she remained unidentified but on the 15th a diver located the nameplate while investigating the partly submerged hull. Which, of the eight vessels lost, was she? CHARLES S. PRICE was the name flashed to the world. Eight days after she had capsized, the overturned hull of the vessel finally sank from view. It lies there even today, 10-1/2 miles northeast of Fort Gratiot Light, east of the last buoy marking the channel from Lake Huron.

For many years the wreck was marked by a buoy and a few attempts were made to salvage the vessel, but all proved unsuccessful. Renewed interest in sunken ships came with the advent of skin-diving after World War II. Because of persistent efforts by scuba divers around Port Huron and Sarnia, the hull of the PRICE was located in 65 feet of water. Her cabins and superstructure are completely gone, buried in hard clay mud and the top of the upturned hull is barely 30 feet under the surface of the water.

What happened to the PRICE and her crew of 28 still remains a mystery. Why did she "turn turtle?" Why were the bodies of her master, Capt. W. A. Black, and half of his crew, found on the beach wearing the lifejackets of a steamer named REGINA (also lost in the storm)?

These and many other questions were never answered. Evidence of a long gash on her bottom has been explained as the work of ice over the years, and the trench extending many feet far behind the hull has been explained as the result of her drag through the water on the bottom. But still she remains a mystery. At least two other vessels lost in the Big Storm have been located but far distant from the "mystery ship."

Front page of the Port Huron Times-Herald

BUILT:	American Shipbuilding Company, Lorain, Ohio
HULL NUMBER:	381
LENGTH:	504
BREADTH:	54
DEPTH:	30
GROSS REGISTERED TONNAGE:	6,322
REGISTRY NUMBER:	US 207539
ENGINES:	23½", 38", 63" diameter × 42" stroke Triple Expansion
ENGINE BUILDER:	Shipyard

PRINCE OF WALES

This wooden side wheel passenger steamer was built for the Ottawa River Navigation Co. in the fall of 1859 and delivered May 28, 1860.

On August 31, 1860 she carried H. R. H. Edward Prince of Wales from Ste. Anne de Bellevue (when he had come by Grand Truck train from Montreal) to Carillon on his trip to Ottawa to lay the foundation stone of the new Houses of Parliament. At Carillon the Prince and his party were conveyed by Carillon and Grenville train to Grenville, a distance of 13 miles, where he boarded PHOENIX which took him on to Ottawa.

The PRINCE OF WALES operated on the Montreal-Carillon route for 29 years, running the Lachine Rapids daily except Sundays and was succeeded by the new steel steamer SOVEREIGN in 1889. For the succeeding four or five years she was used in the excursion trade until broken up at Carillon in 1894. Her beam engine and parts of her superstructure were transferred to the new steel steamer DUCHESS OF YORK built in 1895.

PRINCE OF WALES

BUILT:	A. Cantin, Montreal, Quebec	
LENGTH:	153.1	
BREADTH:	23.3	
DEPTH:	7.7	

GROSS REGISTERED TONNAGE:	295
ENGINES:	Vertical Beam Engine 34″ Diameter × 8 Stroke
ENGINE BUILDER:	George Brush, Montreal

PRINCESS

Lachine Rapids, St. Lawrence River.

PRINCESS

This was a wooden side wheel passenger and freight vessel built 1872 for the Ottawa River Navigation Co. She was used on the night service between Montreal and Carillon until 1881. The night service was discontinued at that time, owing chiefly to the opposition provided by a railway on the north side of the Ottawa River connecting Montreal and Ottawa. Thereafter PRINCESS operated between Montreal, Carillon and Pointe Fortune in the market, freight and passenger service and, in addition, made special excursions for picnics and moonlights. At the end of the 1913 season she was laid up at Carillon. The freight and market business had been on the decline especially in the previous 10 years when she had VICTORIA, owned by Captain Mallette of Rigand, Quebec running in opposition to her.

A fire in 1914 which destroyed the Company warehouse, waiting rooms and ticket office on the Carillon wharf, also damaged part of the upperworks of PRINCESS. Over the ensuing years she went to pieces, mostly due to the force of ice moving out in the spring.

BUILT:	P. Girard, Carillon, Quebec
LENGTH:	141.9
BREADTH:	22.4
DEPTH:	7.8
GROSS REGISTERED TONNAGE:	527
ENGINES:	Beam Engine and One Boiler
ENGINE BUILDER:	George Brush, Montreal, Que.

PURITAN (1)

This small wooden passenger and freight propellor was built in 1887 for the Graham & Morton Transportation Company for cross-Lake Michigan service out of Chicago, Illinois. In 1892 the vessel was sold to the Seymour Transportation Company of Chicago and her place with the original owners was taken by the ill-fated CHICORA. Briefly in service for the Northern Michigan Transportation Company and the St. Joseph and Benton Harbor Transportation Company (1894–1895), the PURITAN sailed between Chica-

go and Traverse Bay ports on Lake Michigan.

This good little steamer was totally destroyed by fire shortly after going into winter quarters at the Stokoe & Nelson slip at Manistee, Michigan in the autumn of 1895. The Report of the Steamboat Inspection Service of December 31, 1895 stated that the cause of the fire was unknown and that the damages amounted to $30,000. The PURITAN was a complete loss.

PURITAN at Benton Harbor-St. Joseph.

BUILT:	J. H. Randall, Benton Harbor, Michigan	*GROSS REGISTERED TONNAGE:*	289.67
LENGTH:	172	*REGISTRY NUMBER:*	US 150396
BREADTH:	23	*ENGINES:*	Unknown
DEPTH:	12.8	*ENGINE BUILDER:*	Unknown

PURITAN

PURITAN in 1905

The PURITAN was a very handsome ship, having four decks and ample accommodations for her prospective passengers. The ship was designed for overnight passenger service and built on speculation by the Craig Shipbuilding Company in 1901; within weeks it was sold to the Holland and Chicago Transportation Company, who intended to name the vessel OTTAWA. Before completion, however, the assets and goodwill of the Holland and Chicago Line were purchased by the Graham and Morton Transportation Company, who named the new vessel PURITAN.

Graham & Morton lengthened the vessel in 1908 to 259 × 40.5 × 26.6, 1,762 gross registered tons, and kept her until the first World War in 1918. Because of the necessity for smaller passenger vessels in naval service, the Puritan was requisitioned for war duty.

It was brought back to commercial service in 1920, but under the ownership of the Chicago, Racine and Milwaukee Line. In 1924, the PURITAN was sold to the Michigan Transit Company, under whose ownership the vessel remained until the firm was restructured and renamed Michigan Transit Corporation in 1927. PURITAN sailed for this line until 1933.

In 1933, the vessel was sold to the Isle Royale Transportation Company, a subsidiary of Duke Transportation Co.

of New Orleans, Louisiana. They renamed her GEORGE M. COX in honor of Duke's chief executive. The vessel was painted all white and refurbished for the cruise trade to Lake Superior.

An accident on May 27, 1933 ended her career after only one-half trip for these owners. While steaming to Port Arthur, Ontario from Houghton, Michigan, in heavy fog with a complement of 121 passengers, crew and several package articles, the COX slammed into the Rock of Ages Reef, Lake Superior at a speed of 17 miles per hour. The sudden stop flung the passengers to the decks, hurled the package freight into the bulkheads, and caused a brief panic by both passengers and crewmen. Moderate calm was restored, the lifeboats were quickly lowered and the passengers taken off. No lives were lost in this peculiar accident, and it is fortunate that all the passengers and crew were promptly rescued. The presence of mind of some of the crewmen and a few of the officers prevented a complete disaster. The ship, however, was doomed. She rode so high out of the water and at an acute angle that she presented quite a sight to photographers shortly following the accident. Before any salvage attempts could be made, and not long after the stranding, the COX slid off the reef into deep water, during a storm, where it still remains.

PURITAN after second rebuild

GEORGE M. COX

PURITAN,
b) George M. Cox

BUILT:	Craig Shipbuilding Company, Toledo, Ohio	*DEPTH:*	21.9
		GROSS REGISTERED	
		TONNAGE:	1,547
HULL NUMBER:	82	*REGISTRY NUMBER:*	US 150898
LENGTH:	233	*ENGINES:*	Triple expansion
BREADTH:	40.5		21″, 34″, 58″ diameter × 40″ stroke
		ENGINE BUILDER:	Shipyard

On the rocks

PUT-IN-BAY

Designed by the eminent ship-designer Frank E. Kirby, the day excursion liner PUT-IN-BAY was commissioned in 1911 as soon as completed for her proud owners, the Ashley & Dustin Steamer Line. It replaced the FRANK E. KIRBY on the Detroit to Sandusky, Ohio route which Selah Dustin began in 1862 with the steamer DART. Regular voyages to the Lake Erie Islands from Detroit were a popular feature of the summer months. Daily, throngs who desired to leave the hot city for the cool expanse of the lake would clambor aboard the PUT-IN-BAY for a pleasurable cruise. Put-In-Bay, Ohio, with its delicious wines and elegant vineyards, was the usual destination of many passengers. The amusement park at Cedar Point, Ohio was another attraction. To accommodate those whose interest was either a day of relaxation or a day enjoying the thrill-rides the park had to offer, the "BAY" stopped at the park before it arrived at Sandusky, Ohio.

The PUT-IN-BAY was once known for its great dance bands. Among the most popular was George Finzel's, whose playing of the hit tunes of the day afforded the dancing crowds with such favorites as "On Moonlight Bay." Toward the end of the ship's career, other bands took Mr. Finzel's place, but he remained the crowd's favorite.

In the spring of 1949, the steamer was sold to Nicholas Constans of Detroit. For this owner the vessel alternated its runs to Lake Erie with trips up the Detroit and St. Clair Rivers to Port Huron, Michigan on Wednesdays and Sundays. She very quickly became the favorite of the ship picturetaking enthusiasts. Because ships on this trade route pass so closely, photographers lined the upper decks whenever another ship would gracefully approach and pass by. The beautiful ride to Port Huron, with a stop at the remains of Tashmoo Park on Harsen's Island, Michigan, had been a favorite for people since the initiation of service by various steam vessels in the early 1830's. From 1949 to 1953 the PUT-IN-BAY serviced this route, but was laid up in Detroit in 1953 because, although enjoyed by many, her economic viability had come to an end. Under the direction of Captain Frank Becker this remembered craft was taken out into lake St. Clair where her upperworks were burned off on October 3rd, 1953. Her hull was then towed to River Rouge where it was scrapped. Too many people abandoned the pleasure of that day for the more convenient self-propelled automobiles.

PUT-IN-BAY in the Detroit River

PUT-IN-BAY upbound past Amherstburg

BUILT:	Detroit Shipbuilding Company, Wyandotte, Michigan	*GROSS REGISTERED TONNAGE:*	1,182
HULL NUMBER:	186	*REGISTRY NUMBER:*	US 208636
LENGTH:	226	*ENGINES:*	25″, 40″, 45″, 45″ diameter × 36″ stroke
BREADTH:	46.5		4 cyl. triple expansion
DEPTH:	17.6	*ENGINE BUILDER:*	Shipyard

PUT-IN-BAY at Port Huron

QUEEN VICTORIA

This wooden beam-engined side wheeler was built in 1860 for the Ottawa River Navigation Company to run between Ottawa and Grenville as a replacement for PHOENIX. With the advent of PEERLESS in 1873, QUEEN VICTORIA was used as a night steamer on the same route connecting with PRINCESS operating on the lower portion of the route between Montreal and Carillon. Connection was made between Carillon and Grenville by the Carillon and Grenville Railway, owned and operated by the Ottawa River Navigation Co., to overcome the small canal between these two places.

In 1881 the night service was discontinued and the QUEEN VICTORIA was sold to a syndicate in Toronto to run to Victoria Park. QUEEN VICTORIA was too large for the Carillon-Grenville Canal and was brought down the Long Sault Rapids of the Ottawa River in spring high water, piloted by a rafting pilot. She was the only large steamer ever to come down the rapids. By 1883 QUEEN VICTORIA was owned by Captain St. Amour and others of Chatham, Ontario and placed on the route between Chatham, Windsor and Detroit. She replaced the steamer J. W. STEINHOFF. QUEEN VICTORIA's running mate on the route was the new steamer C. H. MERRITT. QUEEN VICTORIA commenced operating on this route on August 22, 1883. On September 13, 1883 QUEEN VICTORIA was found to be on fire at about 4 a.m. She was tied up six miles down river from Chatham and had been loading wood. The ship burned to a total loss. The crew escaped injury but lost most of their belongings. It was thought that a spark from the passing wood burning barge MANITOBA was the cause of the fire.

QUEEN VICTORIA

BUILT:	A. Cantin of Montreal Hull, Quebec	*GROSS REGISTERED TONNAGE:*	651.63
LENGTH:	169.5	*ENGINE:*	vertical beam
BREADTH:	23.3	*ENGINE BUILDER:*	Bartley & Gilbert,
DEPTH:	7.6		Montreal

RUFUS P. RANNEY (2)

RUFUS P. RANNEY leaving the locks at the Soo

In the spring of 1961, a singular vessel was purchased by a Genoa, Italy scrap dealer and started a long journey toward Europe. The steel RUFUS P. RANNEY, one of the smallest Upper Lakes freighters built that year, was christened by Miss Elizabeth Ranney on April 25, 1908. Captain Henry Stone took command of her, and on her first trip she carried her capacity load of 7,500 gross tons of iron ore. Rufus Ranney himself had financed the ship, but she was owned and operated by the Triton Steamship Co. The RANNEY was managed by various fleets the first few years of her life, among them being J. R. Davock & Co. in 1911; A. E. Williams from 1912–1915. In 1916 Triton placed the RANNEY under the management of G. A. Tomlinson, and her colors were changed to those of the Tomlinson Fleet, except that she carried the emblem of the Triton Company on her stack until 1955, when she became part of the Tomlinson Fleet Corporation.

On July 9, 1961 the steamer RUFUS P. RANNEY was towed down the Welland Canal to keep a date with the shipbreakers, and for the first time in 80 years there was no vessel bearing that name on the Upper Lakes. This vessel was not 80 years old, but she bore the same name as a wooden freighter which had come out in 1881. Strangely enough, the two vessels, although bearing the identical name, were not named for the same man. (The wooden ship honored Judge Rufus P. Ranney and the steel ship was named for his grandson, a prominent Cleveland citizen.) For several seasons both ships operated simultaneously: the wooden vessel for the Bradley Fleet, and the steel boat as the one and only vessel of the Triton Steamship Company.

The last journey of the RANNEY ended at Genoa on September 9, 1961 where the vessel was scrapped.

Downbound in Lake St. Clair

BUILT:	Superior Shipbuilding Co., Superior, Wisconsin
HULL NUMBER:	520
LENGTH:	425
BREADTH:	52
DEPTH:	28

GROSS REGISTERED TONNAGE:	4,797
REGISTRY NUMBER:	US 205088
ENGINES:	22″, 35″, 58″ Diameter × 40″ Stroke Triple Expansion
ENGINE BUILDER:	Shipyard

JAMES H. REED

JAMES H. REED at a lower lake port

A typical steel bulk freighter for the iron ore and grain trade, the JAMES H. REED was originally owned by the Provident Steamship Company when commissioned in 1903. At the amalgamation of the Interlake Steamship Company in 1913, the REED was one of more than a dozen ships that were purchased from various fleets. During the World War II rush for iron ore, this vessel joined others in the Interlake fleet in very early Spring runs so that the fleet could move its maximum tonnage to the steel mills to help in the defense effort.

A dense fog settled down upon Lake Erie on the night of April 26, 1944. The advantages of radar were still not available to commercial vessels, so there was no warning when the REED collided with the ASHCROFT of CSL at 5:30 a.m. April 27, 1944 about 20 miles North of Conneaut, Ohio. The REED was downbound with a cargo of iron ore from Escanaba, Michigan for Buffalo, New York; the ASHCROFT was in ballast. The usual fog signals (three short blasts every minute) were blown by both vessels, but fog can and often does distort sound, and the warning blasts went unheard.

The collision was so sudden that many of the seamen on board the REED had no chance to escape. The lives of twelve men were snuffed out that early morning as the ship went down quickly. The loaded REED was almost completely severed by the ASHCROFT, but the ships held together for a brief time, enabling the other 24 men of her crew to be rescued by the ASHCROFT and a Coast Guard vessel, which happened to be in the vicinity. The hull of the REED sank in 66 feet of water, near the navigation channel, so it had to be dynamited later that Fall to allow 45 feet of clearance over her wreck.

JAMES H. REED upbound at Belle Isle

BUILT:	Detroit Shipbuilding Company, Wyandotte, Michigan	
HULL NUMBER:	154	
LENGTH:	448	
BREADTH:	52.2	
DEPTH:	29	

GROSS REGISTERED TONNAGE:	5,598
REGISTRY NUMBER:	US 77589
ENGINES:	15″, 23¾″, 36½″, 56″ diameter × 40″ stroke Quadruple expansion
ENGINE BUILDER:	Shipyard

REGINA

REGINA in 1908

The steel canaller REGINA was launched September 3, 1907 for the Canadian Lake Transportation Co., Ltd., Toronto for operation in the package freight and grain trade. She began regular service in the spring of 1908. In 1911 the Canadian Lake Transportation Co., Ltd. merged with the Merchants Mutual Line, Ltd. to form the Canadian Interlake Line, Ltd. A further reorganization took place in 1912 when the corporate name of the existing company was changed to Canada Interlake Line, Ltd. The new Company was absorbed into Canada Steamship Lines, Ltd. in 1913.

REGINA's career in the Montreal-Fort William package freight trade was uneventful until she met disaster on November 9th, 1913. She sailed out into Lake Huron about noon under command of Captain E. H. McConkey, having been preceded about 1 hour by the upbound coal laden CHARLES S. PRICE. Both ships succumbed to the Great Storm some 10 miles above Fort Gratiot Light and east of the Huron Light Ship. The bodies of Captain W. A. Black of the PRICE and some of his crew were found on the Canadian shore wearing life jackets bearing the name REGINA. The REGINA was valued at $125,000 at the time of her loss and carried a crew of 15. It would appear she sank somewhere between Point Edward, Ontario and Grand Bend. No one will ever know for sure how the men from the PRICE came to be wearing life preservers from the REGINA.

Wreckage washed ashore

BUILT:	A. McMillan & Sons, Ltd., Dumbarton, Scotland	
HULL NUMBER:	419	
LENGTH:	249.3	
BREADTH:	42.6	
DEPTH:	23	

GROSS REGISTERED TONNAGE:	1,979	
REGISTRY NUMBER:	C 124231	
ENGINES:	17″, 28″, & 46″ diameter × 33″ stroke Triple expansion	
ENGINE BUILDER:	Muir and Houston, Ltd.	

RESCUE

The wooden, twin screw freighter RESCUE was built in 1855 but no U.S. registry number was assigned. In 1858 the vessel was sold to Captain James Dick and other Toronto citizens who organized the Northwest Trading and Colonization Company and the ship was registered (C. 33528).

The RESCUE was fitted with passenger accommodations and sailed from Collingwood on July 12, 1858 with passengers and freight. Passing through the Soo Locks the next day, she became the first registered Canadian steamer to navigate Lake Superior. She arrived outside the river mouth of Fort William on July 15th. On the following morning she proceeded to Grand Portage where the mail was put in a canoe and eventually delivered to the Red River Settlement over the old fur trade route. The RESCUE continued in this service until 1874, but with competition after 1864 from the sidewheeler ALGOMA (a) RACINE, b) CITY OF TORONTO, built in 1839), operated by the Lake Superior Royal Mail Line.

In 1874 the RESCUE was sold to the St. Lawrence Steam Navigation Company and taken to Montreal. She was dismantled in 1877 and her registry closed.

RESCUE

BUILT:	Bidwell & Banta, Buffalo, New York		
LENGTH:	123.5	*GROSS REGISTERED TONNAGE:*	285
BREADTH:	28	*ENGINES:*	Unknown
DEPTH:	10	*ENGINE BUILDER:*	Unknown

GRANVILLE A. RICHARDSON

GEORGE J. GOULD in 1908

The steel package freighter GEORGE J. GOULD was built in 1893 for the Lake Erie Transportation Co. (Wabash Railroad). Having three tall raked masts, and one stack, this vessel was used on the regular route between Toledo, Ohio and Buffalo, New York.

In 1911 she was sold to the Union Steamboat Line (Erie R.R.) and was renamed GRANVILLE A. RICHARDSON, losing her mizzen mast in the meantime. She sailed in the Erie Fleet until 1915, when the railroad fleets were dissolved. The RICHARDSON went to the Great Lakes Transit Corporation in 1916, and then to Playfair's Great Lakes Steamship Co. of Midland, Ontario on May 2, 1917, being assigned Canadian official #138216. Playfair renamed her GLENCAIRN in 1919. Sometime in this series of changes, her round pilot house was replaced by a box-like affair which survived until the end of her days.

In 1926 she was sold back to American owners, the Nassau Ship and Dredge Company of Chicago, converted to a self-unloading sandsucker at Manitowoc Shipbuilding Corp., Manitowoc, Wisconsin, and renamed NASSAU. Her gross tonnage was changed to 2,098, and much dredging equipment was placed on her decks. For some years thereafter she was a regular visitor at Chicago, where this vessel brought in many loads of sand-fill for the South Shore Outer Drive and park. In 1937 she belonged to the FitzSimons & Connell Dredge and Dock Co., for which firm she ended her days. NASSAU was used in many major construction jobs in and around Chicago for many years thereafter.

A few years after World War II her days became numbered. She lay idle for some time and was finally removed from documentation in December of 1950. One of the last survivors of the great package freight fleets, the old NASSAU saw the rise, zenith and decline of this trade. The hull was cut up for scrap in 1951.

GRANVILLE A. RICHARDSON in 1916

GLENCAIRN in 1924

George J. Gould, b) GRANVILLE A. RICHARDSON, c) Glencairn, d) Nassau

BUILT:	Union Dry Dock Company, Buffalo, New York	*GROSS REGISTERED TONNAGE:*	2,237
HULL NUMBER:	71	*REGISTRY NUMBER:*	US 86267
LENGTH:	265.6	*ENGINES:*	Triple expansion
BREADTH:	40.6		18″, 30″, 48″ diameter × 42″ stroke
DEPTH:	25	*ENGINE BUILDER:*	King Iron Works, Buffalo, New York

NASSAU

ROCHESTER

ROCHESTER in R & O colors

The steel twin-screw passenger steamer ROCHESTER was built in 1910 for the Richelieu and Ontario Navigation Company of the United States, a firm incorporated especially to operate her. This subsidiary of the Richelieu and Ontario Navigation Company Ltd. was taken over by Canada Steamship Lines Ltd., Montreal, in 1913, at which time ROCHESTER was transferred to the C.S.L. American subsidiary, the American Interlake Line. Fitted with 120 staterooms and 16 parlors, she originally operated between Youngstown and Ogdensburg, N.Y., with stops at way ports. The western terminus of the route became Toronto in 1913.

In 1915, ROCHESTER was chartered to the Indiana Transportation Company for service on Lake Michigan and, in 1916, she was to operate on the Northern Navigation route for C.S.L. She was kept in lay-up, however, as a result of litigation arising from an episode of typhoid fever aboard in 1913. On May 1, 1917, she was sold to the Northern Navigation Division, C.S.L., but she remained in U.S. registry even though she operated to Georgian Bay ports.

By 1919, ROCHESTER was back on the Toronto-Ogdensburg route. Placed on the Montreal-Saguenay River service of C.S.L. in 1920 after being renamed CAPE ETERNITY, she ran this route until 1925, when she was operated from Toronto to the Thousand Islands via the Bay of Quinte. Even though she had been renamed in 1920, she remained on the U.S. register until 1922 as ROCHESTER.

CAPE ETERNITY was laid up at Toronto in July 1929 due to declining business and there she remained until sold in 1935 to Seaway Lines of Windsor, Ontario, and renamed GEORGIAN. With her stacks rebuilt, she entered service between Windsor and Georgian Bay ports, with post-season cruise service which frequently took her to Toronto. Her owner's corporate name was changed in 1939 to Lakeway Lines.

The ship was requisitioned by the Royal Canadian Navy in 1941 for use as a floating barracks, first at Halifax, Nova Scotia, and later at St. John's, Newfoundland, as AVALON II. In 1945, she was taken to Sorel, Quebec, and reverted to her former name of GEORGIAN. She was sold on July 19, 1946 to the Wah Shang Steamship Company Ltd. which registered her at Shanghai as HA SIN. Caught up in the Chinese Revolution, she was severely damaged by aircraft bombs while lying at Shanghai. She was then taken to the West Coast of Africa and remained there into the late 1960's as a grape carrier and processor.

ROCHESTER on Lake Michigan

CAPE ETERNITY

ROCHESTER, b) Cape Eternity, c) Georgian, d) Avalon II, e) Ha-Sin

BUILT:	Detroit Shipbuilding Company, Wyandotte, Michigan	*GROSS REGISTERED TONNAGE:*	1,603
HULL NUMBER:	180	*REGISTRY NUMBER:*	US 207073
LENGTH:	246.6	*ENGINES:*	(2) 4 cylinder 16″, 25″, 31″, 31″
BREADTH:	42		diameter × 22″ stroke
DEPTH:	14.9		Triple expansion engines
		ENGINE BUILDER:	Same at Detroit, Michigan

GEORGIAN

THEODORE ROOSEVELT

BUILT:	Toledo Shipbuilding Company, Toledo, Ohio
HULL NUMBER:	107
LENGTH:	275.6
BREADTH:	40
DEPTH:	23.4
GROSS REGISTERED TONNAGE:	1,955
REGISTRY NUMBER:	US 202941
ENGINES:	4 cylinder—30″, 48″, 56″, 56″ diameter × 40″ stroke Triple expansion
ENGINE BUILDER:	Shipyard

THEODORE ROOSEVELT

This day-excursion steel passenger vessel was built in 1906 for the Indiana Transportation Company. The vessel had a 5,000 horsepower engine which drove this speedy vessel at a top speed of 24 mph. Her regular service was two round trips daily between Chicago, Illinois and Michigan City, Indiana with a capacity of 3,500 passengers. During World War I (1917–1918) the ROOSEVELT was an officers' training ship for the U.S. Navy. In 1919 she returned to her former service.

From this time on the Roosevelt saw varied service, all in the excursion trade. 1920–1926 she was owned by the Cleveland-Erieau Steamship Company and ran on Lake Erie. 1927–1944 the vessel was owned by the Chicago-Roosevelt Steamship Company and operated again on Lake Michigan.

Many firms chartered this vessel in other years. These were: Goodrich Transit Company 1927–1930; Bob-Lo Excursion Company, Detroit 1942–1943; Cleveland and Buffalo Transportation Company of Illinois, 1944–1945; sold to Cleveland and Cedar Point S.S. Company in 1945; sold to Cleveland and Buffalo Transit Company of Illinois 1946.

From 1946 to 1950 the vessel was in the U.S. Navy as USS THEODORE ROOSEVELT S.P. 1478. She lay idle from 1947–1950 in the ship canal at Benton Harbor, Michigan until towed to Milwaukee, Wisconsin on May 20, 1950. Here the rusting vessel was scrapped by the Cream City Wrecking Company, ending quite a varied career of the once proud flyer of Lake Michigan.

In BOB-LO colors

SAGAMORE (2)

DAVID Z. NORTON

Steel barges were much in vogue at the turn of the century, and the DAVID Z. NORTON was one of this type. Built in 1898, she sailed for the Wilson Transit Company only a few years and was sold in 1904 to the Huron Barge Line, a subsidiary of Pickands, Mather.

Her new name was SAGAMORE, the same name as the whaleback barge that was lost in 1901. When the Interlake Steamship Company was formed in 1913, the SAGAMORE went into this fleet (also managed by Pickands, Mather). Interlake sold the SAGAMORE to the Pringle Barge Line in 1922 and, although continuing under the same name, the barge's trade shifted primarily to the coal trade between Toledo and Detroit. Never converted to a self-unloader by

Pringle (as were the MAIDA and CONSTITUTION), the SAGAMORE was sold Canadian at the end of World War II.

SAGAMORE was sold in 1947 to N. M. Paterson of Fort William, Ontario and renamed KENORDOC (2) in honor of a ship of the same name that had been lost in World War II (C. 173182; 366 × 44.2 × 22.4; 3045 gross tons). Now her cargoes consisted chiefly of grain and pulpwood transported from the Canadian lakehead to lower lake ports. ALTADOC (2) normally was the KENORDOC's towing steamer. As barges of this type rapidly went out of existence in the 1950's, KENORDOC was taken to Hamilton, Ontario and scrapped in 1957.

SAGAMORE in 1916

SAGAMORE in 1923

David Z. Norton (1),
b) SAGAMORE (2),
c) Kenordoc (2)

BUILT: Globe Iron Works,
Cleveland, Ohio
HULL NUMBER: 73

LENGTH: 369.4
BREADTH: 45
DEPTH: 22.5
GROSS REGISTERED
TONNAGE: 3,250
REGISTRY NUMBER: US 157506

KENORDOC in Lake St. Clair

SAND MERCHANT

This steel sand sucker was laid down at Collingwood on April 28, 1927 and was delivered to her owners—Interlake Transportation Co., Ltd., Montreal—Mapes and Fredon, Managers.

As originally built her cargo was carried in two open hopper sided holds. Sand and gravel was pumped aboard by two centrifugal pumps. Unloading was accomplished by two swinging stiff-legged derricks, each one equipped with a two yard grab bucket. One derrick was mounted aft of the forecastle, while the other was placed in front of the stack. In 1930 the derricks were removed and in their place was fitted an elevator system and a conveyor belt discharge to the dock over a swinging boom mounted aft in front of the stack.

Mapes and Fredon operated SAND MERCHANT until 1931. In that year the Royal Trust Co., Montreal, took possession. They chartered her to National Sand and Material Co., Ltd., Toronto. She operated intermittently in 1932 and not at all in 1933. She returned to service in 1934 and in the following years operated on the Lakes and also at times on the Canadian east coast.

On October 17, 1936 she took on a load of sand off Point Pelee in Lake Erie and cleared for Cleveland. By 8:30 P.M. she had developed a list to port. In a freshening wind, the lake became choppy and the list increased until SAND MERCHANT finally rolled over and sank at 10 P.M. October 17, when about 17 miles northwest of Cleveland. Nineteen of her 26 man crew were lost in the sinking.

No attempt has ever been made to salvage the hull.

SAND MERCHANT

BUILT:	Collingwood Shipbuilding Co., Ltd., Collingwood, Ontario	GROSS REGISTERED TONNAGE:	1981
HULL NUMBER:	79	REGISTRY NUMBER:	C 153443
LENGTH:	252	ENGINES:	Triple Expansion
BREADTH:	43.5		15½", 26" × 44" diameter × 26" stroke
DEPTH:	17.5	BUILDER:	Hewes & Phillips, Newark, New Jersey (1919)

SARANAC

The single screw steel package freighter SARANAC was built in 1890 for the Lehigh Valley Railroad. Constructed in the days when both speed and beauty were factors in design, SARANAC and her four sister ships were considered by many to have been the finest looking steamers on the Great Lakes. Their colors were black hull, white cabins, yellow spars, black stack with maroon band and white letters "L.V." on a black diamond. The usual route of the five ships, the E. P. WILBUR of 1888, SENECA of 1889, CAYUGA, TUSCARORA and SARANAC of 1890, was between Buffalo, New York and Chicago, Illinois in the fast merchandise trade. Occasionally, they made trips to Lake Superior as well.

SARANAC and her sisters were requisitioned by the U.S. Shipping Board for war duty in 1917 and were bulkheaded at Buffalo, by the Buffalo Dry Dock Company. Each half of the steamers was towed through the canals in late 1917 or early 1918. After the war SARANAC was sold to Chilean buyers and renamed MINGEIA in 1919. Less than a year later, in March, 1920 MINGEIA foundered in heavy weather in the Atlantic 100 miles off the coast of Georgia.

SARANAC in the St. Clair River

SARANAC,		*DEPTH:*	13.6
b) Mingeia		*GROSS REGISTERED*	
		TONNAGE:	2,669
BUILT:	Globe Iron Works,	*REGISTRY NUMBER:*	US 116318
	Cleveland, Ohio	*ENGINES:*	24″, 38″, 61″ diameter × 42″
HULL NUMBER:	29		stroke
LENGTH:	290.2		Triple expansion
BREADTH:	40.8	*ENGINE BUILDER:*	Shipyard

CAPTAIN C. D. SECORD

CHARLES R. VAN HISE in 1918

The steel bulk freighter CHARLES R. VAN HISE was launched on June 29, 1900, originally owned by the Bessemer Steamship Co., Cleveland, and absorbed by the Pittsburgh Steamship Co., Cleveland, in 1901. She was taken over by the U.S. Shipping Board in 1918 for salt water service, and went to the Lake Shipbuilding Co., at Buffalo where she was deepened and cut in two sections and bulkheaded. The two sections were then rolled over on their sides to permit passage through the Welland and St. Lawrence Canals.

Neither of the sections got to salt water in 1918, although the bow section did reach Port Colborne in December. Owing to the ending of World War I, the plan to take her to the east coast was abandoned. The two sections were towed to Ashtabula and joined together in the yard of the Great Lakes Engineering Works at the same time a new mid-section (increasing the overall length to 542.4) was fitted in 1919.

She returned to service in 1920 as the A. E. R. SCHNEIDER under ownership of the Morrow S.S. Co., and operated under charter to Cleveland Cliffs Iron Co., with an increased gross tonnage of 6,874. In 1926 she passed

to the management of the Valley Camp Steamship Co., Cleveland, and later operated as S. B. WAY (2). In 1935 she was sold to Columbia Transportation Co., Cleveland, but did not operate as the J. M. OAG.

Sold in 1936 through Captain C. D. Secord to R. A. Campbell's Mohawk Navigation Co., Ltd., Montreal, this unique laker—with her forward house about amidships—returned to service as CAPTAIN C. D. SECORD (C. 158644). In 1953–54 she was given diesel power (built originally in 1942 by Harland and Wolfe, Ltd., Belfast) at Port Weller Dry Docks, Ltd. These diesel engines had originally been installed in the "OCEAN" class tanker EMPIRE METAL of 9,200 tons, which was sunk by bombs at Bona Harbor, Algeria on January 2, 1943. The engines were salvaged in 1950.

The SECORD began to show her age in the 1960's but she kept going until the end of the 1967 season. She was sold in the Spring of 1968 to Steel Factors, Ltd., Montreal for scrapping at Santander, Spain where she arrived under tow on September 13, 1968.

A. E. R. SCHNEIDER in 1920

S. B. WAY

CAPTAIN C. D. SECORD in Lake St. Clair

Charles R. Van Hise, b) A. E. R. Schneider, c) S. B. Way, d) J. M. Oag, e) CAPTAIN C. D. SECORD

BUILT:	Superior Shipbuilding Co., West Superior, Wisconsin	*GROSS REGISTERED*	
HULL NUMBER:	144	*TONNAGE:*	5,117
LENGTH:	458	*REGISTRY NUMBER:*	US 127426
BREADTH:	50.2	*ENGINES:*	20½″, 30″, 43½″ & 63″ diameter × 42″ stroke Quadruple expansion
DEPTH:	25	*ENGINE BUILDER:*	Chicago Shipbuilding Co.

CAPTAIN C. D. SECORD passing under the Blue Water Bridge

SEEANDBEE

SEEANDBEE

SEEANDBEE

Widely acclaimed for many years as "The Great Ship" or "The Largest Sidewheel Steamer in the World," the SEEANDBEE was the third and last ship built for the Cleveland and Buffalo Transit Company. Mr. Frank E. Kirby was the naval architect and she was launched in November, 1912. The steel hull was painted dark green and the cabins were white. She had two masts and four stacks, 510 staterooms and 24 parlors, and could sleep 1,500 passengers or carry 6,000 day passengers. The huge side-wheeler had a total of 7 decks and could cut through the water at 22+ knots.

SEEANDBEE began overnight service between Cleveland and Buffalo in 1913, and in 1921 began post-season cruises to Mackinac Island and Sault Ste. Marie. In subsequent years these were extended to Chicago. In 1937, she was damaged slightly when fire destroyed her sister ship in the fleet, the CITY OF BUFFALO, at their Cleveland docks. Later, SEEANDBEE became a regular cruise ship, operating between Buffalo and Chicago and way ports.

In 1941, she was sold to the C & B Transit Co. of Illinois. World War II brought drastic changes to SEEANDBEE. In 1942, the US Navy took her over, renamed her U.S.S. WOLVERINE and converted the ship at Buffalo into a training aircraft carrier. All superstructure above the main deck was removed and a wooden "flight deck" installed. The pilot house and stack were placed on one side of the flight deck and she took on the job of training pilots on Lake Michigan from the Great Lakes Naval Training Base. WOLVERINE performed this task for the War effort ably.

In August of 1945 she was retired and lay idle until decommissioned in 1946. The vessel fitted no further commercial purpose, and in November, 1947 was taken to Milwaukee where she was scrapped. Her official US Navy number was IX. 64, with displacement of 7,200 tons. Her dimensions were: 500' × 58-1/4' × 15-1/2'.

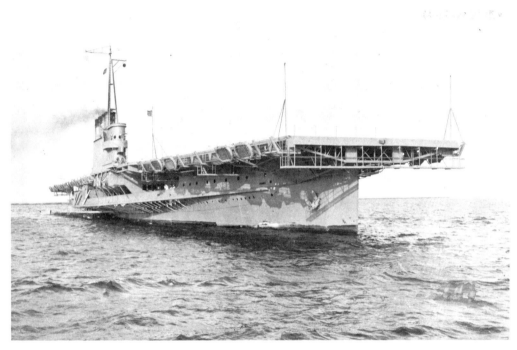

USS WOLVERINE

SEEANDBEE,
b) USS Wolverine

BUILT:	Detroit Shipbuilding Company, Wyandotte, Michigan
HULL NUMBER:	190
LENGTH:	484.5
BREADTH:	58.1
DEPTH:	24
GROSS REGISTERED TONNAGE:	6,381
REGISTRY NUMBER:	US 211085
ENGINES:	66", 96", 96" diameter × 108" stroke Inclined compound
ENGINE BUILDER:	Detroit Shipbuilding Co., Detroit, Michigan

SENATOR

SENATOR in the St. Mary's River

The SENATOR was launched on Saturday, June 20, 1896, amid the cheers of the usual christening crowd, including the proud owners of the new ship, Alexander McVittie, and his entourage. Her career was varied for she had many owners in her short life. These were: Alex McVittie of Detroit, 1896 to 1907; Wolverine Steamship Company, McMillan of Detroit, owner, 1908 to 1916; The Bristol Transportation Company, Richardson of Cleveland, Ohio, manager, 1917 to 1920; Columbia Transportation Company, 1921 to 1923; Fontana Steamship Company, A. E. R. Schneider of Cleveland, manager, 1924 to 1928; and the Spokane Steamship Company of Detroit, a unit of the Nicholson-Universal Steamship Company, during the 1929 season.

The SENATOR was almost lost when she collided with the steamer NORMAN B. REAM on August 22, 1909, one mile above Pipe Island in the St. Mary's River, and sank. There were no casualties, but the ship lay submerged with her masts above water until salvagers could raise and recover her from the relatively shallow water. The hull was towed to the shipyard and was returned to service a short time later.

During her last year, the SENATOR was engaged in the auto trade between Detroit and various ports on the Lakes. It was on such a trip that the ship was lost on Lake Michigan off Port Washington, Wisconsin, on October 31, 1929. On this day she again collided with a ship, this time the MARQUETTE of the Cleveland-Cliffs Steamship Company, during a dense fog, and went down along with 20 of her 29.

As an auto carrier

BUILT:	Detroit Dry Dock Company, Wyandotte, Michigan	GROSS REGISTERED TONNAGE:	4,048
HULL NUMBER:	122	REGISTRY NUMBER:	US 116725
LENGTH:	410	ENGINES:	22", 35", 58" diameter × 44" stroke
BREADTH:	45.4		Triple expansion
DEPTH:	23.9	ENGINE BUILDER:	Dry Dock Engine Works, Detroit, Mich.

JOHN SHAW

The wooden three-masted schooner JOHN SHAW was launched on October 28, 1885 for the Eddy-Shaw Lumber Company, of Bay City, Michigan, (Captain John Shaw and Charles A. Eddy). This attractive looking schooner was first enrolled at Port Huron, Michigan, on October 30, 1885, and for the first eight years of her life engaged basically in the lumber trade. In 1891 her bottom was recaulked. In 1893 she was sold to the Detroit-Saginaw Forwarding Company (Captain Moses M. Humphrey), of Bay City.

On November 10, 1894, in heavy weather and in a snow squall while off Oscoda, Michigan, the tow line parted between the schooner and her towing steamer, the JOHN F. EDDY. The time was three in the morning and she had a cargo of coal. About two hours later, the propeller H. E. RUNNELS picked up the SHAW's crew of seven in a yawl, including Captain Andrew Gustavison of Detroit. He reported that she had sprung a leak just forward of the mainmast and simply filled up. Crew members also reported that on her prior trip, from Chicago to Buffalo, her cargo of wheat was severely damaged by water. And so ended a Davidson-built schooner with only a nine-year life span.

JOHN SHAW

BUILT:	James Davidson, Bay City, Michigan	*DEPTH:*	14.3
HULL NUMBER:	11	*GROSS REGISTERED*	
LENGTH:	205.7	*TONNAGE:*	928
BREADTH:	37.1	*REGISTRY NUMBER:*	US 76601

SHELTER BAY

The veteran canaller NEW YORK NEWS (1) was built in 1922 for the Chicago Tribune Transportation Co. (later Quebec and Ontario Transportaion Co., Ltd.). Designed primarily for the pulpwood and newsprint trade, she was renamed b) SHELTER BAY (1) in 1933. During World War II she saw active service on salt water. She returned to her owner's service after the war.

The vessel was sold in 1958 to N. M. Paterson & Sons,

Ltd., Fort William and renamed c) LABRADOC (1). Due to the opening of the Seaway and the resulting demand for larger and more economical ships, this vessel operated for only part of the 1959 season. She laid up at Kingston, Ontario in the Fall of 1959, never to run again. In August 1961 she was towed to Port Dalhousie, Ontario where she was cut up in the dry dock by A. Newman Co., Ltd., St. Catharines.

NEW YORK NEWS at Montreal-Str. DRUMAHOE behind

New York News (1),		
b) SHELTER BAY (1),		
c) Labradoc (1)		
BUILT:	North of Ireland Shipbuilding Co., Ltd., Londonderry, Ireland
HULL NUMBER:	101
LENGTH:	250.2
BREADTH:	43
DEPTH:	16.8
GROSS REGISTERED TONNAGE:	1,670
REGISTRY NUMBER:	C 146581
ENGINES:	Triple Expansion 16″, 27″ & 44″ × 30″ Two Scotch Boilers
ENGINE BUILDER:	J. G. Kincaid & Co., Ltd., Greenock, Scotland

SHELTER BAY in the Welland Canal

LABRADOC

SIR WILLIAM SIEMENS

SIR WILLIAM SIEMENS in 1908

Originally built for the Bessemer Steamship Company, the SIR WILLIAM SIEMENS and all her sister ships went to the Pittsburgh Steamship Company in 1901. In 1928, the "Steel Trust" sold the SIEMENS to the Paisley Steamship Company, who renamed the vessel the WILLIAM B. PILKEY the following year. When the Columbia Transportation Company (formerly Columbia Steamship Company) was formed in 1935, Oglebay-Norton Company, managers, transferred the PILKEY into their fleet.

The advent of World War II meant that all the available hulls, no matter whether old or new, were pressed into the service of the war effort. The PILKEY was rebuilt into a crane vessel at Fairport, Ohio in 1941 by the Fairport Machine Shop. There, two huge cranes were installed on her decks, to enable her to load and unload scrap steel and iron products more easily. The new trade was begun and she was renamed FRANK E. VIGOR. Besides cargoes of scrap steel, the VIGOR could also transport bulk cargoes in her holds.

For the next few years it was actively engaged in the effort to end the war by providing material for more guns, planes, and ships. However, as the VIGOR was downbound on Lake Erie with a cargo of sulphur on April 27, 1944, the ship met its fate, like so many ships before her, in a dense fog. While traversing the ever dangerous Pelee Passage, (the narrow body of water that separates Lake Erie into two parts—the strait between Pelee Island and the northern Canadian mainland), she collided with the steamer PHILIP MINCH at 8:50 a.m. The VIGOR capsized and sank in 75 feet of water, twenty-eight and a half miles, 72 degrees from Southeast Shoal Light. Fortunately, the entire crew of the VIGOR was rescued—thirty-two men were saved by the capable crew who sailed the MINCH—and they were taken to port, none the worst for wetting. The presence of mind of the captain of the MINCH made it possible to end this tune on the right note.

Near the Soo

WILLIAM B. PILKEY in 1930

SIR WILLIAM SIEMENS,
b) William B. Pilkey,
c) Frank E. Vigor

BUILT:	Globe Iron Works, Cleveland, Ohio
HULL NUMBER:	67
LENGTH:	413.2
BREADTH:	48
DEPTH:	24
GROSS REGISTERED TONNAGE:	4,344
REGISTRY NUMBER:	US 116732
ENGINES:	25″, 41″, 66″ diameter × 42″ stroke Triple expansion
ENGINE BUILDER:	Shipyard

FRANK E. VIGOR in Lake St. Clair

FRANCES SMITH

FRANCES SMITH at Duluth

This wooden passenger and freight steamer was built in 1866–67 and launched on April 30, 1867 as the a) FRANCES SMITH. It was originally owned by Capt. W. H. Smith and was named in honor of his wife. All the timber and planking used in her construction was hand sawn. She came out as a day steamer with two stacks and operated between Collingwood and Owen Sound replacing CLIFTON whose engines and boilers she inherited. During one of her rebuilds the original two stacks were replaced by a single funnel. In the fall of 1868 she stranded near Byng Inlet on a reef which became known as Frances Smith Shoal. The vessel was salvaged in the spring of 1869 and was rebuilt as a night boat for service between Owen Sound and the Soo. This route was later extended to Prince Arthur's Landing. After Capt. Smith's death in 1872, the ship was commanded by Capt. Lute Robertson, a well known Georgian Bay mariner.

In 1874 the vessel began her service to Lake Superior, operating independently. After three years, she entered the fleet of the Canada Lake Superior Transit Company (Smith and Keighley, wholesale grocers of Toronto, were largely interested in this venture). FRANCES SMITH was rebuilt again in 1879 at Owen Sound. Her companions on the Lake Superior run were the side-wheelers CUMBERLAND and CHICORA. In 1882 FRANCES SMITH operated under charter to the Canadian Pacific Railway between Owen Sound and Port Arthur.

In 1887 or 1888 the vessel was sold to the Great Northern Transit Company and received an extensive $36,000 rebuild at Collingwood during which she was renamed b) BALTIC. She re-entered service on the Collingwood, Soo and Mackinac route along with the propellers ATLANTIC and PACIFIC. The vessel remained on this run until 1893 when it was transferred to the Collingwood & Chicago Worlds Fair service. At the close of the 1893 season she was laid up at Collingwood and did not operate for the next three years. On September 5, 1896 at 2:30 a.m. she mysteriously caught fire and burned to the water's edge. Later the machinery was removed and BALTIC's burned-out hull was towed out of the harbor and cut adrift in a strong north-west wind. She soon drifted ashore on an unused section of beach. For a number of years her rotting timbers remained a visible reminder of the "Golden Age" of steamboating on Georgian Bay.

BALTIC

FRANCES SMITH,
b) Baltic

BUILT:	Melancthon Simpson, Owen Sound, Ontario
LENGTH:	181.8
BREADTH:	27.9
DEPTH:	11.9
GROSS REGISTERED TONNAGE:	627
REGISTRY NUMBER:	C 92310
ENGINES:	Beam engines came from GILDERSLEEVE (1839) and CLIFTON (1854) 42″ Diameter × 132″ stroke
ENGINE BUILDER:	Macklem Iron Works, Chippewa, Ont.

SOUTHERN BELLE

**Rothesay Castle,
b) SOUTHERN BELLE**

BUILT:	Wm. Simons & Company, Renfrew, Scotland
LENGTH:	191
BREADTH:	28.9
DEPTH:	8.4
GROSS REGISTERED TONNAGE:	428
REGISTRY NUMBER:	Br. 29290
ENGINES:	Twin 40″–47″, 40″–85″ diameter × 54″–66″ stroke on one shaft Diagonal Oscillating
ENGINE BUILDER:	Shipyard

ROTHESAY CASTLE

The first Clyde steamer built by William Simons was the iron paddle Steamer ROTHESAY CASTLE built in 1861 for service on the Clyde and adjoining waters for Alex Watson. The name she bore was the fourth of five well known steamers on the Clyde to bear the name and the ship was one of the fastest. One historian cites her run between Rothesay and Broomielaw (approximately 60 miles) in 2 hours and 28 minutes as "a performance never equalled before or since." (McQueen—"Echoes of the Old Clyde Paddle Wheels"). In 1863 the ROTHESAY CASTLE was sold for 8,500 pounds to Confederate interests. (David McLutt in 1863 and Heron & Leach of Halifax in 1864 represented the South and are listed as the owners.) She was used as a blockade runner in the Civil War. In 1866 the vessel was purchased by Mitchell & McKay and Thomas Leach successively. The ROTHESAY CASTLE was refurbished as a passenger vessel for service between Toronto, Canada and the Niagara River on Lake Ontario in conjunction with the Canada Southern Railway.

From 1867–1873 the ship ran on the Gulf of St. Lawrence but returned to Lake Ontario at the end of the 1873 season.

After a small fire on February 10, 1884 the vessel was repaired and ran out of Toronto. In 1876 she was given a complete rebuild with sponsons on the hull, paddles lifted 20″ and the engines overhauled. The hull work was done by Messrs. Neil Currie and Company, and the engine adjustments were done by her chief engineer, Mr. A. J. Cameron. In the following years, the vessel generally ran as an opposition boat to another former blockade runner, the CHICORA, under the ownership of D. S. Keith of Toronto. Now named SOUTHERN BELLE, the side-wheeler was chartered for a time to the Canada Southern Railway for excursions from Toronto to Hamilton, Ontario. Her greatest speed and efficiency was demonstrated once late in the Seventies, when she made the trip from Toronto to Lewiston, Ontario on the Niagara River in 1 hour and 57 minutes, running with a head of steam at only 25 to 30 pounds of pressure. The SOUTHERN BELLE gave a quarter century of good service on Lake Ontario before she finally wore out and had to be retired. The BELLE was scrapped in 1889 at Mill Point near Picton, Ontario.

SOUTHERN BELLE in later years

SOVEREIGN

This steel hulled beam engined passenger steamer was built 1888–89 at Montreal, Quebec for the Ottawa River Navigation Company of Montreal. She was built on the banks of the Lachine Canal above the St. Gabriel Lock and was launched on November 14, 1888 by Mrs. Shepherd. She was christened QUEEN but before the superstructure was completed at Tate's Dock in Montreal her name had been changed to SOVEREIGN. She had accommodations for 700 day passengers and her dining room seated 60. She also had 10 staterooms and was fitted with feathering wheels. She entered service between Montreal and Carillon and shot the Lachine Rapids daily except Sundays on her return trip to Montreal.

On the night of March 17, 1906 while in winter quarters at Lachine, her upper-works were destroyed by fire and the hull sank below the ice. The hull was abandoned to the underwriters on payment of the insurance claim of $40,000.

In the spring of 1906 the hull was raised and towed to Sorel, Quebec where it was lengthened to 200'. The upper works were rebuilt and her overall beam was now 41.9 with gross tonnage of 1098. During 1907 and 1908 she operated for the new owners—St. Lawrence Canadian Navigation Co., Ltd., Montreal in opposition to the Richelieu and Ontario Company's Montreal-Quebec service as c) IMPERIAL.

After 1908 she operated from Montreal to King Edward Park on an island a few miles down the St. Lawrence from Montreal. Her managing owner in 1914 was Charles Mignault, Montreal. In 1918 her manager was Alexander Desmarteaux, Montreal. She was sold in 1928 to the Georgian Bay Tourist Company, Midland, for service on Georgian Bay. However after arrival at Midland, Ontario her boilers and hull failed to pass inspection and she was then broken up for scrap.

SOVEREIGN in Lake St. Louis

Queen,		*DEPTH:*	7.4
b) SOVEREIGN,		*GROSS REGISTERED*	
c) Imperial		*TONNAGE:*	636
		REGISTRY NUMBER:	C 94887
BUILT:	W. C. White Shipyard, Montreal	*ENGINES:*	Beam
			34″ Diameter × 96″ Stroke
LENGTH:	162.4	*ENGINE BUILDER:*	George Brush, Eagle Foundry,
BREADTH:	25.5		Montreal

JESSE SPALDING

JESSE SPALDING downbound at the Soo

In 1899, the JESSE SPALDING was named for the owner of the Spalding Lumber Company who had ordered this canal-sized, steel lumber hooker. From her launch she was to prove a most traveled ship. During the First World War, it was sent to the East Coast to engage in the carrying of war material. The canaller was purchased in 1916 by the Coastwise Steamship Company, a Moore-McCormack affiliate, and was renamed MOOREMACK that same year. After the cessation of hostilities, the steamer was purchased by the Vindal Steamship Company in 1921, brought back to the Lakes, and renamed VINDAL. In 1923, after a brief time in the fleet of the Calumet Steamship Company, she was owned by the Detroit Sulphite Transportation Company. This Detroit-based paper firm renamed their new unit CORDOVA and it became a familiar sight on the Detroit River. As the CORDOVA, the ship was again transporting paper products, the purpose for which it had originally been built.

In 1925, the F. D. Gleason Coal Company bought the vessel and renamed it JAY A. PEARSON. Having been converted to a self-unloading sandsucker at Great Lakes Engineering Works, Ecorse, Michigan in 1925, the vessel spent the next 10 years in the Gleason Fleet. In 1935, the vessel was purchased by the Tri-Lakes Steamship Company, a division of Nicholson Transit Company in River Rouge, and was given its sixth and final name—ROCKWOOD. In 1947, she was sold to the Kelley Island Lime & Transport Co., then to the Rockwood Steamship Company, managed by the Erie Sand Steamship Company in 1955 and finally to the Erie Sand & Gravel Company, in 1960. She had 10 owners in all, 5 renames, 2 engines (the steam plant was removed in 1952 and replaced by a diesel) and plenty of captains. She was a lumber hooker, a coal carrier, and a sand dredge, and was finally laid to rest by being scrapped at Ashtabula, Ohio in 1963.

CORDOVA in 1923

JAY A. PEARSON

JESSE SPALDING, b) Mooremack, c) Vindal, d) Cordova, e) Jay A. Pearson, f) Rockwood

BUILT:	F. W. Wheeler Shipbuilding Company, West Bay City, Michigan	*GROSS REGISTERED TONNAGE:*	1,043
HULL NUMBER:	127	*REGISTRY NUMBER:*	US 77362
LENGTH:	220	*ENGINES:*	17″, 28′, 47″ diameter × 36″ stroke
BREADTH:	40		Triple expansion
DEPTH:	14	*ENGINE BUILDER:*	Shipyard

ROCKWOOD

SPARTA

FRANK W. HART in the St. Clair River

At one time the Gilchrist Transportation Company was one of the largest fleets on the Lakes. Among the many steel bulk carriers built by the company at the beginning of the 20th century was the FRANK W. HART, built in 1902.

In 1914 the ship was sold to the National Steamship Company, one of the many fleets managed and operated by the Tomlinson group. In 1929 she was renamed SPARTA and moved iron ore, coal and grain. She experienced no serious difficulties in her life except the very last.

In the Armistice Day storm of November 11, 1940, the SPARTA was having her problems on Lake Superior. The 60 mph winds that rampaged over Lake Superior that day were perhaps not as violent as those that struck Lake Michigan, but they were all that the SPARTA needed to settle her career. About 15 miles East of Munising, Michigan

are the beautiful Pictured Rocks. On this stretch, the SPARTA came to grief.

On a rocky ledge near Miner's Castle, the pinnacle that juts into the air, some 50 feet above the lake, the SPARTA stuck hard and remained pinned. She held fast pinioned to the rocks and would not budge. The crew remained aboard and were hard pressed to secure safety. They were rescued but the vessel remained fast. No lives were lost, but the ship refused attempts at salvage that fall. The next Spring it was finally released by that master of salvage, Captain John Roen, who purchased the steamer when the owners had abandoned all hope of her salvage, and towed her to his dockyard at Sturgeon Bay, Wisconsin. He began reconstruction but abandoned that due to the ship's condition. The hull was redesigned as a drydock which still remains at Sturgeon Bay as part of the Bay Shipbuilding Company.

SPARTA

	Frank W. Hart,
	b) SPARTA
BUILT:	American Shipbuilding Company, Lorain, Ohio
HULL NUMBER:	313
LENGTH:	380
BREADTH:	50
DEPTH:	28

GROSS REGISTERED	
TONNAGE:	4,307
REGISTRY NUMBER:	US 121219
ENGINES:	Triple expansion 22″, 35″, 58″ diameter × 40″ Stroke
ENGINE BUILDER:	American Shipbuilding Company, Cleveland, Ohio

STARBUCK

SCRANTON

The iron package freighter SCRANTON was built in 1888 for the Lackawanna Transportation Co., operated by Captain M. M. Drake. In the very early 1900's Mutual Transit Co. took over management for the Lackawanna Railroad. About 1907–08 SCRANTON was chartered to the Anchor Line—The Erie and Western Transit Co. She was later sold to the Buffalo Transit Co., and operated for a short time by Brown Co., Buffalo. In 1913 she passed to Sydney C. McLouth's River Transit Co., Maine City. McLouth placed her in the bagged cement trade carrying for the Huron Cement Co. In 1924 SCRANTON was chartered to the Minnesota Atlantic Transit Co. (The Poker Fleet) and was purchased by the company in 1927.

The vessel operated as both TEN (1) and later NINE for the Poker Fleet. In 1941 it was sold to the Steel Company of Canada, Ltd., Hamilton for scrapping. Because of the demand for vessels brought on by World War II, however, it was sold to Powell Transports, Ltd., Winnipeg and returned to service in the Canadian Grain Trade as STARBUCK. The vessel was sold by Powell Transports to Western Iron and Metal Co., Ltd., Fort William in 1957 for scrapping. As her iron hull presented demolition problems, she was towed to Superior in 1958 and broken up there.

TEN in 1928

NINE

Scranton, b) Ten, c) Nine, d) STARBUCK

BUILT:	Cleveland Shipbuilding Co., Cleveland, Ohio	*GROSS REGISTERED TONNAGE:*	2,015
HULL NUMBER:	2	*REGISTRY NUMBER:*	US 116235 (later C 173515)
LENGTH:	260	*ENGINES:*	19″, 30″ & 52″ diameter × 40″ stroke
BREADTH:	38.3		Triple expansion
DEPTH:	25	*ENGINE BUILDER:*	Cleveland Shipbuilding Co.

STARBUCK passing Sugar Island

STATE OF NEW YORK

CITY OF MACKINAC—old timetable

The iron sidewheeler CITY OF MACKINAC was launched in 1883 for the Detroit and Cleveland Steam Navigation Company. Designed by the famous naval architect Frank E. Kirby, she was intended for service on the company's new Lake Huron Division between Detroit, St. Ignace, and way ports, along with the CITY OF ALPENA. Both ships were sold in 1892 to the newly organized Cleveland and Buffalo Transit Company for overnight service between those cities. She was renamed STATE OF NEW YORK in 1893.

In 1892 a new line operated jointly by the D & C and C & B firms to run from Cleveland and from Toledo to Put-in-Bay was started. STATE OF NEW YORK and CITY OF THE STRAITS (US 125662) were placed on these routes. In 1907 the STATE OF NEW YORK was chartered to the Lake Erie Excursion Company, of Buffalo, and in 1909, to the D & C company. Also, in 1900, she received four new Scotch boilers (9'8" × 11') built by the Detroit Shipbuilding Company.

In 1909, D & C purchased the vessel outright to run from Detroit to Saginaw and way ports. This route lasted for only two years and in 1911, she was transferred back to the Toledo to Put-in-Bay run. In 1918 Goodrich Transit Company obtained her for cross-lake service on Lake Michigan and renamed her FLORIDA. Then, in May, 1922, they disposed of her to the Western Transportation Company of Chicago, for the short run between downtown Chicago and Jackson Park, on the city's south shore. She remained in this route until 1932, except for a one-year charter stint (1929) to the White Star Line between Detroit and Port Huron.

In 1932 ownership went to the Columbian Transportation Company, of Chicago, and in 1933–34 she carried passengers from downtown to the Century of Progress Exposition. After lying idle from 1934 to 1936 her cabins were dismantled, machinery was removed, and she was converted to a clubhouse for the Columbia Yacht Club. Ownership was transferred to George F. Benedict in 1935, and to the yacht club the next year. She was removed from documentation in 1935. In her clubhouse status, she lay at the foot of Randolph Street, Chicago, until 1954, when a fire destroyed her upper works. However, new houses were built on the old iron hull, and she continues in her clubhouse capacity as this is written.

City of Mackinac, b) STATE OF NEW YORK, c) Florida, d) Columbia

BUILT:	Detroit Dry Dock Co., Wyandotte, Michigan	REGISTRY NUMBER:	US 126150
HULL NUMBER:	61	ENGINES:	Beam Condensing Triple Expansion
LENGTH:	203'		36", 44" & 80" Diameter × 120"
BREADTH:	32'4"		Stroke
DEPTH:	10'5"	ENGINE BUILDER:	W. & A. Fletcher Co.,
GROSS REGISTERED TONNAGE:	807		Hoboken, New Jersey—1883 (#108)

STATE OF NEW YORK

FLORIDA in Goodrich colors

COLUMBIA at Chicago

STEEL KING (2)

STARRUCCA in Erie colors

The steel package freighter STARRUCCA was built in 1897 for the Union Steamboat Line which was the Great Lakes subsidiary of the Erie Railroad. The colors of this line were a black hull, yellow-orange cabins, red stack with black top and a black and white Erie diamond. The ships pilot house and Texas deck were located behind No. 1 hatch and the vessel was operated in the owner's fast freight service, largely between Buffalo, New York and Chicago, Illinois, with occasional trips to Lake Superior.

In 1912 the vessel's name was changed to DELOS W. COOKE. In the winter of 1915–1916 it became part of the fleet of the Great Lakes Transit Corporation. When the package freight trade began to slack off in the middle thirties, the vessel was laid-up. In 1938 she was sold to a Chicago junk dealer, M. Cohen, and taken to South Chicago. After

nearly a year it was resold to the Nicholson Transit Company and rebuilt in 1940 as a bulk carrier by the Nicholson Terminal & Dock Co. for the grain trade with provisions for carrying autos on the upper deck. The vessel's dimensions were changed to: 336.3 × 43.8 × 24.5 and she was renamed STEEL KING (2).

For six years (1945–1950) the STEEL KING was equipped as a crane ship and used in the finished steel scrap and pig iron trades. In 1951 the cranes were removed and she reverted to a bulk freighter. In 1953 the vessel was withdrawn from service and in 1954 the forward section was made into the barge PB-12. The stern portion, cut down to a barge was named "AFT". Enroute for scrapping in 1971 the stern section sank in Lake Erie near Port Colborne.

DELOS W. COOKE in 1917

STEEL KING in the Detroit River

	Starrucca,	*DEPTH:*	14.9
	b) Delos W. Cooke,	*GROSS REGISTERED*	
	c) STEEL KING (2)	*TONNAGE:*	3,114
		REGISTRY NUMBER:	US 116786
BUILT:	Union Dry Dock Company,	*ENGINES:*	23″, 38″, 64″ diameter × 42″
	Buffalo, New York		stroke
HULL NUMBER:	80		Triple Expansion
LENGTH:	326.5	*ENGINE BUILDER:*	King Iron Works,
BREADTH:	44		Buffalo, New York

With cranes

GRAEME STEWART

GRAEME STEWART

In order to upgrade the Chicago Fire Department, two identical steel fire tugs—the GRAEME STEWART and a sister, the JOSEPH MEDILL (2)—were built in 1908. Two General Electric turbine engines powered these tugs, the world's first electrically driven vessels. STEWART was stationed at the Franklin Street Bridge and was quickly available when the Steamer EASTLAND capsized in 1915.

Sold in 1941 to Sincennes—MacNaughton of Montreal, the vessel was converted to a regular towing tug in 1942. Her engines were replaced with a triple expansion steam engine (with cylinders of 15″, 25″ and 42″ diameter and a 26″ stroke) built in Collingwood in 1914. Her superstructure was altered to include two decks for the salvage business. The Canadian registry number was 174156 and her dimen-

sions were: 116.8 × 28 × 14.2 with a gross tonnage of 348.

In 1960, the McAllister Towing Co. took over the fleet, and the STEWART continued her regular towing jobs in Montreal Harbor plus occasional wrecking jobs as a salvage tug. This unit often worked with the former Detroit Fire tug, JAMES BATTLE, which also had been sold for use in the salvage business.

Ironically, it was the BATTLE that towed the STEWART from Montreal to her final destination at Hamilton, Ontario, for the scrappers torch in September, 1970. The vessel was cut up in 1971, thus ending a varied and interesting tug career.

GRAEME STEWART at Montreal

BUILT:	Manitowoc Dry Dock Company, Manitowoc, Wisconsin	*GROSS REGISTERED TONNAGE:*	309
HULL NUMBER:	43	*REGISTRY NUMBER:*	US 206149
LENGTH:	104	*ENGINES:*	Turbine Electric
BREADTH:	28.2	*ENGINE BUILDER:*	General Electric Co., Lynn, Massachusetts
DEPTH:	16		

TASHMOO

TASHMOO

Of all of Detroit's famous ships, perhaps none is better remembered than the TASHMOO. Built in 1900 for the White Star Line, TASHMOO was of steel hull and side-wheel propulsion with an inclined engine of 3,150 horsepower which gave her a speed of more than 20 miles per hour. She operated on the Detroit and St. Clair Rivers for nearly thirty-five years, mostly on the Port Huron run, while also making frequent trips to Toledo. This ship definitely was part of the tradition of the Detroit waterfront. Her arrivals and departures were so regular during the summer months that in the communities along the St. Clair River and lower Detroit River, the inhabitants checked their watches by the sounding of the whistle of the "Glass Hack" as she was popularly called. Captain Baker was her first and best known commander.

In 1901, the TASHMOO voyaged to Cleveland to compete with the Steamer CITY OF ERIE in the now-famous Cleveland-to-Erie race. The CITY OF ERIE was successful over the TASHMOO by only forty-five seconds over the hundred mile course!

The TASHMOO ended her days on June 18, 1936, when she struck an obstruction in the Amherstburg Channel while upbound in the lower Detroit River. The hull had only recently been strengthened with sponsons, and it is thought that one of these was torn loose in the grounding because the hull took water so swiftly. Captain Donald McAlpine successfully docked the vessel near Amherstburg, Ontario and passengers and crew disembarked safely before the ship settled in 21 feet of water. The wreck was scrapped soon afterward, although her pilot house served as a summer cottage near Wallaceburg, Ontario for many years and the ship's bell is preserved in Greenfield Village Museum at Dearborn, Michigan. Such a "flyer" of the lakes will probably never be seen again.

In the St. Clair River

TASHMOO sunk at Amherstburg

BUILT:	Detroit Shipbuilding Company, Wyandotte, Michigan	*GROSS REGISTERED TONNAGE:*	1,344
HULL NUMBER:	131	*REGISTRY NUMBER:*	US 145843
LENGTH:	302.9	*ENGINES:*	33″, 51″, 82″ diameter × 72″ stroke
BREADTH:	37.6		Triple Expansion-Inclined
DEPTH:	13.6	*ENGINE BUILDER:*	Shipyard

THOUSAND ISLANDER

THOUSAND ISLANDER

This day excursion steamer was built in 1912 for the Thousand Island Steamboat Company's connection with the New York Central Railroad and operated initially under U.S. registry to the Thousand Islands out of Clayton, New York. A twin screw vessel, she was designed to operate at 18 M.P.H. with a capacity of 1,000 passengers.

She entered service in July 1912. During her first season, the Thousand Island Steamboat Co. was taken over by the Richelieu and Ontario Navigation Co., Ltd., Montreal. The R. and O. was absorbed into Canada Steamship Lines Ltd., in 1913. However, THOUSAND ISLANDER continued to operate in the Thousand Islands area under U.S. Registry until 1918. In that year, she came under Canadian Registry

(C. 141756) and was placed by C.S.L. on the Detroit-Wallaceburg Line. She continued in this service till the middle 1920's and was then laid up at Sarnia.

On November 25, 1927, she left Sarnia in tow of the bulk carrier COLLINGWOOD enroute to Collingwood, Ontario, for refitting, having been sold to the Georgian Bay Tourist Company for $50,000 (subject to delivery at Midland, Ontario). The tow was caught in a heavy gale on Lake Huron and portions of THOUSAND ISLANDER's upper-works were carried away by the seas. She eventually became unmanageable and was cut adrift and foundered soon afterward.

BUILT:	Toledo Shipbuilding Co., Toledo, Ohio
HULL NUMBER:	123
LENGTH:	166.4
BREADTH:	31.9
DEPTH:	8.3
GROSS REGISTERED TONNAGE:	587
REGISTRY NUMBER:	US 209906
ENGINES:	Twin Compound fore and aft 15″ × 30″ Diameter × 20″ Stroke
ENGINE BUILDER:	Shipyard

In the Detroit River

THREE BROTHERS

THREE BROTHERS

The three-masted wooden schooner THREE BROTHERS was launched in 1874. She was built by the veteran ship-builder Henry D. Root in his yard just south of the present modern highway bridge crossing the Black River across from the American Shipbuilding Company. On April 29, 1874, the vessel was enrolled at Cleveland to James, Julian, and A. Porter, of Black River, George Miller, of Ashland, Ohio, and H. Peachey, of New York.

She led a relatively quiet life so far as oak-hulled schooners of her day were concerned. Perhaps the most noteworthy things that occurred were internal ownership shuffles as George E. Porter replaced A. Porter in March, 1884, and Julian and George E. Porter bought the interest of the others in 1886. Finally, in March, 1889, Julian Porter became the sole owner of the THREE BROTHERS. He also doubled as her master, as she engaged in the lumber trade.

On June 8, 1906, the aging vessel shook some of her lethargy when she was dismasted by a sudden squall on Lake Erie between East and West Sister Islands. The next morning, she was sighted by the sidewheeler STATE OF OHIO. Her plight was reported and the tug A. W. COLTON picked up the mastless schooner and towed her to Lorain for drydocking and repairs. Julian Porter still was her master at that time.

In June, 1911, her ownership changed to Theobald Emig, of St. Clair, Michigan, and her enrollment was transferred to Port Huron. The remainder of her days would be spent at the end of a tow rope in the lumber trade. In 1914, she was sold to Horatio N. Jex, of Toledo, Ohio. She was abandoned at Toledo in 1916, where, after fifty-two years of faithful service, she became a resident of Gillmore's bone yard.

BUILT:	Henry D. Root,	*DEPTH:*	12'
	Black River (Lorain), Ohio	*GROSS REGISTERED*	
LENGTH:	136' 6"	*TONNAGE:*	349
BREADTH:	25' 9"	*REGISTRY NUMBER:*	US 24987

As a tow barge

TIOGA

TIOGA in Erie colors

The TIOGA's first five years of operation were uneventful, but in 1890, she made the headlines in the papers around the Lakes. This 1885-built vessel, while at berth in the Chicago River at Chicago, Illinois, on July 11th, sustained a violent and sudden explosion which ripped apart her stern and caused severe damage to both the ship and the dockside. The accident killed an estimated 21 people and worked havoc among the ships in the nearby harbor. Huge fires spread rapidly from the explosion, and the Chicago Fire Department, both on shore and with fireboats, was kept busy throughout the next few hours. The cause of the explosion was later attributed to the cargo of naptha that the TIOGA had in her hold. How the naptha caught fire was not determined, but the resultant disaster caused by the fires and the explosion was a topic of discussion and lawsuits for many months. After the fires were extinguished, the ship was carefully probed for the bodies that had been unaccounted for, but the explosion had been so severe that some were never found.

The TIOGA was towed down the lakes to Buffalo, New York, where it was repaired and returned to service. Her engine was rebored to cylinders of 22″ and 42″ diameter and a stroke of 48 inches. Until 1915, she remained with the Lake services of the Erie Railroad. The railroads were

forced at that time to divest themselves of their package freighters. The TIOGA lay idle at the dock for a couple of years, until it was purchased in 1917 by C. A. Massey's Superior Transit Company.

The end of her career came only a few years later, on November 26, 1919, when she stranded on Eagle River Reef, Lake Superior. The storm that had raged over the lake for two days pounded the ships that were brave enough to travel out in the fury. The TIOGA hit the reef off the Keweenaw Peninsula hard and stuck fast. For hours the trapped crew was at the mercy of the gale force winds and giant grey combers smashed the vessel, coating her with inches of ice and snow. The survivors huddled together to obtain any warmth their bodies could give. The usual warmth of the engine room afforded but little comfort because the ship had struck and ruptured her steam lines leaving little hope of rescue. As the winds abated, however, rescue once again became possible. After many attempts, the entire crew of the TIOGA was saved. The vessel, however, later slid beneath the cold waves to be buried forever in the deep waters of Lake Superior. Her upper pilothouse was preserved and is still in private use as a recreational building near the wreck site.

BUILT:	Union Dry Dock Company, Buffalo, New York
HULL NUMBER:	39
LENGTH:	285.5
BREADTH:	38.9
DEPTH:	25.7

GROSS REGISTERED TONNAGE:	2,085
REGISTRY NUMBER:	US 145405
ENGINES:	23½″, 39½″ diameter × 48″ stroke Steeple Compound
ENGINE BUILDER:	King Iron Works, Buffalo, New York

TIONESTA

TIONESTA in the St. Clair River

Tionesta was the first of three palatial steel passenger and freight ships built in the early years of the 20th century for the Anchor Line, a division of the Pennsylvania Railroad. Like her sisters, TIONESTA, built in 1903 for service between Buffalo, New York and Duluth, Minnesota, carried the name of a Pennsylvania River.

In 1916, she became a part of the newly formed Great Lakes Transit Corporation. For a few years in the early 1930's TIONESTA operated between Buffalo and Lake Michigan ports. All three ships were withdrawn from service in 1936 and lay idle at Buffalo thereafter. TIONESTA, the oldest of the triplets, was sold for scrap in 1940 and towed to Hamilton, Ontario where she was broken up.

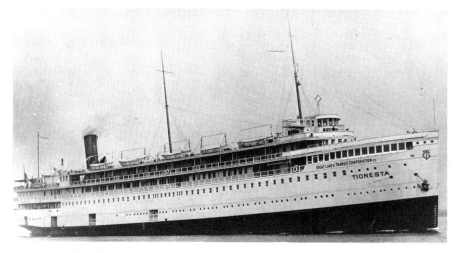

In Great Lakes Transit colors

BUILT:	Detroit Shipbuilding Company, Wyandotte, Michigan	*GROSS REGISTERED TONNAGE:*	4,329
		REGISTRY NUMBER:	US 145958
HULL NUMBER:	150	*ENGINES:*	22″, 31½″, 45″, 65″ diameter × 42″ stroke
LENGTH:	340		Quadruple expansion
BREADTH:	45.2	*ENGINE BUILDER:*	Shipyard
DEPTH:	28		

TORONTO

The steel paddle passenger TORONTO was built in 1899 for the Toronto-Thousand Islands-Prescott run of the Richelieu and Ontario Navigation Co., Ltd., Montreal. She was absorbed into Canada Steamship Lines, Ltd., Montreal in 1913. The famous KINGSTON became her running mate in 1901. TORONTO was retired from service in 1938, partly because her wooden main deck did not conform to new safety regulations for overnight passenger vessels.

Her life was one of dependable service marred by few accidents. One of these occurred on July 5, 1924 when she was in collision with MODJESKA off the C.S.L. Terminal in Toronto Bay. TORONTO'S bows were damaged but MODJESKA was held at fault. From 1938 TORONTO lay in reserve at Toronto. She was sold for scrapping at Hamilton in 1947.

TORONTO in R & O colors

BUILT:	Bertram Engine Works Co., Ltd., Toronto, Ontario	*GROSS REGISTERED TONNAGE:*	2,779
HULL NUMBER:	29	*REGISTRY NUMBER:*	C 107412
LENGTH:	269.4	*ENGINES:*	28″, 44″ & 72″ diameter × 72″ stroke
BREADTH:	36 (over guards 68′)		Triple expansion, Inclined
DEPTH:	13.8	*ENGINE BUILDER:*	Shipyard

C. 1930

TURBINIA

TURBINIA leaving Toronto harbor

The triple screw day passenger steamer TURBINIA was built for the Turbine Steamship Co., in 1904. With 4,000 H.P., her maximum speed was approximately 30 M.P.H. She left Newcastle on June 1, 1904 and crossed the Atlantic in six days. After a stop at Kingston, Ontario for inspection, she arrived at Hamilton on June 19, 1904. She made a special V.I.P. cruise to Toronto on June 29, 1904 and entered regular Toronto-Hamilton service the next day.

TURBINIA immediately entered into stormy competition with the Hamilton Steamboat Co.'s MODJESKA and MA-CASSA. Early in 1906, control of the Turbine Steamship Co. passed to the T. Eaton Co., Ltd., Toronto. In 1909, the Eaton interests also acquired control of the Hamilton Steamboat Co., but the two lines operated independently until both were absorbed by the Niagara Navigation Co., Ltd. in 1911.

The Richelieu and Ontario Navigation Co., Ltd. swallowed up the Niagara Navigation Co., in 1912 and was itself absorbed by Canada Steamship Lines, Ltd. in 1913. TUR-BINIA left the Lakes late in 1917 for waters around the British Isles, being employed as a troop carrier and hospital ship. She returned to the Lakes in 1922 and resumed Toronto-Hamilton service in 1923. In 1926, she was transferred to C.S.L.'s Montreal-Quebec City day line. This service was dropped about 1929 and TURBINIA was then laid up at Sorel. In 1937, she was sold to Les Chantiers Manseau, Ltee., Sorel for scrapping.

TURBINIA

BUILT:	Hawthorne, Leslie Co., Hebburn on Tyne, Scotland	*GROSS REGISTERED TONNAGE:*	1,064
HULL NUMBER:	393	*REGISTRY NUMBER:*	C 112201
LENGTH:	250	*ENGINES:*	One high pressure turbine and two low pressure turbines
BREADTH:	33.2	*ENGINE BUILDER:*	Parsons Marine Steam Turbine Engine Co., Newcastle, England
DEPTH:	12.6		

TWIN CITIES

These twin screw, diesel electric drive steel package freighters of the barge canal type were built in 1923 at Ashtabula by the Great Lakes Engineering Works. TWIN CITIES was laid down as *Hull 517* while TWIN PORTS was *Hull 516*. Dimensions for both vessels were 250.6 × 42.2 × 17.5. Gross tonnage 1,460; net 840. They were built for the Minnesota Atlantic Transit Co. and were designed for service between Duluth, Buffalo and New York during the lake navigation season, and for service to the West Indies and the Gulf of Mexico during the winter months. Ownership was later transferred to the Detroit-New York Transit Co.

In 1931 TWIN CITIES was renamed b) DETROITER

and TWIN PORTS became b) CLEVELANDER. In 1931 both ships were sold to the National Motorship Corporation. In 1946 they were transferred to the Island Dock Co. and in 1947 both were purchased by Cleveland Tankers, Inc. It was intended to convert both vessels to tankers for the Company's Canadian subsidiary, Lakeland Tankers, Ltd., Toronto, but the conversion never took place. Both vessels saw little service except that DETROITER a) TWIN CITIES operated under charter to the T. H. Browning Interests in 1950. In 1951 both ships were supposedly sold to Moran Towing and Transportation Co., but they remained idle at Port Weller until scrapped by A. Newman & Co., St. Catharines in 1954.

DETROITER

TWIN PORTS at the Soo

CLEVELANDER

UNIQUE

UNIQUE truly lived up to her name. Designed by Crockett McElroy, the wooden passenger propellor was launched on June 16, 1884 with a hull of the finest oak. The designer made the model and wrote the specifications himself. The UNIQUE was built with the idea of monopolizing the passenger trade on the St. Clair River. She was to make two round trips daily between Detroit and Port Huron, with scheduled stops at Algonac, Marine City, St. Clair and Sarnia, Ontario and flag stops in between. The line was called the "Rapid Transit Line" but was not a success due to regular failures of UNIQUE's boilers and engines, all of which caused her owners considerable loss.

From the beginning, the vessel was to prove a completely unique ship. She was launched stern first, a novelty in those times. She was berated by poets (so-called) who wrote such ditties as the following, quoted from the Port Huron Daily Times of Monday, June 18, 1894:

> "The new steamer UNIQUE,
> Made a beautiful snique,
> On a direction oblique,
> Into a big Crique,
> So to spique.
>
> (by) Unknown Frique."

The vessel was painted a bright yellow up to her promenade deck, with white cabins and upper works. Her engines were reportedly the first of the quadruple type on the lakes. When the vessel made its first trips to Port Huron it encountered the first of many mishaps. She made it to Port Huron on September 3, 1894, but there-after had many troubles. On the 14th of September, a man lost his life when something on her boilers gave way, scalding him to death.

In 1895, the UNIQUE came out with new boilers and a completely white paintjob, but troubles were still with her. In 1896, she was reportedly sold to Eastern parties but nothing materialized until 1900 when the vessel was sold to Ogdensburg, N.Y. owners who ran the vessel in the Thousand Islands trade. Again in 1901, she was sold, this time to Philadelphia parties, who ran her in service on the Delaware River. New boilers again were installed, some alterations made in her machinery, and her name changed to DIAMOND STATE.

In 1904, the vessel was selected from a list of 30 boats by agents of August Belmont, a businessman who had ordered a fast yacht. The upper cabins were removed, her lines were changed to yacht style, and she was renamed again, this time to SATELLITE. The unlucky ship was destroyed by fire in New York Harbor on November 20, 1915, thus ending the brief career of the unique UNIQUE.

UNIQUE

UNIQUE,		
b) Diamond State,		
c) Satellite		
BUILT:	Alex Anderson, Marine City, Michigan	
LENGTH:	163	
BREADTH:	20.5	
DEPTH:	11	

GROSS REGISTERED TONNAGE:	381
REGISTRY NUMBER:	US 25299
ENGINES:	15", 22½", 30", 42" diameter × 18" stroke Quadruple Expansion
ENGINE BUILDER:	Frontier Iron Works, Samuel F. Hodge, Detroit

UNITED EMPIRE

UNITED EMPIRE

This wooden passenger and freight propeller was built in 1882–83 by James H. and Henry Beatty for the Northwest Transportation Co., Sarnia. Familiarly known to lake men as "OLD BETSY," her picture appeared on the Canadian four dollar bill issued in 1902. The Northwest Transportation Co. was absorbed into the Northern Navigation Co., Ltd. in 1899 but UNITED EMPIRE continued on the Sarnia-Lakehead service, although she was renamed SARONIC in 1905.

The pattern was broken in 1913 when she operated in the Montreal-Lakehead package fright service. Also in 1913, Canada Steamship Lines, Ltd. absorbed Northern Navigation Co., Ltd. In 1914 "OLD BETSY" operated on C.S.L.'s Quebec, North Shore Gulf of St. Lawrence route. She

returned to her old Upper Lakes run in 1915. She was damaged by fire at Sarnia on December 15, 1915. This same fire destroyed the MAJESTIC. She was rebuilt in 1916 as a steam barge and operated by C.S.L. in the grain trade. On August 20, 1916 she stranded on Cockburn Island, Lake Huron and was damaged amidships by fire which broke out after the grounding. As a result she was abandoned to the Underwriters as a total loss.

The hull was sold in 1917 to W. Schlosser of Milwaukee and converted into the barge W. L. KENNEDY, registered at Marquette, Michigan (US. 215206) with gross tonnage of 1,014. She was used to carry pulpwood for the Detroit Sulphite Company, and was finally abandoned in 1924 in the Detroit River near Amherstburg, Ontario.

SARONIC in 1911

UNITED EMPIRE,	*DEPTH:* 15
b) Saronic,	*GROSS REGISTERED*
c) W. L. Kennedy	*TONNAGE:* 1,961
	REGISTRY NUMBER: C. 80776
BUILT: Dyble and Parry, Sarnia, Ontario	*ENGINES:* Fore and Aft Compound 34″ & 60″ Diameter × 42″ stroke
LENGTH: 252.8	*ENGINE BUILDER:* George H. Ouille,
BREADTH: 36	St. Catharines, Ontario

UTICA

UTICA,	
b) Quintay	
BUILT:	Detroit Shipbuilding Company, Wyandotte, Michigan
HULL NUMBER:	157
LENGTH:	325
BREADTH:	44.2

DEPTH:	30.9
GROSS REGISTERED TONNAGE:	3,533
REGISTRY NUMBER:	US 200954
ENGINES:	19″, 27½″, 40″, & 58″ diameter × 42″ stroke Quadruple expansion
ENGINE BUILDER:	Shipyard

UTICA in 1928

Another package freighter for the New York Central controlled Western Transit Company was built in 1904 by the Detroit Shipbuilding Company at Wyandotte. The UTICA served this owner until the railroad steamer divisions were ordered sold by government decree in 1915. This was the result of anti-trust suits brought against the railroads. The UTICA was one of several ships that were absorbed in the newly formed Great Lakes Transit Corporation in 1916.

In 1933, when the formidable Great Depression hit the United States, many of the lake ships were laid up due to lack of business. Especially hard hit were the package freight shippers. The UTICA however, had already been diverted in 1927 to another growing aspect of shipping on the Lakes, the automobile carrying business, and was not affected. From 1933 to 1936 she was chartered to the D&C Fleet to carry cars between Detroit, Michigan, and other Lake ports, especially Cleveland, Ohio and Buffalo, New York.

World War II arrived before the shipping firms on the seas or the Lakes could provide enough hulls, or the builders could provide new ones. Consequently, the vessels which could be taken to the coasts without too much difficulty were requisitioned by the United States Maritime Admin-istration or the War Shipping Board. Some of the ships could transit the St. Lawrence canals but others had to be floated on pontoons through the Chicago Drainage Canal and the Mississippi River. One such vessel to transit to the coast by the latter means was the UTICA. In 1942, she was taken over by the War Shipping Board and made it to New Orleans, Louisiana that same year. Curiously, she was returned to the Lakes the following year, as she was needed here instead. Before the conflict was over, the governmental heads again decided to take this vessel to the ocean by way of Chicago, Illinois. The UTICA made her final passage past Detroit, Michigan, on June 22, 1945, in tow of her fleet-sister, the ALRED H. SMITH, enroute to Chicago. The war was ended before she could be used, so the Great Lakes Transit Corporation sold her to Chilean buyers.

The Compania de Muelles de la Publacion Vergara pur-chased the UTICA and renamed her QUINTAY. After she had been converted to ocean service in 1945 at Manitowoc, by the Manitowoc Shipbuilding Company, she served this firm on the Pacific until April 28, 1949, when she was wrecked on Penguin Island in the Messier Channel. She had been bound from Callao, Peru to Punta Arenas, Chile. None of her crew was lost.

VICTORY

VICTORY

	VICTORY,		*DEPTH:*	22.5

VICTORY,
b) Victorious

BUILT: The Chicago Shipbuilding Company, Chicago, Illinois

HULL NUMBER: 14
LENGTH (original): 387.5
BREADTH: 48.3

DEPTH: 22.5
GROSS REGISTERED TONNAGE: 3,774
REGISTRY NUMBER: US 161758
ENGINES: Triple expansion 22″, 38″ & 63″ diameter × 40″ stroke
ENGINE BUILDER: Cleveland Shipbuilding Company

VICTORIOUS

This bulk carrier was built in 1895 for the Interlake Company, an affiliate of Pickands Mather & Co., Cleveland. Although one of the giants of the Lakes when launched —the first 400 footer together with ZENITH CITY—she was soon eclipsed by the 580′ carriers. Therefore the hull was lengthened at Superior, Wisconsin in 1905 by 72′ increasing her gross tonnage to 4527. The ship was reboildered in 1912. In 1913 the Interlake Company was absorbed into Pickands Mather & Company's Interlake Steamship Co., Cleveland. Interlake Steamship Co. gave her a rebuild at Fairport, Ohio in 1926.

In 1940, the ship was purchased by Upper Lakes and St. Lawrence Transportation Co., Ltd., Toronto and renamed VICTORIOUS (C. 172358). This firm became Upper Lakes Shipping Limited in 1961. VICTORIOUS remained in service, usually in the grain trade, until it arrived at Toronto on Friday, December 6, 1968, with a cargo of winter storage grain. The owners did not fit her out in 1969 and sold her to the Government of Ontario for use as a breakwater at Ontario Place, Exhibition Park, Toronto. Actually Upper Lakes Shipping, Ltd., sold her to the Toronto Harbour Commission, which body prepared the hull for its new use as a breakwater and then turned her over to the Government of Ontario.

VIRGINIA

VIRGINIA

Built in 1891 for the Goodrich Line for fast service between Chicago, Illinois and Milwaukee, Wisconsin, this palatial steel passenger express liner was described by the Marine Review of that year as "The finest ship that ever flew the American Flag." VIRGINIA's performance proved beyond doubt all claims made for her speed and seaworthiness. Her chimed whistle's melodious tone was one not soon forgotten.

On May 16, 1918, VIRGINIA was sold to the U. S. Navy for transport service across the English Channel. Parts of the staterooms were removed, side ports and gangways sealed and part of the bow was cut off for canalling. VIRGINIA was taken to the coast, renamed U.S.S. BLUE RIDGE and accepted by the Navy on OCT. 17, 1918. Her

new dimensions and tonnage were: 264.7 × 38.3 × 22.1 —1,985 gross registered tons. During August of 1919 the Navy disposed of the former liner to William Wrigley of Chicago, who owned and operated the Wilmington Transportation Company in 1920. New upper works were put on after the sale and the vessel was sent to the Pacific coast to sail from Los Angeles, California to Catalina Island off the coast. The vessel was renamed AVALON that same year. During the ensuing years she was a fixture, a favorite tourist attraction of the West Coast. Ownership changes occurred in 1954 (Catalina Island Steamship Company) and in 1961 (Alvin Kidman). Sold for scrap in 1964, the AVALON sank while under tow to the scrapyard off Palos Verdes Point, California on September 16th.

VIRGINIA,
b) U.S.S. Blue Ridge,
c) Avalon

BUILT:	Globe Iron Works, Cleveland, Ohio
HULL NUMBER:	42
LENGTH:	269.2
BREADTH:	38.3
DEPTH:	12.8
GROSS REGISTERED TONNAGE:	1,606
REGISTRY NUMBER:	US 161654
ENGINES:	20″, 32″, 52″ diameter × 36″ stroke Twin triple expansion
ENGINE BUILDER:	Shipyard

AVALON

PERRY G. WALKER

PERRY G. WALKER was a steel bulk carrier built in 1903 for the Gilchrist Transportation Company. This ship was involved in one of the most peculiar incidents ever to happen on the lakes, on June 9, 1909. The story of the "accident" that befell the lock at Sault Ste. Marie, Ontario will be retold many times over. Because of the traffic jam at the American locks, the Captain of the WALKER decided to take the Canadian lock across the river in order to speed up his passage. At that time, the master of a vessel had the option of taking any of the existing locks to facilitate his passage to Lake Superior if he was upbound, or to Lake Huron if he was downbound. There was no regulatory system to decide for him.

The steamer ASSINIBOIA of the Canadian Pacific Railroad passenger and freight line and the CRESCENT CITY of the Pittsburgh Steamship Company were downbound, waiting to enter the Canadian Lock. After some other steamers had cleared the lock upbound, the two vessels began their approach. The ASSINIBOIA entered the lock first and maneuvered to tie up at the lock wall before the CRESCENT CITY entered behind her. The WALKER, upbound in the meantime, steered for the wall below the lock. As the WALKER approached, something went wrong with her engine signals, and instead of slowing down, she speeded up. The vessel tore into the lower lock gate which was closed, smashing and tearing it from its hinges. The ASSINIBOIA parted her lines as a giant cascade of water pushed her from astern, sending her tumbling through the now open lower gate, and rushing her down upon the oncoming WALKER. The ASSINIBOIA miraculously escaped hitting the WALKER and plummetted into the lower St. Mary's River. The CRESCENT CITY, entering behind the ASSINIBOIA, could not keep control, and in hot pursuit followed the passenger ship down through the now completely open lock. Here again, an apparant miracle occurred, for the CRESCENT CITY, loaded with iron ore, only scraped the lock still on her way past the now startled crew of the WALKER and countless onlookers and into the lower river at quite a speed. She bashed into the lock wall, dragged over the gateless sill and merely brushed aside the WALKER on her descent. When all these events were later investigated, it was realized that the unlucky crash and the dash of the two ships into the lower river had not taken more than a few minutes. The passengers of the ASSINIBOIA were roughed up but unhurt. The crew and Captain of the CRESCENT CITY were unharmed but dazed, and the Master and crew of the WALKER were completely mystified. The onlookers gaped in amazement and watched the cascade of water thunder through the open lock.

PERRY G. WALKER in the American Locks

PERRY G. WALKER,
b) Taurus

BUILT:	Chicago Shipbuilding Company, South Chicago, Illinois
HULL NUMBER:	63
LENGTH:	416
BREADTH:	50.3
DEPTH:	24
GROSS REGISTERED TONNAGE:	4,470
REGISTRY NUMBER:	US 200377
ENGINES:	22″, 35″, 58″ diameter × 40″ stroke Triple Expansion
ENGINE BUILDER:	Shipyard

The Canadian Lock was soon repaired. ASSINIBOIA and PERRY G. WALKER sustained only minor damage but the bottom of the unlucky CRESCENT CITY was all but completely torn out. The pumps kept her afloat until she had delivered her cargo safely to Conneaut, Ohio on Lake Erie. Then the vessel went to the shipyard for repairs, the second major repair job in less than two years. (She had been in the terrific storm on Lake Superior in 1905, and had been tossed onto the rocky shore in that blow.)

In 1913, the PERRY G. WALKER was sold to the Interlake Steamship Company, whose service she ran for the rest of her life. In the same year, she was renamed TAURUS, perhaps because of her persistency in the lock incident. No more serious accidents befell this ship during the rest of her career and in 1943 she was traded to the U.S. Maritime Administration for newer ships. After World War II, in 1947, she was reduced to scrap at Hamilton, Ontario. Her career had ended, not in mishap this time, but in faithful service. She will always be remembered for the accident to the Canadian Lock of 1909.

TAURUS in the Detroit River

WAR FOX

The three island type of coastal freighter WAR FOX was built in 1917 for the Cunard Steamship Company of Liverpool, England, but never got a chance to prove the truth of Cunard's slogan, "Getting There is Half the Fun," because she was requisitioned by the U.S. Shipping Board when the U.S. entered World War I in the spring of 1917. She was then renamed LAKE FOREST.

Ninety-eight other similar vessels being built in several Great Lakes shipyards were also taken over by the Shipping Board and these became the first of the famous "Lakers." Three hundred and thirty-one more of these small freighters were built under contract to the Shipping Board in 1918, 1919 and 1920, for a total of 430 standard type vessels, a number exceeded only by the renowned "Liberty" ships and "T-2" tankers of World War II.

After a brief duty in World War I, LAKE FOREST, with several other Lakers, was sold by the U.S. Government to Lloyd Royal Belge in 1920 and renamed VENETIER. In 1925, the ship was owned by Cie Gle Aversoise, also Belgian, and was renamed TABAKHANDEL. In 1926, Arm Glysen, Belge sold her to Sud Atlantic, Argentina, who promptly renamed her ESTE. The following owners had possession of the vessel from 1930: Mihanovich of Argentina from 1930 to 1937; Schwager of Chile, who renamed the vessel CHOLLIN, to 1948; El Melon Cement of Chile the season of 1948 when they renamed her, RAFAEL ARITZIA and operated the ship until 1956; Valch & Moncton, Chile who renamed her SAN PATRICIO to 1957; Vatikiotis of Greece who renamed her MARY V in 1957; and Sigalas of Greece who renamed the vessel for the last time, KADIO S. until 1960.

This grand old-timer, which escaped the three common ends of so many Lakers, World War I, the Ford scrap heap of 1928-29, and the "Battle of the Atlantic" in World War II, was finally scrapped at Gijon, Spain in August 1960.

WAR FOX

WAR FOX, b) Lake Forest, c) Venetier, d) Tabakhandel, e) Este, f) Cholin, g) Rafael Ariztia, h) San Patricio, i) Mary V., j) Kadio S.

BUILT:	Detroit Shipbuilding Company, Wyandotte, Michigan	*GROSS REGISTERED TONNAGE:*	1,949
HULL NUMBER:	213	*REGISTRY NUMBER:*	US 215748
LENGTH:	251	*ENGINES:*	20″, 33″, 54″ diameter × 40″ stroke
BREADTH:	43.5		Triple expansion
DEPTH:	18.5	*ENGINE BUILDER:*	Shipyard

S. D. WARRINER

At the turn of the century, many vessel owners tried a system of incorporating the progress made in steel freighters by building steel barges to be towed behind the steamers akin to the old wooden steambarges with their cut-down schooner consorts. The system proved successful because of the powerful engines built at that time, enabling a steel bulk carrier to tow one or two steel barges behind it, with a great reduction in crew expense and total construction cost. In 1901, the Calumet Transportation Company, which was managed by the M. A. Hanna Company of Cleveland, had ordered two such steel barges, one of which was the S. D. WARRINER.

For the next 15 years, she was towed by one of the twin steel steamers, G. A. FLAGG or RANDOLPH S. WARNER. This steamer-barge combination was a frequent visitor to the narrow Portage Ship Canal, otherwise known as the Keweenaw Waterway, separating the Keweenaw Peninsula of Northern Michigan from the mainland.

During the fierce conflict of World War I, many Lake vessels were pressed into duty to serve on the coasts of North America and across the Atlantic to European ports. Because of the dire need of shipping to overcome the new threats of the German U Boats, the ships of the Calumet Transportation Company headed for the East Coast. Each vessel had to be taken through the Welland and St. Lawrence River Canals. For this trip, a ship in excess of 256 feet in length had to be cut in two, bulkheaded (each part sealed against leakage) and taken through the canals in sections. Both parts then would be joined together again at Montreal or Quebec City. The S. D. WARRINER was sold to the Gulf Barge and Towing Company in 1918 and spent the rest of her life in the service of this firm and its successor, the S. D. Warriner Transportation Company.

In November, 1950, the WARRINER was abandoned due to age at Mobile, Alabama, and scrapped in that place. She had served on the Lakes and the Coast for almost 50 years. Her memory is preserved here as another staunch Lake-built vessel that withstood the rigors of salt water exposure for many years.

S. D. WARRINER in 1916

BUILT:	West Bay City Shipbuilding Company, West Bay City, Michigan	*BREADTH:*	41.6
		DEPTH:	21
HULL NUMBER:	600	*GROSS REGISTERED TONNAGE:*	2,279
LENGTH:	300	*REGISTRY NUMBER:*	US 117033

JAMES WATT

JAMES WATT at the Soo

The JAMES WATT was one of seven large steamers and five steel barges built for John D. Rockefeller's Bessemer Steamship Company during the winter of 1895–96. All of the vessels were named for famous inventors, the JAMES WATT carrying the name of the man who perfected the modern steam engine. She was launched in September, 1896 and served the Bessemer Steamship Company until sold to the Pittsburgh Steamship Company in 1901. This ship was very powerful for her size and gained fame as an icebreaker, especially when she broke the CHARLES R. VAN HISE out of 18 inches of solid ice in Gladstone Harbor in the fall of 1904.

The old two-deck system of construction was used in the WATT but the middle decking itself was not placed. In other words, instead of the WATT's holds being large clear areas, as in the modern freighter, she had a steel framework in her hold which could be planked over, thus making two separate levels upon which to carry cargo. This framework made the unloading of bulk cargoes difficult. In 1925, steel arches were built into the holds and the old framing was removed. Later, when a new pilot house and cabins were added, the gross tonnage changed to 3,853.

In 1928, the WATT was sold to the Jenkins Steamship Company for whom she carried a variety of cargoes, including ore, coal, grain and automobiles. Following her sale in 1936 to the Carriers Transport Corporation, the WATT was used more extensively in the auto trade. In 1937, she was owned by the Erie Steamship Company, and in 1938, the WATT was purchased by her final operator, the Nicholson Transit Company.

In many of her later years, the WATT carried new automobiles from Detroit, "the Motor City," to Duluth, Minnesota, on the upbound trip and grain downbound. In her last years, the WATT also transported coal on the winter run from Toledo to Detroit.

In 1961, the WATT was sold to Acme Iron & Metal Company for scrap. They resold the vessel for European scrapping and, on July 16, 1961, the WATT sailed through the Welland Ship Canal under her own power for Quebec, from where she was towed across the Atlantic Ocean, arriving at Gijon, Spain on September 25, 1961.

In Nicholson colors

JAMES WATT in Buffalo harbor

BUILT:	Cleveland Shipbuilding Company, Cleveland, Ohio	GROSS REGISTERED TONNAGE:	4,090
HULL NUMBER:	26	REGISTRY NUMBER:	US 77236
LENGTH:	406	ENGINES:	25″, 40″, 68″ diameter × 42″ stroke
BREADTH:	48		Triple Expansion
DEPTH:	28	ENGINE BUILDER:	Shipyard

Upbound at Mission Point

WAUKETA

BUILT:	Toledo Shipbuilding Co., Toledo, Ohio
HULL NUMBER:	113
LENGTH:	175
BREADTH:	38.4
DEPTH:	14.5
GROSS REGISTERED TONNAGE:	543
REGISTRY NUMBER:	US 206077
ENGINES:	17¼″, 27½″, 43″ diameter × 30″ stroke Triple expansion
ENGINE BUILDER:	Shipyard

WAUKETA on the Lakes

This steel day-excursion steamer was built in 1908 for the White Star Line of Detroit for day trips from Detroit to Port Huron and Toledo. For two decades, she served her first owner, usually running opposite TASHMOO, on the river trip to Port Huron. In 1927, the vessel was owned by the Detroit-Port Huron Steamship Company, serving on the same route as before. In 1930, the vessel was sold to the Meseck Towing Company of New York City (the Steamer Wauketa, Inc.) and used for short cruises on the Hudson, East River and Lower New York Bay, along with AMERICANA, another Lakes ship bought by Meseck. In 1940, WAUKETA was sold to the Sutton Line. In 1945, she was sold to the Chesapeake and Ohio Railway for ferry service on Hampton Roads between Newport News, and Norfolk, Virginia. WAUKETA's dimensions were changed in 1946 to 179.9 × 38.4 × 14.2—588 grt. In 1951, the C&O abandoned the ferry line in favor of busses across the James River Bridge. WAUKETA left Newport News on February 23, 1952 for a Baltimore, Maryland, scrap yard where she lay abandoned for a year before being reduced.

On the East Coast

WAYNE

The steel cross-river Detroit auto/passenger ferry WAYNE was launched on March 17, 1923, by Great Lakes Engineering Works at River Rouge, Michigan. Miss Virginia Walker, youngest daughter of the president of Hiram Walker's Sons, of Walkerville, Ontario, performed the christening honors. The WAYNE operated from the foot of Joseph Campau Street, Detroit, to the ferry landing at Walkerville (now Windsor) for the Walkerville & Detroit Ferry Company until that service was suspended on May 5, 1942. The monotony of the run was broken by an occasional moonlight or picnic excursion. Following this, she lay idle at Walkerville until 1943, when she was sold to the Duluth-Superior Steamship Company, of Duluth, Minnesota, which was controlled by Nick Constans.

After a few more years of inactivity, she finally was towed to Duluth by the tug ATOMIC, of McQueen Marine, Ltd., arriving there on May 4, 1946. She was rebuilt with a large enclosed dance hall on her main deck and used for rides around "the Horn," out through the Superior entry and return via the Duluth Ship Canal. She also ran moonlight excursions on St. Louis Bay. In April, 1950, the WAYNE was transferred to Toledo, Ohio, to run moonlights on Maumee Bay and Lake Erie for Toledo Excursions, Inc., also under the control of Mr. Constans. At the end of the 1950 excursion season, she returned to lay-up at Windsor,

Ontario. This also ended her pleasure service on the lakes.

The WAYNE was removed from documentation in May, 1952, and sold to the Baudhuin Yacht Company at Sturgeon Bay, Wisconsin. The tug JOHN ROEN towed her as far as Detour, Michigan, dropped her while the tug went to Lake Superior on another tow job, then picked her up again on the return trip, bound for Sturgeon Bay. On the return trip to Detour, they found that vandals had smashed all of the windows and done other damage. The former ferry was to serve as a clubhouse at the Wisconsin port, but arrangements were never completed. She remained at Sturgeon Bay until the Bisso Ferry Company of New Orleans, Louisiana, purchased her.

Again, the tug JOHN ROEN attached a tow line to the WAYNE, this time bound for Chicago. There her upper works were removed so that she would pass under bridges. Great Lakes Towing Company delivered her to Lockport, Illinois, where Mississippi River tow boats picked her up for the remainder of the trip south. She was to resume her original career, this time between New Orleans and Algiers, but the completion of a highway bridge made this unnecessary. The Bisso Company converted her to a floating warehouse. At last report, April 15, 1958, she still was in the Bisso yard.

WAYNE as a ferry boat

BUILT:	Great Lakes Engineering Works, Ecorse, Michigan	*GROSS REGISTERED TONNAGE:*	379
HULL NUMBER:	243	*REGISTRY NUMBER:*	US 222835
LENGTH:	134.1	*ENGINES:*	20″, 40″ diameter × 28″ stroke Fore & Aft Compound
BREADTH:	56.6	*ENGINE BUILDER:*	Shipyard
DEPTH:	14.4		

FRANK WILKINSON

	Fairriver,	*DEPTH:*	18
	b) FRANK WILKINSON	*GROSS REGISTERED*	
BUILT:	Barclay, Curle & Co.,	*TONNAGE:*	1940
	Limited,	*REGISTRY NUMBER:*	C. 161524
	Whiteinch (Glasgow) Scotland	*ENGINES:*	Triple expansion 15″, 25″ & 40″
HULL NUMBER:	635		diameter × 33″ stroke
LENGTH:	253	*ENGINE BUILDER:*	Barclay Curle & Co., Ltd.,
BREADTH:	43		Glasgow

FAIRRIVER

This bulk freighter was built in 1929 as (a) FAIRRIVER for Fairport Shipping Company, Ltd., Welland, Ontario, a subsidiary of the Jenkins Steamship Co., Cleveland. Barclay Curle built her under contract for Swan Hunter and Wigham Richardson Ltd. In 1931, Swan Hunter repossessed her. They sold her in 1932 to Capt. R. Scott Misener and he registered her to Huron Steamships Ltd. She was transferred to the parent, Sarnia Steamships Ltd., in 1938. Another change within the Misener organization took place in 1951 when she passed to the Colonial Steamships Ltd. Scott Misener Steamships Ltd. became her owner in 1959. She had been renamed (b) FRANK WILKINSON in 1944. In the spring of 1959, she went into permanent lay up at Port Dalhousie, Ontario, a victim of the demand for larger ships created by the opening of the Seaway. In 1962 she was cut up in the drydock at Port Dalhousie by Newman Steel Co. Ltd., St. Catharines, Ontario.

FRANK WILKINSON

WILLOWDALE

TALARALITE

Talaralite,
(b) Imperial Midland,
(c) WILLOWDALE

BUILT: Collingwood Ship Building
Co., Ltd.,
Collingwood, Ontario
HULL NUMBER: 50
LENGTH: 250
BREADTH: 43.8
DEPTH: 23.5

GROSS REGISTERED
TONNAGE: 2,335
REGISTRY NUMBER: C. 137907
ENGINES: Triple expansion 18″, 30″ & 50″
Diameter × 36″ stroke
Two oil fired Scotch Marine
Boilers 13′6″ × 11′
ENGINE BUILDER: Collingwood Ship Building
Co., Ltd.,
Collingwood

IMPERIAL MIDLAND

Built in 1918 for Imperial Oil Shipping Co., Ltd., Toronto, as TALARALITE, this canal-sized tanker was intended for salt water service in South America. She was renamed b) IMPERIAL MIDLAND in 1947. Her service with Imperial Oil Ltd. ended with lay-up at Port Weller on December 6, 1952.

On December 13, 1952, with steam gone from her boilers, the tugs JALOBERT and PORT WELLER took her in tow bound for Port Dalhousie, four miles to the west. A moderate sea was running off Port Weller at the time and somehow the towline fouled in JALOBERT's wheel. While PORT WELLER towed the JALOBERT to port, the helpless IMPERIAL MIDLAND drifted stern first down Lake On-

tario toward the Niagara Bar. Several miles east of Port Weller piers, IMPERIAL MIDLAND's anchors held fast until the tugs could complete the tow to Port Dalhousie.

On her arrival at Port Dalhousie drydock, work commenced on converting the tanker to a dry cargo carrier for Reoch Steamships Ltd., Montreal. The ship returned to service on November 5, 1953 as c) WILLOWDALE. The next nine years were spent mostly in the scrap trade between River Rouge and the Steel Company of Canada Ltd., plant at Hamilton, Ontario. In August, 1963, she arrived at Toronto where her crew was paid off. Within a few weeks, she was reduced to a pile of scrap by Ship Repair and Supply Ltd., Toronto.

WILLOWDALE in the St. Clair River

Being scrapped in Toronto

U.S.S. WILMINGTON

Armanent: eight 4-inch rapid fire guns; four 6-pounders; four 1-pounders; four Colts; one 3-inch field gun.

Construction of the steel U.S.S. WILMINGTON was authorized by Act of Congress dated March 3, 1893. Her keel was laid on October 8, 1894, and she was launched on October 19, 1895. She was crewed by ten officers and 165 ratings and commissioned on May 13, 1897. Assigned to the North Atlantic Squadron, she served in Cuban waters during the Spanish-American War. Following the war, she was fitted for foreign service and sailed from Hampton Roads, Virginia, on December 24, 1898 for duty with the South Atlantic Squadron. This included a cruise to the heads of navigation of the Orinoco and Amazon Rivers.

On October 16, 1900, she departed Pernambuco for Asiatic waters, via Gibraltar and the Suez Canal. She arrived at Manila, P.I., on January 21, 1901, and departed Cavite on May 10 to join the China Squadron for patrol duty out of Shanghai. On June 30, 1904, she was decommissioned at Cavite.

On April 3, 1906, WILMINGTON was recommissioned and resumed her patrol duties out of Shanghai and Hong Kong. This lasted until she was notified by cable of the United States' entry into World War I in April, 1917. She was assigned to the Yangtze Patrol and became flagship of that force on May 23, 1921. On May 20, 1922, she sailed from Hong Kong for Cavite. She departed the latter port on June 2, and arrived at Portsmouth, N.H., on September 20, 1922.

She was assigned to duty on the Great Lakes and departed on July 19, 1923 on her first cruise for naval reserve units stationed in Ohio and Kentucky. Attached to the Third Regiment, U.S. Naval Reserve Force, Ninth Naval District, she arrived at Toledo, Ohio, on August 1, 1923, where she became a familiar sight moored at the Naval Armory. While on the lakes, she was commonly referred to as "The Battleship Linoleum."

She serviced naval reserve units throughout the Great Lakes for the next eighteen years. With the impending hostilities of World War II, her name was changed to USS DOVER on January 27, 1941. She was placed in active commission again on November 2, 1942, and taken to New Orleans, where she was used to train naval armed guard gun crews.

The USS DOVER was decommissioned on December 20, 1945, and sold on December 30, 1946, to the Hawley Forge and Manufacturing Company of San Francisco. She was used by a barge company there to raise a sunken tug boat and to carry her out to deeper water. Then the old China veteran's sea-cocks were opened and she was scuttled in seventy-five feet of water.

U.S.S. WILMINGTON

U.S.S. WILMINGTON,		*LENGTH:*	250'9" (length load waterline)
b) U.S.S. Dover		*BREADTH:*	40' (Extreme Breadth)
		DEPTH:	9' (Mean Draft)
BUILT:	Newport News Shipbuilding &	*GROSS REGISTERED*	
	Dry Dock Co.,	*TONNAGE:*	1,392 (Displaced Tons)
	Newport News, Virginia	*ENGINES:*	Twin triple expansion
HULL NUMBER:	Gunboat No. 8	*ENGINE BUILDER:*	Shipyard

CAPTAIN THOMAS WILSON

CAPTAIN THOMAS WILSON being towed through Military Street Bridge, Pt. Huron

The Jenks Shipbuilding Company of Port Huron, Michigan, had been in business for a little more than ten years when they received a contract from Thomas Wilson, owner of the Wilson Transit Company, to build a steel bulk freighter. The Jenks firm went to work on the vessel, the longest they had ever built at their yard on the Black River in Port Huron, and launched her on August 30, 1900. This giant was successfully christened and slid into the narrow waters of the Black River where her engine was installed. The engine was also a product of the Jenks family who had built engines under the name of the Phoenix Iron Works since the late 1870's.

Being masters of the art of wooden shipbuilding, the Jenks company easily adapted their talents to establish a well known steel shipbuilding plant. Their first steel vessel had been the RAVENSCRAIG, a small canal-sized vessel, and they were determined to make a name for themselves. However, the problems they faced with the new WILSON were not envisioned at the time of her building. Once they had completed her, the immense problem of getting her out of the narrow confines of the Black River ensued.

The sluggish Black River is very narrow in many spots as it patiently winds its way to the blue waters of the St. Clair River through the city of Port Huron. Besides the narrowness, the river was bisected three times by bridges which spanned the brackish river. The bridges of that time were of the swing-bridge type. The piers were in the center of the stream and the bridge turned on a table-like affair whenever it had to be opened to shipping. Thus the narrow river was even narrower at the bridges. The first bridge lay upstream from the Jenks plant and did not have to be encountered. The next was at 7th Street and the last at Military Street.

The 7th Street bridge was navigated successfully. To traverse the one at Military Street, the oldest and most difficult of them all, was to prove a greater obstacle. The tugs had worked diligently to maneuver the 50-foot wide boat through the winding river and fully expected to pass through their last obstacle without too much trouble. Not so. The huge WILSON stuck fast when she entered the south canal past the bridge. The tugs pulled and pushed but she would not budge. A clever mechanic then suggested that the tugs pull her back through the opening and then widen the opening itself. The mechanic's idea was sound, but the tugs could not move the freighter. Finally, after much discussion, the piling around the center table of the bridge was removed by a now furious tug crew and workers brought from the yard. At last the vessel was released with much profanity and perspiration. The ship was free to sail the lakes, and her trials proved she was truly a masterpiece of shipbuilding technique. The next vessels built at the Black River yard did not have the problem of the WILSON because the river was widened and the center bridge works narrowed to enable these large vessels to pass through.

The CAPTAIN THOMAS WILSON sailed for the next 46 years, with few events as exciting as trying to reach the St. Clair River. In 1943, she was traded to the U.S. Maritime Commission with the A. W. OSBORNE for the new "Maritime Class" THOMAS WILSON. Just before this trade, she was renamed KICKAPOO, so that the new vessel being built could carry on the name of the famous founder of the Wilson Transit Company. The KICKAPOO was sold for scrap and reduced at Hamilton, Ontario, in 1947.

CAPTAIN THOMAS WILSON

CAPTAIN THOMAS WILSON,
b) Kickapoo

BUILT: Jenks Shipbuilding Company,
Port Huron, Michigan
HULL NUMBER 14
LENGTH: 420.5
BREADTH: 50

DEPTH: 24
GROSS REGISTERED
TONNAGE: 4,719
REGISTRY NUMBER: US 127469
ENGINES: 22″, 38″, 63″ diameter × 40″
stroke
Triple expansion
ENGINE BUILDER: Shipyard

KICKAPOO

YANKCANUCK (1)

MANCHESTER at the dock

The composite (iron frames and wooden planking with an iron keel) freighter MANCHESTER, was built in 1889 for the Inter-Ocean Steamship Company. In 1908, it was sold to the Milwaukee-Western Steamship Co., managed by Capt. Denis Sullivan. In 1921, the vessel was renamed JOSEPH W. SIMPSON and the following year she was shortened by 41'1". The new dimensions were: 250.8 × 42 × 20.7 and the ship had a gross tonnage of 1,813. She now entered the coal and grain trade. In 1924, she was sold to the Reiss Steamship Co. of Sheboygan, Wisconsin, and in 1927, to the George Madden Coal Corporation of Ogdensburg, New York. She was converted to a crane vessel at the Buffalo Dry Dock Co., Buffalo, in 1928.

The SIMPSON was sold Canadian in 1937 to Edwin F. Priddle of Gore Bay, renamed MINDEMOYA and given the Canadian official number of 170256. She spent the rest of her life under Canadian registry. Her registered dimensions were: 243.2 × 41.8 × 19.6 and 1,778 gross tons. During the war years she served several owners. In 1939, she ran for the Mindemoya Transportation Co. of Toronto and went to the Albatross Steamship Co. of Montreal in 1941.

The final owner, Captain F. Manzzutti of Sault Ste. Marie, Ontario, bought her in 1945 and renamed her YANKCANUCK in 1946. She had a profitable career for Capt. Manzzutti and his American wife in the following decade. After 70 years of service, the YANKCANUCK was scrapped at Sault Ste. Marie, Ontario in 1959. A new vessel was built to replace the old lady in 1963, and bears the same name to honor the faithful service of the first YANKCANUCK.

In the St. Clair River

JOS. W. SIMPSON

BUILT:	Detroit Dry Dock Company, Wyandotte, Michigan
HULL NUMBER:	91
LENGTH:	281
BREADTH:	41
DEPTH:	23
GROSS REGISTERED TONNAGE:	2,132
REGISTRY NUMBER:	US 92087
ENGINES:	Triple expansion 20″, 32″, 54″ diameter × 42″ stroke
ENGINE BUILDER:	S. F. Hodge & Company, Detroit, Michigan

MINDEMOYA

YANKCANUCK

ZENITH CITY

In 1895, the steel bulk freighter ZENITH CITY was built by the Chicago Shipbuilding Company at South Chicago for the American Steamship Company which was commonly called the "City Line." Each ship of the fleet was christened in honour of a famous city.

When she was launched on Wednesday, August 16, 1895, the ZENITH CITY was one of the longest ships on the Lakes. In 1901, she and the other ships of her fleet were absorbed into the newly organized fleet of the Pittsburgh Steamship Company, the Lake transportation division of the United States Steel Corporation. In 1942, the aging vessel was traded in to the U.S. Maritime Commission as partial compensation for the "Maritime Class" ships which were built during World War II. After the cessation of hostilities in 1945, ZENITH CITY, which had continued in the service of the Pittsburgh Steamship Company, was retired. She was laid to rest in Erie Bay for a year and finally was towed to Hamilton, Ontario, where she was cut up for scrap in 1947.

ZENITH CITY led a notably uneventful life. She is, perhaps, best remembered for her melodious chimed whistle which is said to have been one of the most beautiful ever heard on the Great Lakes.

ZENITH CITY

BUILT:	Chicago Shipbuilding Company, South Chicago, Illinois	*GROSS REGISTERED TONNAGE:*	3,850
HULL NUMBER:	15	*REGISTRY NUMBER:*	US 28129
LENGTH:	387.5	*ENGINES:*	20″, 37″, 63″ diameter × 42″ stroke
BREADTH:	48.3		Triple expansion
DEPTH:	23.3	*ENGINE BUILDER:*	Cleveland Shipbuilding Company, Cleveland, Ohio

ZENITH CITY

EPILOGUE

We remember these vessels and all their sister ships. The freighters and passenger boats of bygone days accomplished their intended purposes and added a touch of man-made beauty to the blue lake waters they plowed so ably for so many years. So often were they seen that they became fixtures, parts of the grand fleet of steel and wooden ships that passed quietly and relentlessly, carrying their burdens of commerce to enhance the progress of industry and benefit the expanding populace of Canada and the United States.

Slowly plodding, nudging the blue water ahead of them, a white comb in their teeth, these blunt-bowed vessels still silently make their way past countless white cottages which dot the shore, past slender skyscrapers and the dull gray industrial vistas. Sometimes, gaily painted salties meet these lumbering giants, exchange cheery whistle hellos, and drift ceaselessly on beneath the azure skies. These steel-armored carriers, these "freighters of fortune," continue their circuits through calm and fury. Nowhere can the still, deep waters turn so quickly into scudding, gray combers in such a short time, yet these ponderous caravels of industry sail the fickle waters, sometimes impervious to tragedy, other times swallowed up in their fury. They continue, even in the icy, midwinter bleakness, through fierce gales and whispery breezes, through impenetrably milky fogs and sheets of sleety snow. They remain undaunted; they remain in our memory.

We remember them and those who sailed them.